FIFTY YEARS OF MUSIC

The Story of EMI Music Canada

FIFTY YEARS OF MUSIC
THE STORY OF EMI MUSIC CANADA

Nicholas Jennings

Macmillan Canada
Toronto

First published in Canada in 2000 by

Macmillan Canada, an imprint of CDG Books Canada

Canadian Cataloguing in Publication Data

Jennings, Nicholas, 1953-

    Fifty years of music : the story of EMI Music Canada

Includes bibliographical references.

ISBN 0-7715-7664-1

1. EMI Music Canada – History. 2. Sound recording industry – Canada – History.

I. Title.

ML3792.J46 2000   338.7'6178149'0971   C00-930409-6

This book is available at special discounts for bulk purchases by your group or organization for sales promotions, premiums, fundraising and seminars. For details, contact:

CDG Books Canada Inc., 99 Yorkville Avenue, Suite 400, Toronto, ON, M5R 3K5.

1 2 3 4 5 FP 04 03 02 01 00

Cover design by Megan Oldfield for Coolaide Design

Text design by Stray Toaster

Front cover photo courtesy of Oliver/TSI Imaging/Stone

Photo research by Klix and Nick Jennings

EMI Project Manager: David MacMillan

Macmillan Canada

An imprint of CDG Books Canada Inc.

Toronto

Printed in Canada

Contents

President's Foreword

I remember my first days on American Drive—I wasn't in the President's chair then. In fact, I was in the Capitol-EMI warehouse packing records to be sent out to stores across Canada.

That was in 1970. Since then I have seen a lot of this company, from the shipping room all the way through to the A & R department. Everywhere I went, I saw that we had one thing in common: a love of music. Everyone throughout the company, from the front office to the back warehouse, shared a passion for the sounds of the times.

And what times they were! This book chronicles an era like no other. From the explosion of pop music in the 1960s to the revolution in audio technology in the '90s, our label has been at the centre of it all. And the template to our success from the very beginning has been the combination of good musical ears and keen business minds.

The early pioneers of Capitol Canada, who you will read about in the pages that follow, forged the mould in a converted wire and nail factory in London, Ontario. When I invited those founding fathers to our 50th anniversary picnic, and heard about their exploits—they built the boiler for the record presses by hand—I realized that the same spirit still drives the company I now lead.

But there's no point in pressing records—or burning CDs—unless you've got something worth listening to at the end of the production line. We started signing some of Canada's first pop acts in the '60s, when Beatlemania raged. Now, from Anne Murray to Tom Cochrane, from The Moffatts to The Tea Party, EMI is home to the best music this country has produced in the last 50 years.

The next 50 are bound to be equally eventful—especially in light of our corporate marriage with Warner Music, which has suddenly made us the world's premier music group with more than 2,500 artists, 2,000 albums a year and over 2 million song copyrights. But that's another story. This one is about our roots, where it all began and what has led up to this point in our impressive history.

Don't just take my word for it. Read this book and share our incredible ride

Deane Cameron
January 2000

Author's Acknowledgements

Just before I hit my teenage years, around the age of 10, I found myself torn between sports and music. Should I spend my weekly allowance on hockey cards or pop records? Having just returned from England, where I'd been swept up in the first wave of Beatlemania, music— perhaps predictably—won out. Every Saturday, then, for the next few years, I'd cycle over to my neighborhood shopping centre in suburban Toronto and visit the Eaton's record department. There, I'd plunk down 66 cents for the latest 45 by whatever group had caught my fancy. Usually, it was something by The Beatles, The Animals, Manfred Mann or some other British band. But I also remember buying singles by Canadian groups, including The Staccatos, The Ugly Ducklings and Jack London & the Sparrows. More often than not, those 45s all bore the same distinctive looking centre-piece: the bright orange and yellow swirl of Capitol Records.

I still own many of those precious pieces of vinyl. And I fondly revisited them when I undertook the research and writing of this book tracing the history of Capitol Records of Canada through to its emergence as EMI Music Canada. In many ways, the evolution of this record company mirrors the growth of Canadian music itself, since the label has always been in the forefront of developing homegrown talent. There are too many people at the company to thank for their role in helping to shape this project. Their names, however, can be found throughout these pages. But I would like to single out two individuals, beginning with Deane Cameron, whose vision and passion gave birth to this book in the first place. Deane never wavered in his belief that his company's story was an important piece of Canadian music history— and, therefore, a story worth getting right. David MacMillan, my point person at EMI, oversaw the book's production from start to finish and handled all my requests with diligence and humor—even as he juggled massive marketing campaigns for Moist and The Tea Party.

Thanks must go out to May Darmetko, Larry Delaney, Christopher Doty, *The Record*'s David Farrell, Richard Flohil, Jeanine Hollingshead, *RPM*'s Walt Grealis, CHUM's Brad Jones, *Billboard*'s Larry LeBlanc, Discovery Records' Jim Levitt, Steve McLean, Denise Magi, All That Rocks' Gerry Mikolczki, Bill Munson, Richard Patterson, Robin Selz and Doug Thompson, who all aided me in my research, either by answering simple queries or by giving me generous access to their archives. I am grateful to company founders Harvey Clarke, Johnny Downs and Ken Kerr for their inspiring stories and for the interviews granted by Al Andruchow, Bill Banham, Bill Bannon, Rob Brooks, Eddie Colero, Frank Davies, Pierre Dubord, Arnold Gosewich, Ed Leetham,

Sharon MacDonald, Bill Rotari, Tim Trombley, Paul White, Hugh Wiets and Maurice Zurba. I also want to commend Susan Girvan, senior editor at CDG Books, for keeping it all together and Todd Fujimoto, designer at Stray Toaster, for the ultra-cool style he gave to the look of the book, and Dolores Gubasta, for covering the waterfront in her photo research.

I am indebted to three friends for their personal encouragement: Gilbert Bélisle, Roger Gibbs and Kirk Makin. Finally, special thanks to my sons, Callum and Duncan, and my wife, Carol Hay. Without their unconditional love and constant support, this book would simply not have been possible.

Nicholas Jennings
December 1999

CHAPTER ONE

CANADIAN DREAMS:

1949 - 1959

The London Evening Free Press

TUESDAY, JULY 12, 1949

JOBS FOR 75 PERSONS AT NEW RECORD FIRM

CHAPTER ONE

CANADIAN DREAMS:
1949 - 1959

Perhaps it's fitting that the first disc pressed by Capitol Records of Canada in June 1949 was a song by Hollywood's Gordon MacRae. After all, Capitol's parent company had been formed in Tinseltown seven years earlier by a triumvirate made up of record-store owner Glenn Wallichs, singer-songwriter Johnny Mercer and Paramount Pictures executive Buddy DeSylva. And MacRae, an actor-singer who had successfully made the transition from radio to film, was then one of Hollywood's brightest stars.

It's significant that within a year or so of releasing MacRae's "24 Hours of Sunshine," Capitol Canada also issued "Yodeling Cowboy," a song written and sung by Canadian country-and-western artist Jack Kingston. With Kingston's cheerful tune about

Hooray for Hollywood: Johnny Mercer, Glenn Wallichs and Buddy DeSylva give birth to Capitol Records of America in Tinseltown, 1942

"yodeling under Ontario skies," the fledgling label took its first step in supporting domestic talent. It was a gesture that grew into a commitment. Over the next 50 years, the company's support of Canadian music was to deepen with each passing decade.

Overleaf: Capitol Canada's founders Scotty McLachlan (left) and Johnny Downs (right), watch as an unknown jack-hammer operator digs an opening for what would become Capitol Canada's first home, in a rundown wire and nail factory in London, Ontario (note the Canadian Pacific Railway siding in the background, critical for shipping and receiving), spring 1948

While those two discs, both 78 rpm recordings, were milestones in the history of Capitol Canada, they reveal little about the record company's difficult birth during the late 1940s. At the time, Canada, like most countries, was recovering from the trauma of the Second World War. Music seemed to be the tonic everyone needed. Radio stations flourished, jukeboxes were everywhere and phonographs became as common in homes as electric toasters.

Three major record companies were operating in Canada in the mid-1940s: Columbia, RCA Victor and Decca. The fledgling Capitol U.S. label was well aware of the Canadian market's potential if buyers could purchase

Ken Kerr (left) and Johnny Downs take a break from building what would become Capitol Canada's boiler house (the upright steam boiler and smokestack can be seen in the background), spring 1948: pioneer spirit

domestic product instead of expensive imports. In the summer of 1947, the company contacted Ken Kerr, sales manager for Sparton of Canada, in London, Ontario, which had been pressing records for Columbia since 1939. How would he like to run a Canadian operation? Kerr jumped at the chance and began working for the American label as its only Canadian employee. Almost immediately, however, the idea ran afoul of Canadian government restrictions on foreign investment that were in place at the time. Capitol dropped its plans and paid Kerr off—but not before telling him to keep in touch.

The failure of Capitol's venture left the label without access to the Canadian market. Kerr wasted no time in contacting Johnny Downs and Scotty McLachlan, two bandleaders who had both been inspired by the success of London's musical hero, Guy Lombardo, and had each done stints in the local record business: Downs had run the record bar at Simpson's (now The Bay), McLachlan had

TONIGHT---8.30
The BIGGEST SHOW of '52
FALL EDITION
NAT "King Cole"
STAN Kenton & his Great ORCHESTRA
the divine SARAH Vaughan
ALL IN PERSON...PLUS
STUMP and STUMPY
GEORGE KIRBY
TEDDY HALE
The CONGAROOS
Prices: $1.00 - $1.75 - $2.50 - $3.00
Box office open 10 a.m. to 9 p.m.
MAPLE LEAF GARDENS

worked for the Musicana label. The three hit upon the idea that if they could drum up enough local investment and start a record company, maybe they could win the contract to press Capitol's records in Canada.

It was clearly a gamble. With the help of Allan Aysworth, the London-based representative of Cochran Murray, a Toronto investment company, Kerr, McLachlan and Downs raised $25,000 from a diverse group of businesspeople from the printing, bookbinding, restaurant and agricultural product fields. The group included Bob Robarts, whose brother John became the premier of Ontario in 1961 and L.C. Bonnycastle, vice-president of the John Labatt Brewing Company. They called their enterprise Regal Records and began searching for a property in London.

Commercial properties were hard to come by in London, especially with buildings that backed on to the Canadian Pacific Railway line, critical for shipping and receiving. Eventually, a site was found, a run-down wire and nail factory at the corner of St. George and Ann Streets. In true pioneer spirit, Kerr and his cohorts set about converting the building themselves,

Downs, sales manager for Capitol Records of Canada, in his London, Ont. office, 1952: imaginative promotion

constructing a boiler house and installing all the necessary equipment, including two record-pressing machines. By August 1948, with a staff of 12, they began producing 10-inch, 78 rpm records.

Fortunately, the first Regal pressing, a recording called "You Call Everybody Darling" by Al Trace and his Orchestra, became a hit in Canada and the United States. Before long, Regal began making 78s for U.S. companies like Regent and the prestigious Savoy jazz label.

Within a year, the gamble had paid off: in June 1949, Regal landed a five-year contract to press Capitol releases in Canada. The deal was clinched by Lockwood Miller, the American founder of London's Occidental Life Insurance Company, who had invested in Regal a few months earlier. As luck would have it, Miller had been a college friend of Glenn Wallichs's in Los Angeles.

U.S. bandleader Stan Kenton, hugely popular in Canada, plays for RCAF airwomen Catherine 'Bunty' Well and Joan Creed, June 30, 1953

With Miller as president, Kerr as general manager and McLachlan and Downs in charge of the plant and sales departments, respectively, the newly formed Capitol Records of Canada (which supplanted Regal) immediately announced plans for expansion.

On July 12, the *London Free Press* reported that the company would be purchasing 8 more pressing machines, hiring up to 100 workers and increasing production from 200,000 to 2 million records a year. "For the present," the newspaper added, "only standard 78 rpm records will be made here. Records playing at 45 rpm and the firm's new Telefunken classical catalogue will be available in both standard and slow-play records later in the year."

Everything went smoothly at first, as Capitol Canada began releasing a steady stream of records by such Capitol U.S. artists as Nat King Cole, Tex Ritter and Stan Kenton, who had a dazzling young Canadian trumpeter named Maynard Ferguson in his band. After setting up distribution offices in Montreal and Toronto, Kerr headed out across Canada to develop a network of independent distributors. Then came the challenge of switching production from 78s to LPs and 45s. "It was an exciting time," recalls Kerr, now retired and living on Vancouver Island. "But it was also a bit of a nightmare, because we were pressing records at three different speeds and sizes (12-inch, 10-inch and 7-inch) all at the same time in a pretty small plant. Our press operators really had to keep their wits about them."

They certainly did. Paid by the number of discs they

Montreal-born trumpeter Maynard Ferguson hits the high notes for an audience at the University of Rochester, New York, 1958: dazzling

The recordings of husband-and-wife team Mary Ford and Les Paul were among Capitol Canada's biggest sellers in the 1950s

turned out, press operators had to contend with sometimes difficult conditions and distractions. Former press operator Corinne Morgan remembers how hot it got during the summer. "The machines heated up the shellac, or the plastic 'biscuit,' so it would soften and you could mash it down with the stamper," explains Morgan. The stamper, in turn, imbedded the grooves that carried the recorded sounds. "It was like operating a hamburger grill." Meanwhile, there was no air conditioning. With the shipping doors open to try to cool things down, passing CP freight steam engines would occasionally spew clouds of black smoke into the plant. Admits Kerr: "It was pretty noisy and smelly when that happened."

More often than not, however, the good times outweighed the bad—especially when sales were good. One of Capitol Canada's first major-selling records was Nat King Cole's "Mona Lisa." The tender ballad, with Cole's liquid vocals pouring over a velvety backing of lush strings, transcended all the usual musical boundaries in the fall and winter of 1950. "We sure pressed a lot of those," recalls Kerr, who adds that the single sold well over 100,000 copies—enough for a platinum award by today's standards.

Other big sellers in the early 1950s included "How High the Moon" by the husband-and-wife team Les Paul and Mary Ford, "Wheel of Fortune" by torchy pop vocalist Kay Starr and "I Yust Go Nuts at Christmas" by Scandinavian jokester Yogi Yorgesson. Although jazz and country sides by the likes of Stan Kenton and Tex Ritter never sold as well nor received nearly

Cole, backstage at Theatre Rochester in New York, 1958: almost everything the ultra-smooth singer touched turned to gold

HOW HIGH THE MOON

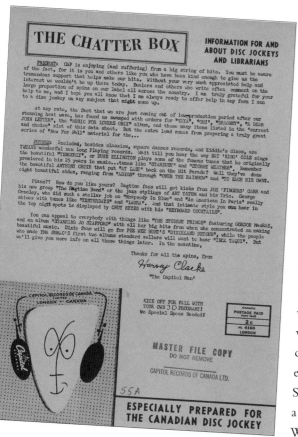

Canadians Guy Lombardo and Gisele MacKenzie, seen here in a CBC radio studio, found a happy home on Capitol

THE CHATTER BOX

INFORMATION FOR AND ABOUT DISC JOCKEYS AND LIBRARIANS

ESPECIALLY PREPARED FOR THE CANADIAN DISC JOCKEY

as much airplay in Canada as those pop hits, tunes like Kenton's "Peanut Vendor" and Ritter's "High Noon" (the theme song of the Gary Cooper western of the same name) enjoyed brisk business with jukebox operators.

Kerr and Downs, working with branch managers Lee Mendel in Montreal and Jack Earthy in Toronto, often came up with imaginative promotional ideas for the company's releases. One such gimmick was reported in the *Toronto Star*'s "Turntable Talk" column on November 18, 1950. Columnist Hugh Thomson wrote: "Just this minute a young lady visited us with an intriguing carton from Capitol Records. It contains generous samples of biscuits and the enclosed note reads, 'underneath is June Christy's newest Capitol biscuit,' the songstress's latest 45 rpm single of 'He Can Come Back' and 'A Mile Down the Highway.'" Added Thomson whimsically: "We haven't sampled the disc, but we never knew we had so many friends in the office till we started in on the cookies."

Whenever Capitol artists came to Canada, Kerr and his staff kept them busy with radio-station interviews and record-store signings. CBC Radio and Jack Kent Cooke's CKEY station in Toronto were regular stops on such visits, as were the Eaton's and Simpson's department stores, both major players in the record retail business. Sometimes the visiting artists led to a few eyebrow-raising encounters. When Tex Ritter came through, Kerr found his views extreme—even by Cold War standards. "Ritter had made a record called 'The Fiery Bear,'" recalls Kerr, "about Russia and the communists. He was very anti-communist, a real Joseph McCarthy type, but otherwise a heck of a nice guy, and very easy to work with."

In the early 1950s, radio was the best showcase for music. Harvey Clarke, Capitol's energetic advertising and promotion manager, kept disc jockeys informed with a chatty newsletter called, appropriately, *The Chatter Box*. Each issue thanked the DJs for "all the spins," and always carried the signature "Harvey Clarke, The Capitol Man." Numerous Canadian singers launched their careers with radio programs, including Winnipeg's Juliette and Gisele MacKenzie. In fact, Clarke wound up working with the vivacious MacKenzie, whose "Meet Gisele" show on CBC Radio eventually led to her getting work on "Club 15" radio show in Hollywood in 1951 and a recording contract with Capitol. After enjoying hit singles like "Don't Let the Stars Get in Your Eyes," MacKenzie went on to even bigger fame as a TV star.

Audio experiments by adventurers like Les Baxter produced eyebrow-raising results—known in the ironic '90s as "exotica"

Gleason's hilarious characters, well known to television viewers, moved over to vinyl, complete with the comedian's accompanying songs

By early 1954, Capitol Records of Canada had pressed more than 5 million discs. Even more significant was the company's share of the market: 12 per cent in Canada, compared to 10 per cent in the United States. None of this was lost on the Los Angeles–based company, which saw the profit potential, especially in light of word that restrictions on foreign investment had by then been lifted. The board of directors promptly voted to create a wholly owned Canadian subsidiary. The contract with its London, Ontario, partners would not be renewed and all future pressing and distribution would be arranged by the company itself. This news spelled the end of London's recording industry. Earlier in the year, Columbia had announced that it was transfer-

Legendary EMI recording artist Edith Piaf, with a debonair Dean Martin in the late '50s

ring its franchise from Sparton in London, to Quality Records in Toronto.

In September, the newly incorporated Capitol Record Distributors of Canada opened an office at 318 Richmond Street West in Toronto and hired Harold Smith as general manager. RCA was contracted to press all Capitol releases from its plant in Smiths Falls, Ontario. While Harold Smith built a sales and distribution network, he was aided by the fact that Capitol U.S. was launching a new breed of singers led by Frank Sinatra. This was the pre-rock 'n' roll era and Sinatra, who had already been a bobby-soxer and sung novelty pop songs, had just moved into the next phase of his recording career: saloon ballads and swing tunes. Smith had plenty of material to work with. From February 1954 to September 1955, Capitol released two Sinatra albums and seven singles, beginning with "Young at Heart."

In January 1955, Britain's EMI (Electric and Musical Industries) bought a controlling interest in Capitol Records, including Capitol in Canada. The company had a long and celebrated history in the recording business, dating back to the invention of the gramophone in the late nineteenth century. Although EMI's acquisition of Capitol had little effect on the Canadian operation at first, a strong cultural affinity with the English owners would become advantageous in a decade's time, during the so-called "British Invasion."

Doo-woppers The Four Freshmen had a supportive fan in Stan Kenton

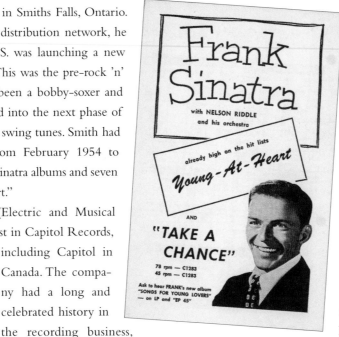

Aside from Sinatra and EMI's takeover, 1955 was the year of doo-wop. While Columbia and Mercury had signed Toronto's The Four Lads, The Diamonds and The Crew-Cuts, Capitol landed California's The Four Preps, described as the "Pat Boone" of vocal groups because of their clean-cut image, and The Four Freshmen, a vocal outfit from Indianapolis. The

Freshmen had a big fan in Stan Kenton, who was so impressed by their sound that he telephoned Capitol and arranged a recording contract. The group scored several hits, including "Day by Day" and "Graduation Day."

Rock 'n' roll shook and shimmied its way into Canada the following year. In April 1956, Bill Haley and the Comets performed the first rock concert at Toronto's Maple Leaf Gardens. That same month, Elvis Presley topped the Canadian charts with "Heartbreak Hotel" on RCA. Presley enjoyed two other number one hits that year in Canada with "Hound Dog" and "Love Me Tender." By April 1957, he headlined his own sold-out shows at the Gardens and was a bona fide superstar.

Capitol didn't immediately leap into the rock revolution. But the label did sign Gene Vincent, a rockabilly hellcat from Norfolk, Virginia, whose dark, denim-and-leather looks were featured in the movie *The Girl Can't Help It*. Like Presley's sultry "Hound Dog," Vincent's sizzling "Be-Bop-a-Lula" was the rock 'n' roll shot heard around the world in 1956. No other artist captured rock's rebellious spirit quite like Vincent.

Late in '56, Capitol Canada's Harold Smith found new quarters for

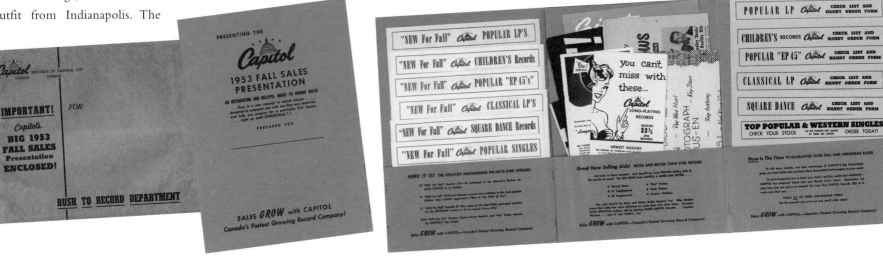

Sparky's discs were leaders among long-playing albums in the famous line of children's records on Capitol

Bozo, the Capitol Clown, was an icon of the times and his recordings remained popular with children and adults alike throughout the 1950s

the company: a warehouse on Toronto's Queen Street, just east of the Don River. It was a good move. The building, which Capitol shared with Coca-Cola, had plenty of space for future expansion and was conveniently located across from a friendly watering hole, the Edwin Hotel, where Capitol employees often gathered after work.

Soon, there were indeed signs of growth for the Canadian company. First, it landed a prestigious artist via Hollywood: Guy Lombardo. It was fitting that Lombardo, Canada's best-selling artist at the time, should join a record label that had Canadian roots in his hometown. Fitting, too, that the first single the celebrated bandleader waxed for Capitol was the song for which he became best known: "Auld Lang Syne." Then, the following year, the company formed the Capitol Record Club of Canada, as a way of attracting more consumers to its many

releases, which by now numbered in the hundreds.

Meanwhile, Smith unwittingly hired someone that year who would play a significant role in the company's growth over the next decade. For the time being, however, Paul White would have a humble beginning in the shipping department. A journalist "straight off the boat" from England, White wasn't used to

Lewis and Martin translated their buddy movie roles into hotly sought-after 7-inchers such as this wacky disc

loading and unloading boxes in a warehouse. He soon got the hang of it and stacked the boxes of records according to the catalogue numbers printed on the sides. "In shipping, you quickly learned which were the best-sellers," recalls White. "It was great experience."

White still remembers the catalogue number of Capitol's best-seller at the time. "It was SW740," laughs White, "the soundtrack to *The King and I.* Boy, I stacked a lot of those." Other top-selling releases included soundtracks to *Carousel* and *Oklahoma*, pop releases by Nat King Cole, Frank Sinatra and Dean Martin, and the latest country releases from Faron

Lombardo: the first single he recorded for Capitol, 'Auld Lang Syne,' was the song for which he became best known

Young, Ferlin Husky and Tennessee Ernie Ford. One of the hippest releases was Miles Davis's *Birth of the Cool*, featuring the groundbreaking, orchestrated jazz arrangements of Canada's Gil Evans. "There was a pretty wide range of music coming through, and we listened to all of it in the back as we worked," admits White.

A hard-working self-starter, White soon found himself promoted from the backroom to the front office, where he worked on the order desk. He still had to keep track of catalogue numbers, but now he could see where the hits were coming from. "Our Ontario salesmen would

MUSIC world

MARCH 1958

Volume 1, Number 19 25¢

The story of ED SULLIVAN

Special illustrated article in this issue

CANADA'S ONLY POPULAR MUSIC PUBLICATION

return on Fridays," recalls White, "after going all over the province during the week. Then the orders would start pouring in." He adds: "In those days, there weren't retail chains. You still had individuals from stores calling up to place orders. They'd want so many boxes of this 45 or 20 copies of that LP. You could quickly see which things were becoming hits."

Harvey Clarke (second on right), Capitol Canada's advertising and promotion manager, sits in on an interview with John Dickens (left), of London, Ont.'s CFPL, bandleader Ray Anthony and singer Marci Miller

In the spring of 1957, Toronto radio station CHUM began publishing a chart, the first of its kind in Canada. Presley's "All Shook Up" on RCA topped the inaugural chart, but it wouldn't be long before Capitol artists were enjoying the same honour. That year also saw the debut of *Music World*, a biweekly magazine which billed itself as "Canada's Only

Publication Devoted to Popular Music." Published by Ray Sonin, a radio DJ at Toronto's CFRB, it carried industry news, artist features and a review section with picks by a columnist known only as "The Spinner." The magazine became an instant source of advertising for Capitol Canada, as national promotion manager Sterling "Whitey" Haines ran notices for the label's latest singles and albums recommended by local DJs.

Over the next two years, Capitol went from strength to strength in Canada. In 1958, the label hit the number one spot on the influential CHUM chart with The Kingston Trio's "Tom Dooley," the song that sparked the folk boom in which Canadians would play such a large role. Other Capitol hits at the time included

CHUM HIT PARADE CHART: Week of Nov. 3, 1958

	TITLE	ARTIST	LABEL	POSITION LAST WEEK	No. OF WEEKS ON CHART
1.	TOM DOOLEY	Kingston Trio	Capitol	2	5
2.	IT'S ONLY MAKE BELIEVE	Conway Twitty	MGM	1	6
3.	I GOT STUNG/ONE NIGHT	Elvis Presley	RCA Victor	Pickhit	1
4.	TOPSY (Part II)	Cozy Cole	Sparton	3	5
5.	THE END	Earl Grant	Decca	5	6
6.	MEXICAN HAT ROCK	Apple Jacks	Cameo	12	5
7.	FOR MY GOOD FORTUNE/GEE BUT IT'S LONELY	Pat Boone	Dot	7	7
8.	QUEEN OF THE HOP	Bobby Darin	Atco	17	5
9.	IT'S ALL IN THE GAME	Tommy Edwards	MGM	4	10
10.	COME ON LET'S GO	Ritchie Valens	Apex	15	5
11.	The Day the Rains Came	Jane Morgan Raymond Lefevre	Kapp Barkley		
12.	Forget Me Not	Kalin Twins	Decca		
13.	Chantilly Lace	Big Bopper	Mercury		
14.	Stairway to the Sea/Call Me	Johnny Mathis	Columbia		
15.	I Got A Feeling/Lonesome Town	Ricky Nelson	Imperial		
16.	La-Do-Dada	Dale Hawkins	Quality		
17.	Hideaway	Four Esquires	Quality		
18.	Tea For Two Cha Cha	Tommy Dorsey	Decca		
19.	No One But You/Pussy Cat	Ames Brothers	RCA Victor		
20.	Susie Darlin'	Robin Luke	Dot		
21.	Summertime Blues	Eddie Cochran	London		
22.	Guaglione	Perez Prado	RCA Victor		
23.	You Cheated	The Shields	Dot		
24.	Mr. Success	Frank Sinatra	Capitol		
25.	Walking Along	The Diamonds	Mercury		
26.	The Blob	Five Blobs	Columbia		
27.	Fibbin'	Patti Page	Mercury		
28.	What Little Girl/I'll Wait For You	Frankie Avalon	Reo		
29.	Just Young	Andy Rose	Delta		
30.	You Want Love/Once In a While	Clyde Stacy	Regency		
31.	Firefly	Tony Bennett	Columbia		
32.	There Goes My Heart	Joni James	MGM		
33.	With Your Love	Jack Scott	Carlton		
34.	Sweetheart/Light of Love	Peggy Lee	Capitol		
35.	Leave Me Alone	Dicky Doo & The Don'ts	Quality		
36.	Love Makes The World Go Round	Perry Como	RCA Victor		
37.	Non Dimenticar	Nat King Cole	Capitol		
38.	Tears On My Pillow	The Imperials	Quality		
39.	Brand New Heartache (EP)	Everly Bros.	Apex		
40.	Once Upon A Time	Dean Martin	Capitol		
41.	No One Knows	Dione & The Belmonts	Reo		
42.	Love Is All We Need	Tommy Edwards	MGM		
43.	To Know Him is to Love Him	The Teddy Bears	Dore		
44.	I'll Remember Tonight	Pat Boone	Dot		
45.	Need You	Donnie Owens	Reo		
46.	Promise Me Love	Andy Williams	Apex		
47.	Near You	Roger Williams	Kapp		
48.	Beep Beep	Playmates	Apex		
49.	Mocking Bird	Four Lads	Columbia		
50.	Bo Diddley (EP)	Jimmie Rodgers	Apex		
50.	Problems/Love Of My Life	Everly Bros.	Apex		

Dean Martin's "Return to Me" (#5), Frank Sinatra's "Witchcraft" (#9) and Ray Anthony's "Peter Gunn Theme" (#12). By 1959, Capitol had also acquired EMI's distinguished Angel catalogue of classical recordings and the Pathé Marconi catalogue of French pop music. In fact, the company had grown so rapidly that it took over all three floors of its Queen Street building.

Paul White, meanwhile, was moving quickly through the company's ranks. When national promotion manager Whitey Haines needed an assistant, he looked no further than the affable Englishman. Recalls White: "I was involved in a record industry bowling league and used to write this blurb sheet about it that people thought was fun. Haines saw that I could write, so he put me to work writing the blurbs that went out with the singles." Then when Haines, a part-time songwriter in his own right, went to work for BMI Canada, the performing rights society, he recommended White for

Trumpeter Miles Davis: his revolutionary Birth of the Cool *recordings with Canada's Gil Evans forever changed the course of jazz*

his job. Smith didn't hesitate in promoting him. For White, it would prove a most auspicious posting, as the company—renamed, once again, Capitol Records of Canada—looked ahead to the next decade full of confidence and optimism.

GIL EVANS

CAPITOL
1949

Evans: one of the greatest composer-arrangers in the history of jazz

Svengali is an apt anagram of his name. Although usually credited as arranger-composer, pianist or bandleader, Canadian-born Gil Evans played a much larger role for a group of younger musicians at the dawn of the 1950s. The group was the Miles Davis Orchestra, featuring Gerry Mulligan, Lee Konitz and others. Evans presided over them like an *éminence grise*, acting as musical mentor, sage and all-round spiritual adviser. Out of gatherings at Evans's New York apartment came Davis's legendary *Birth of the Cool* recordings on Capitol.

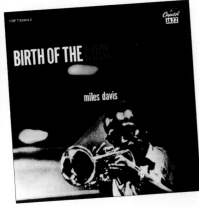

Based on ideas Evans developed for the Claude Thornhill Orchestra, the revolutionary *Birth of the Cool* featured instrumentation and arrangements that were considered wildly unconventional for jazz at the time. Along with French horn and tuba, the recordings incorporated richly textured, almost impressionistic sounds. The creative synergy between Evans and Davis also laid the foundation for the pair's trilogy of majestic albums for Columbia, *Miles Ahead*, *Porgy and Bess* and *Sketches of Spain*, that are now widely regarded as some of the finest recordings in jazz history.

Born Ian Ernest Gilmore Green in Toronto in 1912, he moved early and often as a child. The family eventually settled in Stockton,

California, near San Francisco, where Evans first caught the remote radio broadcasts of Louis Armstrong, Fletcher Henderson, Duke Ellington and other jazz pioneers. A self-taught musician, Evans formed his first jazz group in high school and then led a Stockton band between 1933–38. His band landed a featured spot on Bob Hope's radio show before Claude Thornhill hired him as an arranger in 1941. Except for a three-year stint in the army, Evans remained with the bandleader until 1948.

It was Evans's work for Thornhill, especially his orchestrations of bebop numbers, that first won Davis's admiration. The two met when Evans requested permission to arrange the trumpeter's "Donna Lee" for Thornhill, and Davis, in turn, asked if he could study the musical charts of Evans's arrangement. The exchange led to a series of meetings at Evans's Manhattan apartment, a damp room in the basement of a building behind a Chinese laundry. There, Evans, Davis and a group of musicians from Evans's circle and several bop groups began rehearsing an adventurous brand of jazz. Initially, their efforts were heard only in club performances. But Davis, who had signed with Capitol in 1949, convinced the label to record his "impressions in modern music" project.

The *Birth of the Cool* recordings were released in various formats, beginning as 78 rpm singles in 1949–50 and later 45 rpm singles. An album titled *Classics of Jazz* came out in 1954, featuring eight numbers. Three years later, Capitol released an expanded version, including Evans's arrangement of "Boplicity," written by Evans and Davis under the pseudonym Cleo Henry, the name of the trumpeter's mother. This 1957 release marked the first time the recordings were titled *Birth of the Cool*, a name suggested by Capitol U.S. executive Pete Rugolo. Evans's contribution was singled out by critic Andre Hodeir. "'Boplicity,'" he wrote in 1954, "is enough to qualify Gil Evans as one of jazz's greatest composer-arrangers."

After he and Davis collaborated on *Miles Ahead*, Evans was in constant demand for studio work. A year later, he was a recording bandleader in his own right and performed at New York's Birdland in 1959. Ever the musical explorer, Evans went on to experiment with electronic instruments and rock and r&b rhythms in the 1960s. He and his orchestra recorded *The Music of Jimi Hendrix* for RCA, and often performed the legendary guitarist's material in concert. In the 1970s, he led a series of big-band projects, while

In the studio: taking the music along the path to orchestral maturity

the early 1980s saw him score films such as *Absolute Beginners* and *The Color of Money*. He died in 1988 at the age of 75 and was posthumously inducted into the Canadian Music Hall of Fame in 1997.

A true innovator, Evans took jazz to unprecedented heights. As the respected U.S. jazz critic Leonard Feather put it: "Despite the complexity of his work on every level—melodic, rhythmic, tonal and especially harmonic—Evans, like Duke Ellington, has remained rooted to jazz and as a consequence has succeeded in taking the music a step further along the path to orchestral maturity."

MAYNARD FERGUSON

CAPITOL
1950

With bandleader Stan Kenton at the keyboard

"The sputnik of jazz." That's how jazz critic Leonard Feather described Canadian trumpeter Maynard Ferguson in 1958 in *Downbeat* magazine. "[Ferguson] tore off madly into outer space during 1950," the respected American critic wrote, "using the Stan Kenton orchestra as his vehicle and stratospheric high notes as his fuel."

Feather's imagery may have been a product of the times, but he was right about one thing: Ferguson's rise was nothing short of meteoric. A child prodigy who held his first union card before he entered high school, Ferguson began his career playing alongside fellow Montreal musician Oscar Peterson in Ferguson's brother's band. After moving to New York in 1948, he was soon on a fast track to stardom. Still barely out of his teens, Ferguson began turning heads, first in Boyd Raeburn's big band, then with Jimmy Dorsey and Charlie Barnett. Almost immediately, his dazzling technique and piercing high-note style became the talk of the music world.

In 1949, Stan Kenton, a bandleader known for his adventurous tastes, recruited Ferguson to join his Innovations in Modern Music orchestra. Ferguson's soloing, especially on numbers like "All the Things You Are," soon became a staple of Kenton's shows and his albums on Capitol Records. Ferguson recorded four singles for Capitol himself, including the explosive "Love Locked Out." In 1950, the young man with the horn was honoured with first prize as best trumpeter in *Downbeat*'s annual poll, an achievement he repeated for three successive years.

Ferguson: a meteoric rise from Montreal prodigy to international jazz sensation

His tenure with Kenton wasn't without controversy. For every rave review Ferguson received there seemed to be another that criticized his high-register screeching style. "Ferguson's solo," sniffed one critic, "is a wonderful example of a trumpet man imitating the range of a tin flute." Even Leonard Feather initially believed that Ferguson was "a freak artist to whom the upper register was all."

Ferguson simply forged ahead. After being hired by Paramount Pictures as first-call studio trumpeter, he left Kenton to record a series of film soundtracks, including the biblical epic *The Ten Commandments*.

Then came another breakthrough: a prestigious performance with Leonard Bernstein and the New York Philharmonic Orchestra. Soon, he was leading all-star jazz bands from New York to Los Angeles.

By the time he formed his own 13-piece band in 1957, Ferguson had effectively silenced his detractors. Feather himself was forced to recant: "[Ferguson] was criticized, sometimes with undue harshness, by this writer," he admitted. "He took the criticism like a gentleman and a well-adjusted human being. Today, playing valve trombone as well as trumpet, he reveals a far wider musical scope than we had suspected; his brash, often exciting orchestra has provided some of the best band sounds of the past year." Before the decade was out, *Downbeat* voted the Maynard Ferguson Orchestra first place in the "new star" big-band division.

Ferguson went on to lead many fine bands, and groom some exceptional talent along the way. The list of solo artists who have performed with him reads like a who's who of jazz: Chick Corea, Bob James, Chuck Mangione, Slide Hampton, Wayne Shorter, Peter Erskine and Joe Zawinul. And he achieved mainstream popularity when his recording of "Gonna Fly Now," the theme from the hit film *Rocky*, resulted in a Top-10 single, a gold album and a Grammy nomination in 1978.

Ferguson, who turned 71 in 1999, will always be remembered for his awesome solos on Stan Kenton's records and for rekindling the public's interest in big bands during the '80s and '90s with his own Big Bop Nouveau Band. Now regarded as the world's premier big-band leader, the "sputnik of jazz" launched a legend that will remain in orbit for many years to come.

His dazzling technique and piercing high-note style became the talk of the music world

GUY LOMBARDO

CAPITOL
1956

For many people, New Year's Eve is synonymous with "Auld Lang Syne." And for many years, Canadian bandleader Guy Lombardo was inextricably linked with the Scottish ballad. Lombardo's velvety version of the tune, broadcast annually across North America from The Grill at New York's Hotel Roosevelt (and later from the grand ballroom of the Waldorf Astoria), became as much the signal of a new year as champagne, streamers and the giddy countdown to midnight on December 31.

In fact, for several New Year's Eves, Lombardo's performance could be heard on two rival U.S. radio networks, neither of which could bear to broadcast their celebrations without him. "On these occasions," *The New Yorker* reported in 1957, "CBS bagged him for the last fifteen minutes of the old year, and NBC for the first fifteen of the new." Added the magazine wryly: "Between them, they stretched out the stroke of midnight considerably."

That Lombardo and his orchestra, the Royal Canadians, could have such an impact is not altogether surprising, given their popularity throughout the 1930s, '40s and '50s. They survived the stock-market crash and became the most successful dance band of all time, selling 7 million copies of their recordings in 1947 alone. Within ten years, Lombardo and his brothers—Carmen, Lebert and Victor, all of whom played in the band—were collectively earning

Lombardo with ballroom dancers: the bandleader enjoyed a massive international following playing 'the sweetest music this side of heaven'

Local hero: admiring the street named after him in his hometown of London, Ontario

$1 million a year while performing at presidential balls in Washington and World Series games at Yankee Stadium. Although his detractors dubbed him the "Prince of Wails" and the "King of Corn" for his tremulous, sentimental style, Lombardo was proud that fans and the music industry could count on him to deliver a dependable, popular and profitable product.

Lombardo was eldest of seven children, born in 1902, in London, Ontario, to an Italian tailor and his wife. Gaetano (as he was christened, after his father) proved his musical-leadership ability at an early age. When he was 15, he formed the Lombardo Brothers' Orchestra and Concert Company and soon landed the group a major engagement at an outdoor dance pavilion in Grand Bend, Ontario. After performing in his hometown's Winter Garden, Lombardo and the band, renamed the Royal Canadians, started playing regularly in Cleveland and Chicago. In 1929, they began a 33-year residency at New York's Roosevelt Grill. Already, the group billed its sound as "the sweetest music this side of Heaven," a variation on a tribute paid by Chicago music critic Ashton Stevens.

Lombardo had a knack for knowing what the public wanted to hear. Improvisation was out of the question, a fact that drew scorn from jazz aficionados—as did the band's muted rhythm section. One story went that Lombardo once led his band through a radio broadcast without realizing that his drummer, caught in a traffic jam, was not in attendance. "We've never been able to see much music in a drum," he later confessed. Instead, he insisted that the group's music be easy to dance to, have a catchy melody and bear the identifiable mark of the Royal Canadians. The formula worked: Lombardo's many hits, first on Decca and, beginning in 1956, on Capitol, included "Star Dust," "Easter Parade," "Winter Wonderland" and "*The Third Man* Theme." The Royal Canadians remained a lucrative force right up until Lombardo's death in 1977, with total sales of recordings reaching the $300 million (U.S.) mark.

"I never switch to a fad," Lombardo told *The New Yorker* in 1957. "There's been bop and swing, and there was a time when everybody was on a Latin-American kick, and now there's rock-and-roll. They come and they go, like waves, and we ride them out. The trouble with a fad is that if a band takes it up wholeheartedly, when the fad dies out— as it's bound to, sooner or later—the band dies with it."

GISELE MacKENZIE

CAPITOL
1951

She was Canada's singing sweetheart when Anne Murray was still in diapers. The host of her own CBC radio show in the 1940s, Winnipeg's Gisele MacKenzie went on to become the darling of Hollywood in the 1950s, a star of both stage and screen. "The Girl Who Can Do Anything," *Newsweek* called her when she was the magazine's cover girl in October 1956. Singer, violinist, pianist, comedian, dancer and actress. For a time, she really could do it all.

Born Gisele LaFleche in Winnipeg in 1927, the second oldest of five children, MacKenzie grew up to hate the violin—although it would later prove to be the key to stardom. Her disdain for the instrument was a reaction to music lessons imposed on her by strict parents when she was seven. "I never had the time to play with other kids," she once recalled, "[because] musically, I was the chosen one. Dad always wanted at least one of his children to play the violin well [and] Mother decided it would be me."

Sent at age 14 to study at the Royal Conservatory of Music in Toronto, she quickly discovered that being able to sing and play the piano made her popular at the girls' school she attended. Within five years she was doing it on the air, hosting CBC Radio's "Meet Gisele." When a CBC producer later recommended her to an agency in New York, she got to sing there with Percy Faith's orchestra. A bigger break came in 1951, when she was invited to replace The Andrew Sisters on Bob Crosby's "Club 15" radio show in Hollywood. At the time, an advertising executive for the show suggested she change her name from LaFleche. "It makes you sound like a stripper," he told her. She promptly adopted her paternal grandmother's family name.

MacKenzie began recording for Capitol in Los Angeles during her two years on "Club 15," heard across North America on the CBS network. One of her first assignments was to record a series of duets with actor Gordon MacRae *(Oklahoma, Carousel)*, a prospect that initially terrified the young singer. "After all," MacKenzie told one interviewer, "it's difficult to sing a love song with someone you've just met." But the movie star immediately put her at ease and the pairing proved successful. She also recorded a string of singles herself, including three that made the Top 20 in 1953: "La Fiacre" (#20), "Adios" (#14) and "Don't Let the Stars Get in Your Eyes" (#11).

MacKenzie's radio work came to an end with the cancellation of Crosby's show in the spring of 1953. She hit the road, performing concerts and promoting her singles, some of which, like "Don't Let the Stars Get in Your Eyes," had already made the charts. Then, while performing in Ottawa, opportunity knocked once again: Jack Benny wanted her to join his vaudeville show in San Francisco. MacKenzie jumped at the chance and it led to a spot on Benny's TV program, *The Jack Benny Show*.

Benny discovered MacKenzie could play the violin and worked out a skit in which he pretended to teach her a piece, only to have her turn

Winnipeg-born MacKenzie, with George Burns and Jack Benny

With Groucho Marx

With Lucille Ball and Dezi Arnez: a singing star of stage and screen

around and deliver a virtuoso-like performance. With Benny's trademark egg-on-his-face expression, it brought the house down. The violin routine—as well as MacKenzie's wit and style—quickly established her as a versatile performer and led to a regular spot on TV's popular "Your Hit Parade" program, where she appeared from 1953–57.

In 1955, MacKenzie recorded a top-selling kids' album for Capitol, *Gisele MacKenzie Sings Children's Songs from France*, and later starred in such musicals as *South Pacific, Annie Get Your Gun* and *The King and I*. Her star shone brightest in 1957 when she landed her own television show on NBC, complete with a staff that included orchestra leader Raymond Scott, choreographer Jack Regas and such guests as Jimmy Durante. Suddenly she was a "personality," proclaimed by *Look* magazine as "TV's happy amalgam of beauty and ebullience."

Although "The Gisele MacKenzie Show" lasted only one season, a victim of vocal overdose (it followed two hours of programs hosted by singers Perry Como, Dean Martin and Polly Bergen), it raised MacKenzie's profile and fees substantially. As the decade came to a close, the singer was playing month-long engagements at the prestigious Empire Room of New York's Waldorf Astoria and earning $15,000 for a week at the glamorous Flamingo Hotel in Las Vegas.

Now retired from show business and living in North Hollywood, Gisele MacKenzie will always be remembered as both Canada's "First Lady of Song" and America's "Girl Who Can Do Anything."

SALLI TERRI

CAPITOL
1957

A Canadian by birth, Salli Terri enjoyed considerable fame south of the border in the late 1950s and early '60s, as a singer of stage and screen, as well as numerous recordings for the Capitol label.

Born in London, Ontario, in 1935, the daughter of a career violinist and conductor and his amateur vocalist wife, Terri (née Stella Tirri) moved at a young age with her family to Detroit. There, she studied music at Wayne State University before eventually settling in California. While performing with the Roger Wagner Chorale in Los Angeles, Terri was heard by Laurindo Almeida, a Brazilian guitarist who had come to the United States to play with Stan Kenton. Almeida was struck by her mezzo-soprano voice and suggested a collaboration. The result was *Duets With the Spanish Guitar*, a mixture of classical works and traditional folk songs from the United States and Latin America. The 1957 Capitol release won a prestigious Grammy Award and led to two follow-up recordings.

From there, Terri went on to a successful solo career, recording several popular albums of her own. *Songs of Enchantment* (Capitol) was a collection of children's songs, while *Songs of the American Land* (Angel/EMI) featured such well-known folk tunes as "Red River Valley," "Home on

Terri: a voice that was "sweet and clear, well shaded and carefully controlled"

the Range" and "My Old Kentucky Home." Following a performance in 1961 at the Ashgrove club in Los Angeles, *Variety* described her voice as "sweet and clear, well shaded and carefully controlled."

Terri then took her love of Early American music into the academic field, where she lectured on the subject at various universities. Married to composer John Biggs, creator of the John Biggs Consort, she landed singing roles in several movies, including in the 1960 musical *Bells are Ringing*, starring Judy Holliday and Dean Martin, and the 1962 epic *How the West Was Won*, with John Wayne, Jimmy Stewart and Henry Fonda.

Although she worked with artists ranging from Aaron Copland and

Salli with Brazilian guitarist Laurindo Almeida: together, they won a 1957 Grammy Award for their Duets with the Spanish Guitar

Igor Stravinsky to Danny Kaye and Dinah Shore, Salli Terri will always be best known as the vocalist who accompanied Almeida on those classic collaborations, which *High Fidelity* magazine described as "luscious duets of wide appeal, beguilingly performed."

A gifted mezzo-soprano who excelled in both folk and classical fields

NAT KING COLE

CAPITOL
1943

"Unforgettable," the title of one of his biggest hits, also accurately describes the voice of Nat King Cole, whose warm, ultra-smooth singing style made him one of the biggest stars of the 1950s. As *The Guinness Who's Who of Fifties Music* puts it: "Nat Cole's voice, which floats butter-won't-melt vowel sounds in an easy, dark drawl, is one of the great moments of black music, and no matter how sugary the arrangements he always managed to sing as if it mattered."

Born Nathanial Adams Cole in Montgomery, Alabama, in 1917, Nat King Cole was one of the first artists signed to the newly formed Capitol label in Los Angeles in the early 1940s. Although his instrumental trio was a favourite of jazz fans, it wasn't until he started singing that his popularity really began to soar. After recording "The Christmas Song" with an orchestra in 1946, Cole often added strings to sweeten his trio's accompaniment of his vocals. From that point on, almost everything he touched turned to gold, including "Nature Boy," "Mona Lisa," "Orange Colored Sky" (with Stan Kenton), "Smile," "The Sand and the Sea" and "Dance Ballerina Dance."

A pioneer who cut across racial barriers, Cole was the first black jazz artist to have his own weekly radio show from 1948–49. He appeared on "The Ed Sullivan Show" in the mid-50s and starred in several movies, including *China Gate* and *St. Louis Blues*, in which he played composer W.C. Handy. Cole also landed his own television series in 1956, the first major TV breakthrough for a black performer.

None of these accomplishments were easily achieved. Racism remained a powerful and insidious force within North American society in the 1950s. During his first trip to Las Vegas, segrega-

tion kept Cole and his musicians out of the city's casinos, hotel rooms and swimming pools. When he bought a house in fashionable Beverly Hills, he was met by an outcry of objections from his white neighbours. Even his TV series was tainted by racial prejudice: despite Cole's popularity, the show's advertising agency claimed it could not find a national sponsor (Cole quit in protest after one season). The lowest point came in 1956, when he was attacked by group of white supremacists during a performance in Birmingham, Alabama, with British bandleader Ted Heath's orchestra, forcing an unnerved Cole to cancel several dates to recuperate.

Cole had mostly happier experiences touring Canada in the 1950s, which he did several times. However, discrimination was not unheard of. When Cole arrived to perform in Toronto for the week of November 13, 1950, at the Loew's Uptown theatre, Capitol Canada's Ken Kerr greeted him and arranged to book him into a hotel. But the "finer" establishments in Toronto turned him down. "We wanted to put Cole up at either the Royal York or the King Edward," recalls Kerr, "but they wouldn't take him. We wound up having to go to the St. Regis Hotel over on Sherbourne Street, which was a bit of a dump."

Cole's week-long stand at the Loew's was far more successful. As was customary in those days, theatres booked music and variety shows together with the latest Hollywood movie to create a more attractive, vaudeville-style entertainment package. Following the screening of *Dial 1119*, a thriller starring Marshall Thompson, Cole and his trio headlined a show that included Ellis McLintock's local orchestra, singer Yvette, comedian Jack E. Leonard, a family of dancers and a marionette act. All for the price of 44 cents, plus tax. There were full houses every night.

During Cole's stay in Toronto, Kerr took the singer around for radio station interviews and in-store appearances. It was an unusually busy week. "Every station wanted to see him," recalls Kerr, "and we arranged for him to sign autographs at Sam Sniderman's (Sam the Record Man) and the major department stores. He was very popular." After the final night's performance, Capitol

Singer-pianist Nat 'King' Cole greets a couple of starstruck Ontario Provincial Police officers backstage in London, Ont.

Canada threw a catered party for Cole on the Loew's stage. Says Kerr: "All the local deejays came and Cole's wife, Maria, was there. It was quite an affair."

Cole returned to Toronto in November 1952, performing on a bill with Sarah Vaughan and fellow Capitol artist Stan Kenton at Maple Leaf Gardens. *Toronto Telegram* reviewer Stan Helleur called Cole's "suave balladeering" one of the highlights of the show. With his memorable vocals and genial style, Cole remained a favourite with Canadian audiences until his death in 1965.

STAN KENTON

CAPITOL
1943

In the post-war years of the 1940s and early '50s, Canadians had an unabashed love affair with dance bands. From the Vancouver Hotel's Panorama Roof to Toronto's Casa Loma and Montreal's Mount Royal Hotel, they jitterbugged and swayed to the sounds of one swing orchestra after another. But of all the big bands that toured and recorded in those heady days following the Second World War, few could match U.S. pianist-bandleader Stan Kenton's for popularity or sophistication.

Unlike his more conventional competitors, Kenton displayed a willingness to experiment with the big-band sound. His first single for Capitol in 1943, "Artistry in Rhythm" (the band's theme), featured an introduction, out-of-tempo stretches and a Chopin-like piano solo. And the band became known for its staccato reed-section style as much as

Kenton: few big bands could match his for popularity or sophistication during the 1950s

for its powerful brass-section work and imaginative saxophone voicings. By the mid-40s, Kenton was working with vocalists like Anita O'Day and June Christy on recordings that became some of his best-selling discs.

As he grew in popularity, Kenton maintained his adventurous tastes. In 1947 he tackled "The Peanut Vendor," a sizzling Cuban song recorded in what he called "the new recording technique" of stereo for the album *Kenton in Hi-Fi*. Driven by an authentic Latin rhythm section led by the amazing percussionist Machito, the track featured an incendiary trumpet solo by a hot young Canadian trumpeter named Maynard Ferguson, full of then-revolutionary dischords. Then, in 1950, Kenton ambitiously added strings to his 40-piece Innovations in Modern Music orchestra and took them out on tour. From then on, the bandleader was often praised for his music's grand, symphonic sweep.

When he came up to Canada in the fall of 1952, Kenton left the string section behind, in what was obviously a cost-cutting move. But he did

bring along Ferguson, who had joined the band three years earlier. Billed as "The Biggest Show of '52" and featuring Sarah Vaughan and fellow Capitol recording artist Nat King Cole, the tour—which stopped in Toronto and Montreal, before returning to Ontario for stops in Guelph and London—was by all accounts a smash hit.

"A most entertaining package," wrote *Toronto Telegram* columnist Stan Helleur after the tour's November 20 show at Maple Leaf Gardens. "Kenton is always a welcome visitor to this lakeport," Helleur added, "but when he adds Sarah Vaughan, Nat Cole and an assortment of top vaudeville acts, he's set for an even bigger hello. [Kenton's] band, minus a violin section this year, was as technically perfect as ever."

Capitol Canada's first general manager Ken Kerr remembers working with the tall, elegant bandleader. Kenton and his orchestra, he says, often played an Ontario circuit that included Kingston, Peterborough, Kitchener, Hamilton, Sarnia and Niagara Falls, "wherever there was a decent-size ballroom." Added Kerr: "Anywhere Kenton went, there was a huge crowd. He was really popular with the college kids, who liked their music brash and loud. But they'd come to his shows to listen, not to dance. A few would be jiving around, but most just nodded their heads."

One particular detail that Kerr recalls was Kenton's hands. "He had the longest fingers of anybody I've ever seen," says Kerr. "When he played piano, they could span an octave and a half. It was absolutely astonishing."

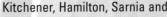

THE KINGSTON TRIO

CAPITOL
1958

*Hang down your head, Tom Dooley/Hang down your head and cry
Hang down your head, Tom Dooley/Poor boy, you're bound to die*

Guard, Grove and Shane: their unlikely hit, about a mountaineer who was hanged for murder, sparked the folk boom of the late 1950s

A century-old Blue Ridge Mountains tune about a mountaineer who was hanged for murder, "Tom Dooley" brought unexpected success to The Kingston Trio when it was released in the fall of '58. The song topped the charts in November, at a time when pop numbers like "Bird Dog," "Rockin' Robin" and "The Chipmunk Song" ruled the day. And it went on to spark the folk boom of the late 1950s, paving the way for Peter, Paul and Mary, Bob Dylan and many of Canada's earliest folk stars.

The Kingston Trio came together in San Francisco in the mid-50s, when college students Dave Guard, Nick Reynolds and Bob Shane began playing coffeehouses and beer parlours around town. They began as Dave Guard and the Calypsonians and later chose the name Kingston Trio because it sounded "collegiate" and yet still conjured up images of Jamaican calypso, which was popular at the time.

Guard and his buddies got their first break in 1957 when they were called in as replacements for comedian Phyllis Diller, who'd cancelled her engagement at San Francisco's Purple Onion coffeehouse. The Trio

Clean-cut image, close vocal harmonies

went over so well that they stayed on for the next seven weeks. One night, Bob Hope's TV agent saw the group and recommended them to Capitol Records' Voyle Gillmore. Promptly, Gillmore signed The Kingston Trio to an album deal.

While still at the Onion, Guard, Reynolds and Shane heard a singer audition for the club with a song called "Tom Dula." They loved the tune and quickly learned the words, but they didn't get the last name

right. Still, after recording it for their first Capitol album, their version began to get heavy airplay in Salt Lake City. When the song's popularity spread to other cities, Capitol released it as a single. "Tom Dooley" eventually hit the coveted number one spot at *Billboard* and went on to sell more than a million copies.

The song's success caught the music industry completely by surprise. In fact, there was no folk category at the Grammy Awards at the time of the group's breakthrough. "Tom Dooley" won for Best Country and Western Performance in 1958.

The Grammys played catch-up the following year, honouring the Trio with an award in the newly formed Best Folk Performance category. With their clean-cut image, close vocal harmonies and gentle guitar and banjo accompaniment, the group's members were suddenly the darlings of the industry.

It's difficult to overstate the influence of "Tom Dooley." Across North America, coffeehouses like The Inquisition in Vancouver, The Gate of Horn in Chicago and Gerde's Folk City in New York began springing up in the wake of the song's success, presenting hootenannies and a host of folk singers. And record companies, from independents like Vanguard to majors like Capitol, began scouting for the next major folk stars.

In Canada, the folk boom's impact was especially strong—and led to a flood of acoustic talent. When Ian Tyson first arrived in Toronto from Vancouver, "Tom Dooley" was all over the radio; it wasn't long before he teamed up with Sylvia Fricker and they became the first stars of Canadian folk. Many others followed, including Gordon Lightfoot (initially in a duo called The Two Tones), Denny Doherty (beginning with his group The Halifax Three and later as a founder of The Mamas and the Papas), and future EMI recording artist Buffy Sainte-Marie. All of them owed at least some measure of their success to The Kingston Trio's unlikely hit of '58.

FRANK SINATRA

CAPITOL
1953

Frank Sinatra at the 1954 Academy Awards with his children, Frank Jr. and Nancy (before her boots were made for walking): saloon ballads and swing tunes

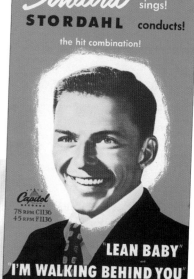

When Frank Sinatra signed on with Capitol Records in 1953, after leaving the Columbia label, he was back in the limelight as an actor, starring in the film *From Here to Eternity*, for which he would win an Oscar. But his star as a singer had all but faded to a flicker.

Several years earlier, *Modern Television & Radio* magazine had tackled the topic of the crooner's career slide with a headline that boldly asked the question "Is Sinatra Finished?" The accompanying article went on: "'Frankie is on the skids! Sinatra is all washed up! Frank is finished!' That old refrain is being bounced around more and more. It started a couple of years ago with people in the music business. Now it has spread to the fans themselves."

Ol' Blue Eyes: 'his voice was never better than it was during his Capitol years'

However, within months of stepping into Capitol's studios in 1953 with arranger Nelson Riddle (a magical pairing on the label's part), Sinatra began staging one of pop music's most dramatic comebacks. Their first sessions together produced such gems as "South of the Border," "My One and Only Love" and "I've Got the World on a String," which hit the pop charts in the summer of 1953. The hits continued through the mid-'50s, with "Someone to Watch Over Me," "Learnin' the Blues" (#1, *Billboard*), "Love and Marriage" (#5) and "Hey! Jealous Lover," which reached the number three spot late in 1956.

By the time Sinatra pulled into Canada the following June, there was a level of excitement reminiscent of the singer's thrilling concerts in the 1940s. Sinatra had been booked to perform two sold-out shows at the Vancouver Forum, during his only Canadian stop. In a special report for *Music World*, the Canadian music trade magazine that began publishing that year, correspondent Bob Turner

The Sultan of Swoon, the Svengali of Swing

described the giddy scene around Sinatra, both onstage and off:

"Right from the opening number through his famous 'beat' songs to the ballads that set young girls swooning fourteen years ago, the audience was in the palm of his hand. In what turned out to be the highlight of the evening, "One More for My Baby," with just one baby spot[light] on his head and shoulders and a complete blackout, the proverbial pin, dropped, would have resounded like a cannon."

What happened after the Vancouver shows resembled the hysteria that surrounded Sinatra in his bobby-sox-idol days. The 41-year-old singer was rushing to get to the Vancouver airport to catch his chartered DC-6B flight to Portland for his next show. When he tried to leave the Forum, he found a mob scene outside, with more than 2,000 people waiting between him and his limousine. Reported Turner: "Finally, after some brief problems which left him without a hat or a handkerchief, loot of some rather avid fans, police broke a path through the wildly cheering crowd to his car."

For the next several years, Sinatra's presence on the Canadian airwaves remained a constant. Songs such as "Chicago," "All the Way" and "Talk to Me" made many playlists from 1957–60, while "Witchcraft," "High Hopes" and "Nice 'n' Easy" all hit the Top 10 on the influential CHUM chart during the same period. Paul White, Capitol Canada's young promo man at the time, remembers the anticipation that surrounded releases by the man the media dubbed, in a blaze of alliteration, the "Sultan of Swoon," the "Bony Baritone" and the "Svengali of Swing."

"You always waited for the latest Sinatra," recalls White, "because they were always so well produced. And Sinatra's voice," he added, "was never better than it was during his years at Capitol."

Novelties

Voice of the Xtabay

In the conservative 1950s, singer Yma Sumac was the queen of exotica, the ethnic-tinged, easy-listening genre that enjoyed a revival (along with lounge music) in the ironic '90s. Born high in the Peruvian Andes, a descendant of the last of the Incan kings, Sumac was also a publicist's dream. Besides an image tailor-made for the media, she possessed a five-octave vocal range that created a sensation in the music world. "There is no voice like it today," wrote the *Washington Times Herald*. "It has a greater range than any female voice of concert or opera. It soars in the acoustic stratosphere, or plumbs the depths of pitch with equal ease. Such voices happen only once in a generation."

Discovered in New York's Blue Angel nightclub by Capitol Records talent scout Walter Rivers, Sumac was quickly signed to the label, which issued her debut album, *Voice of the Xtabay*, in 1950. The original 10-inch recording took full advantage of the singer's exotic background, featuring a front-cover photograph of her dressed as an Incan princess. The back cover text read: "The Xtabay is the most elusive of all women. You seek her in your flight of desire and think of her as beautiful as the morning sun, touching the highest mountain peak. Her voice calls you in every whisper of the wind. The lure of her unknown love becomes ever stronger, and a virgin who might have consumed your nights with tender caresses now seems less than the dry leaves of winter. For you follow the call of the Xtabay…though you walk alone through all your days."

The recording itself was a drum-laden, string-drenched collection of tracks like "Jungla," "Kon Tiki" and "Goomba Goomba" on which Sumac's voice did indeed soar the acoustic stratosphere and plumb the depths of pitch. Fuelled by Sumac's image as an unusual artistic phenomenon, the album became a best-seller and led to several other Capitol releases, including *Legend of the Sun Virgin*, *Legend of the Jivaro*, *Mambo!* and *Fuego del Ande*. Sumac later appeared in two movies, *Omar Khayyam* and *Secret of the Incas*, with Charlton Heston. She also later recorded an album with Les Baxter, a Capitol recording artist who pioneered the exotic lounge style with such albums as *Jungle Jazz* and *Tango of the Drums*.

Sumac continues to be an artistic force, cited as an influence by such diverse singers as Diamanda Galas, Nina Hagen and Kate Pierson, among many others. And *Voice of the Xtabay* (reissued on CD in 1995) remains a classic: an adventurous oddity of the Eisenhower-era '50s.

I Yust Go Nuts at Christmas

One of Capitol's top-selling artists in the early 1950s, Yogi Yorgesson was actually Harry Stewart, an American comedian who thought he could make a name for himself as a Swede. Pronouncing every "j" sound with a "y," Yorgesson recorded an entire album of holiday songs, including "Yingle Bells," "That Yolly Holiday" and "I Yust Go Nuts at Christmas," which became a major hit.

Capitol released many of Yorgesson's singles through the decade and compiled them on the album *The Great Comedy Hits of Yogi Yorgesson*. Included in that compilation were such unforgettable titles as "Who Hid the Halibut on the Poop Deck," which many years later had the dubious honour of being featured on Rhino Records' *The World's Worst Records: Vol. 2*. Not content with his Scandinavian persona, Stewart also pretended to be Japanese, recording briefly under the name Harry Kari. He died in a car crash in 1960.

Calypso is Like So…

Actor Robert Mitchum was an icon of cool, 1940s film noir, a Hollywood tough guy as hard-boiled as the heroes he played. The movie star was also a lover of calypso—a taste he acquired while shooting on location in Trinidad during the '50s. Having fallen under the music's spell, absorbing the works of Lord Melody and Mighty Sparrow, Mitchum took his own stab at the island's lilting songs. The resulting *Calypso is Like So…* never matched Harry Belafonte's chart-topping *Calypso* album in commercial terms, but it did deepen Mitchum's cool mystique, and became both a rarity of celebrity recordings and one of the true oddities in the Capitol catalogue.

Released in 1957, the album featured a rum-soaked Mitchum on the cover, in all his heavy-lidded, insolent glory. Inside, the actor tackled such songs as Sparrow's "Jean and Dinah," Roaring Lion's "Tic Tic Tic" and the hilarious "Mama, Looka Boo Boo," about a man so ugly that his children make fun of him. A master of accents, Mitchum even sang them all in his own, West Indian-style patois. However, the album failed to catch the calypso wave triggered by Belafonte's seismic success, and Mitchum returned to the screen, starring in such classics as *Cape Fear*, *Five Card Stud* and *The Big Sleep*, among many others. Still, as a glimpse into the legendary tough guy's gentler side, *Calypso is Like So…* remains a surprising, little-known gem.

C A P I T O L

POPULAR - DIXIELAND
WESTERN AND FOLK
RHYTHM AND BLUES
SQUARE DANCES - CHILDREN

February *Capitol* 195

FIRST IN THE FIELD BY FAR!

THE BRITISH INVASION:

1960 - 1969

CHAPTER TWO

THE BRITISH INVASION:
1960 - 1969

t the dawning of its second decade, Capitol Records of Canada was well established as one of the major labels in the country. The company had grown considerably through the previous ten years, relocating to Toronto, expanding its catalogue and increasing its staff. Despite these advancements, the label was still in its

infancy and hadn't yet shown much independence. It didn't even have its own Artists and Repertoire (A&R) department. All that would change dramatically in the early 1960s, as Capitol began to develop a homegrown roster.

It all began with an English jazz saxophonist named Freddy Gardner. Although Capitol's new promotion manager Paul White had never heard of him, Gardner was obviously popular with older British immigrants, because his recordings were in demand from dealers. White first heard about it from one of the salesmen, who mentioned that Gardner had apparently released some 78s on their par-

Capitol Canada's first-ever sales convention at Toronto's Guild Inn in 1960, with general manager Harold Smith (second from right)

ent EMI label. Then company president Harold Smith instructed White to find out how many tracks Gardner had recorded and put together an album. Laughs White: "I guess everyone figured that because I was from England, I'd know how to do all this. But actually, I didn't have a clue."

A transatlantic correspondence led White to the master tapes of Gardner's recordings. Then he found someone in EMI's London office who was willing to write liner notes. All that was left was to come up with a cover. A trip to the British tourism office in Toronto turned up a photograph of Lord Nelson's column in Trafalgar Square. With all the elements in place, White produced *Freddy Gardner the Unforgettable*, Capitol Canada's first domestic album in 1960. To everyone's surprise, it became one of the label's best-selling titles.

Realizing there was more potential gold in those vaults, White began poring through EMI's catalogue and picking other artists he thought might sell in Canada. The label's next Canadian releases were albums by comedian George Formby, the Glasgow Orpheus Choir and singer Lois Marshall. Later came The Band of the Irish Guard and Andy Stewart singing songs of Scotland. An especially big seller was the playfully titled *Hits of the Blitz*, wartime songs sung by Vera Lynn. Long-playing records had been around since 1948,

but as White noted, "Some of these artists had no albums out, just 78s. So I'd decide on the track listing and produce our own collections. That's how our A&R department started."

One morning over coffee, Harold Smith told White about a local pianist-bandleader he'd just signed. Smith was a member of Toronto's Granite Club, where Frank Bogart's orchestra was in residence. White recalls: "Obviously, over a few scotches, Frank convinced Harold that he should record him. One thing led to another and suddenly we're producing his album." Released in 1961, Frank Bogart's *Society Dance Date* became the label's first all-Canadian album in the 6000 Series.

Bogart, born in Woodstock, Ontario, in 1915, led several orchestras that were in constant demand at country clubs, annual balls and weddings. He recorded a second album for Capitol two years later called *Steppin' in Society*, for which Canadian broadcaster Elwood Glover penned the liner notes. "Frank Bogart has kept abreast of the dancing public," wrote Glover. "Although the swing bands no longer appeal, people still like to dance and this album gives you an idea of the flexibility of the Bogart adaptation to dancing tastes."

Not content to release only records that appealed to the older generation, White looked at what else was available. There certainly wasn't much rock 'n' roll coming from the United States at the time. As Red

Robinson, legendary DJ and then program director at Vancouver's CFUN radio station, puts it: "Elvis had gone into the army, Chuck Berry had been arrested and Dick Clark's *American Bandstand* came on and brought us Bobby Darin, Bobby Rydell and Bobby Vinton. Suddenly, everyone was a Bobby—we even had Bobby Curtola in Canada!" Added Robinson: "They were watering down rock 'n' roll and making it acceptable to mum and dad. As we all know, that ain't rock 'n' roll."

England was no different. By 1962, however, White had discovered some fabulous pop music by going through the EMI catalogue. Neither Harold Smith, nor his successor that year, an American named Geoffrey Racine, were much impressed by youthful singers such as Helen Shapiro, Frank Ifield and Cliff Richard, but they did allow White to release singles and albums by those artists. And, much to their surprise, all three artists had hits that year.

White sensed that big things lay in store, especially for Richard, who was already a major teen idol in Britain. Like Elvis Presley, to whom he was often (and unfairly) compared, Richard had successfully made

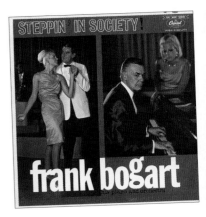

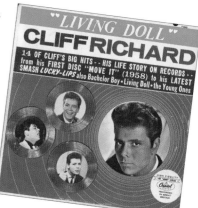

the transition from the recording studio to the movie screen, and films like *Summer Holiday* boosted his popularity considerably. In the meantime, White started publicizing all of Capitol Canada's releases in a newsletter he wrote and began publishing called *The Sizzle Sheet*. Printed weekly, it went out to all radio DJs and program directors and quickly became a popular, and effective, promotional tool.

Red Robinson remembers just how effective Capitol Canada's promotional tactics could be. "What Paul White did," recalls Robinson, "was get CHUM playing something that I wasn't playing and then say in his *Sizzle Sheet*, 'well, they're playing it at CHUM…' Or, conversely, he'd get me playing something and say to CHUM, 'look, they're playing it out on the west coast at CFUN.' Paul knew that if he could get both us and CHUM on a song, he could connect the whole country because we were such big, influential stations. And he often did."

Besides British pop music, Capitol also began hitting the mark with comedy records. In 1963, the label released *Bridge on the River Wye*, featuring British Goon members Spike Milligan and Peter Sellers. Capitol also issued *That Was the Week That Was*, based on the popular BBC television show starring David Frost. The label's biggest comedy successes were the recordings of Rolf Harris. Aside from his best-known *Tie Me Kangaroo Down, Sport*, the Aussie funster released several other hit albums, including *At the Cave*, which was recorded in a Vancouver nightclub.

Canuck humour made its debut with albums by Rich Little. The Ottawa-born comedian tackled indigenous topics on *My Fellow Canadians*, spoofing everything from parliament and the Queen to the Grey Cup and "Hockey Night in Canada." The man of a thousand voices also released *Scrooge and the Stars*, in which he played 22 well-known personalities in his modern version of Charles Dickens's *A Christmas Carol*. Little went on to become a major star of American television, with regular appearances on talk shows and variety specials.

Meanwhile, Capitol's Toronto offices on Queen Street East were bustling with activity. Paul White hired Bill Bannon, who remained with the company for more than 15 years, to help put his many promotional ideas into action. Salesmen Joe Woodhouse and Maurice Zurba, who became two other long-serving employees, went out into the field to sell the product, while Al Mair, the future manager of Gordon Lightfoot and owner of Attic Records, took orders over the phone. All were kept busy by a release schedule that saw the label issue an average of a dozen albums a month.

In addition to the American and British catalogue items, Capitol Canada was beginning to release more domestic product. President Geoffrey Racine, although not a lover of pop, did have a distinct fondness for the classics. He took it upon himself to sign a number of light classical performers, including pianists Margaret Ann Ireland and the husband-and-wife

Helen Shapiro: in the vanguard of the British Invasion

Cliff Richard & the Shadows: from the recording studio to the movie screen

team of Margaret Parsons and Clifford Poole, as well as Paul Brodie, now regarded as Canada's foremost classical saxophonist. While not huge sellers, such releases did add to the workload for Capitol's still quite small staff. But it was nothing, compared to what the company's employees were about to have on their hands.

Aside from such perennial major sellers as Nat King Cole, Frank Sinatra and The Kingston Trio, a new American act had joined the Capitol roster and was about to become one of the label's biggest success

The Beatles meet the press at Toronto's Maple Leaf Gardens, August 17, 1966

stories. Made up of brothers Brian, Dennis and Carl Wilson, their cousin Mike Love, and Al Jardine, The Beach Boys roared onto the scene in 1963 with uptempo sunny songs about California obsessions: surfing, hot rods and girls. Through most of the year, the group released a flurry of hits, including "Surfin' U.S.A.," "Little Deuce Coup" and "Be True to Your School."

British pop erupted in 1964. Not even the early successes of Helen Shapiro and Cliff Richard and his group, The Shadows, who all enjoyed bigger breakthroughs in Canada than in the United States, could have prepared Racine's staff for the volcanic effect that English bands had on the Canadian marketplace. Led by The Beatles, the British Invasion, as it came to be known, landed on Canada's shores and launched an all-out musical assault. And The Beatles and most of the other "invading" groups all came to Capitol through its EMI affiliation. According to Maurice Zurba, those days were a mixture of excitement and chaos. "Once The Beatles hit, it was sheer pandemonium," recalls Zurba. "We could barely keep up with the orders."

The Beatles, however, didn't hit right away. Capitol Canada had begun releasing the group's singles in the spring of 1963. "Love Me Do," "Please Please Me" and "From Me to You" were distributed in the first six months of the year and nothing much happened, despite Paul White's best promotional efforts. In a February issue of The Sizzle Sheet, White advised his readers to "give ['Love Me Do'] a couple of spins and you'll be

hooked." He added earnestly: "Don't neglect this side." Then in June, when "From Me to You" was released, White wrote assuredly: "It was England's No. 1 disc and it could be a No. 1 in Canada too. This group has it." And yet by November, White was still predicting: "Be warned— Beatlemania is going to take over Canada in the same way it captured Great Britain and Europe."

The initial sales of the singles (78 of "Love Me Do," 180 of "Please Please Me" and 500 of

The Beatles appear on Ed Sullivan's TV show, February 9, 1964

"From Me to You") were paltry enough to make Geoffrey Racine and vice-president Edward Leetham skeptical. Leetham eventually went to White and told him that he was striking out and would have to abandon the project. "Give me one more chance," White urged him. "They're huge in England, they've got another great single coming and an album on the way."

White's faith was rewarded with the release of The Beatles' first album in Canada, which was called, naturally, *Beatlemania! With the Beatles*. The company arranged to have the master tapes flown over as soon as they were available and rushed a package together, using the now-famous shaded Beatles' portrait shot on the cover. Released in early December *Beatlemania!* sold more than 50,000 copies before Christmas. That figure would multiply many times over the next few months.

Maurice Zurba, whose accounts included Simpson's in downtown Toronto, remembers having to make repeated trips to the department store's fifth-floor record bar to replenish its stock of *Beatlemania!* "Initially, they'd only ordered 100 copies before Christmas, which wasn't even enough to take care of special orders," says Zurba. "Then they took

another 100 and then another and another. I was bringing these boxes in on a dolly and they were grabbing and selling the records almost before I got them unloaded. It was absolutely crazy."

Everyone at Capitol's Toronto offices sensed something strange and wonderful was happening. Mail was pouring in from fans requesting photographs and autographs, while others were phoning in asking for any tidbit of Beatle-related news. At one point, the label's receptionist started answering the phone with, "Hello—

Capitol Records, home of The Beatles." Meanwhile, sales were going through the roof. The phenomenon escalated rapidly after the group made its now-famous appearance on "The Ed Sullivan Show" in February 1964. Watched by more than 73 million people in North America, the program helped turn the band into instant icons—much

the way it had done for Elvis Presley seven years earlier. Pop music would never be the same.

Beatlemania was like a runaway train. And it was all Capitol Canada could do to keep up with it. Eventually, the company had to look beyond the RCA facility in Smith Falls and engage nearly every pressing plant in Canada to meet the demand for Beatles records. In February 1964, the company rushed out *Twist and Shout*, using the cover of an English

extended play. Featuring "Please Please Me," "She Loves You" and the raucous title track, it sold even better than the first Beatles album. At that point, the label was releasing singles that were not yet available in the United States. When the Canadian releases of "Roll Over Beethoven" and

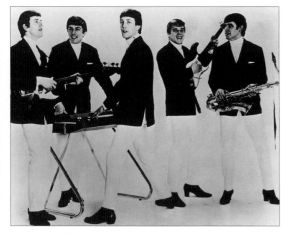

The Dave Clark Five: The Beatles' rivals generated their own hysteria

Gerry & The Pacemakers: the first British Invasion group to tour Canada

"All My Loving" were imported into the States and made the *Billboard* charts, it ruffled some feathers. The final straw came when Capitol Canada issued a third album, *Long Tall Sally*, using the same cover as the second U.S. album but with different tracks. "That's when Geoff Racine got a memo from head office saying from now on all Capitol releases were to be released simultaneously," recalls White. "Of course, we obliged."

While the new, coordinated-release edict made good sense from a business point of view, it couldn't erase the fact that the British Invasion had established a North American beachhead in Canada first, months before it was able to move into the United States. Capitol Canada had released more Beatles singles than any other country, and in the process White had helped to fill the company's coffers with consecutive hits by other English acts as well, especially The Dave Clark Five and Gerry & the Pacemakers. In fact, at its commercial peak, from 1964–65, Capitol boasted a whopping 45 per cent share of the Canadian market. White's reward? Racine, as president, gave him the go-ahead on signing Canadian talent. On top of his work as national promotion manager, White was now functioning as the company's A&R director. It wasn't until 1967, however, that he was given that title, overseeing A&R activities for the entire country, including a small, French-language department in Quebec.

The first domestic pop act White signed was The Esquires, a band that initially mimicked the sound of Cliff Richard and his group almost too closely. In fact, the band's first single for Capitol was a note-perfect cover of the Shadows' "Atlantis." But The Esquires built a strong following and soon evolved into a distinctive group in its own right. Then in 1964, White signed Toronto's Malka & Joso, a singing duo that was charming coffeehouse audiences with its exotic repertoire of international folk songs. Suddenly, Capitol had two of the country's brightest new acts, a fact not lost on *RPM Weekly*, the flag-waving music trade magazine founded that year by ex-Mountie Walt Grealis. "Beginning with groups like The Esquires, Capitol showed a commitment to Canadian talent that other labels simply didn't have," says Grealis. "We admired that and gave their artists all the support we could."

In fact, *RPM* acknowledged Capitol's efforts in December 1964 at its inaugural awards honouring the country's top recording artists and industry figures. The forerunner to the Junos, RPM Awards for that year went to The Esquires and new Capitol signing Jack London, while the label won for Top Record Company, Top Canadian Content Record Company and Top National Record Promotion Man (Paul White). Capitol would continue to win

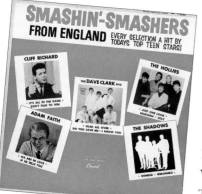

in many of those same categories throughout much of the decade.

It's a wonder that White had any time to sign new Canadian talent, with all the EMI product he was releasing. But along with Beatles albums and repackaged collections like *The Cliff Richard Souvenir Album*, *Across Canada with The Dave Clark Five* and the British Invasion compilation *Smashin' Smashers from England*, White also managed to release debut albums in 1965 by Toronto's Jack London & the Sparrows and Edmonton's Wes Dakus & the Rebels, and Malka & Joso's second album. To say Capitol was busy would be an understatement. "Shirley Jackson was the girl who did all the production ordering," recalls White. "I'd go in to see Shirley with my latest project and she'd kick me out of her office because she was so far behind. She didn't want to know. And yet we all worked long hours. That's just the way it was."

White discovered Wes Dakus during a promotional tour of western Canada. "Radio guys would tell me who people were listening to and going to see," says White. "Then I met Barry Allen and Stu Mitchell, who were both in Wes's band, and signed them to separate contracts. Barry was our first Canadian breakthrough act, the first artist that I signed who had songs on the charts in Vancouver, Toronto and Halifax. Edmonton became quite a scene for a while."

Indeed, *RPM* saluted Edmonton in a special issue in 1966 titled "Canada's Music City in the West." According to the article, Edmonton at the time had "nine 'in town' radio frequencies, two TV channels and at least 50 regularly working bands, several orchestras and hundreds of soloists." White, who was now officially called Capitol's A&R director, took out an ad in the issue: "The Best Talent in Edmonton is on Capitol Records," listing Allen, Dakus & the Rebels, Mitchell and a group called James & the Bondsmen. Later that year, the label signed another promising band from the city, Willie & the Walkers. Like Allen and Dakus, the Walkers were recorded and produced in Clovis, New Mexico, by Norman Petty, Buddy Holly's former manager-producer. "Edmonton had everything but recording studios," Allen recalls. "Fortunately, we had a connection with Norman. And it was a pretty close community, so we let others in on it."

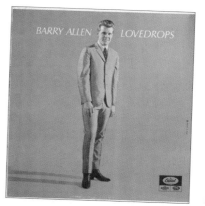

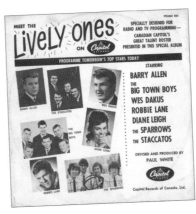

Television played a major role for Allen and other Capitol artists in the mid-1960s. Stations across Canada, catering to the growing teen market, began broadcasting a number of weekly shows that featured folk and pop music. The best of these was CBC's "Music Hop" (later renamed "Let's Go"). Weekdays at 5:30 p.m., the program presented a cross-country roundup of local talent from five different cities: Halifax (Monday); Montreal (Tuesday); Toronto (Wednesday); Winnipeg (Thursday); and Vancouver (Friday). For White and his A&R departments in Toronto and Montreal, it gave them a quick and easy window into the country's music scenes.

The CBC offered folk duo Malka & Joso enviable exposure with their own show, "A World of Music," which ran on Saturday nights for 13 weeks in the fall of '66. Meanwhile, the CTV network gave another Capitol artist, Toronto singer Robbie Lane, a starring role in the weekly dance program "It's Happening." In those pre-video days of Canadian music, appearances on such programs were invaluable tools for artists to broaden their audiences and showcase their latest records. When Capitol released Lane's debut LP that year, the label naturally named the album *It's Happening*.

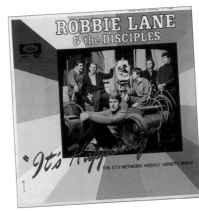

Lane's association with Capitol began through its licensing and distribution deal with Hawk Records, a small label owned by Ronnie Hawkins, on which both Lane and Hawkins recorded several singles. Hawk was one of several local labels that Capitol struck deals with at the time. While the labels retained control of their A&R, Capitol got their records into stores and did their promotion.

In 1965, The Paupers' Chuck Beal, Denny Gerrard (standing), Bill Marion and Skip Prokop came to Capitol via Roman Records

Through Roman Records, owned by Toronto disk jockey Duff Roman, Capitol handled early recordings by The Paupers, David Clayton Thomas and his band, The Shays. And by cutting a deal with the newly formed Yorktown label, Capitol Canada got involved with The Ugly Ducklings, one of the most popular bands then playing in Toronto's Yorkville district.

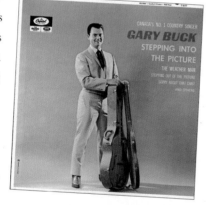

Capitol rounded out 1966 with another unprecedented number of hit singles. The Beach Boys, The Beatles and many of the other British Invasion acts, including The Hollies, The Yardbirds, Manfred Mann and Peter & Gordon, were the biggest sellers. Up there, too, was Barry Allen's "Lovedrops." Allen, along with Dakus and a new Capitol signing from Ottawa, The Staccatos, were among the pop winners at the RPM Awards. On the country side, Capitol's Gary Buck and Diane Leigh took the best male and female vocalist honours, establishing a new musical presence for the label. Buck, a native of Sault Ste. Marie, Ontario, proved to be a versatile and valuable member of the Capitol family. Besides his success as a recording artist, he ran the company's publishing division, Beechwood Music, which soon began reaping dividends.

Sgt. Pepper's Lonely Hearts Club Band. The Monterey Pop Festival. The Summer of Love. Nineteen sixty-seven was shaping up to be a watershed year for rock 'n' roll and anyone under 30 (whether they went to San Francisco with a flower in their hair or not). In Canada, a love-in on a national scale broke out with the opening of Expo '67 (Man and His World) in Montreal. Coinciding with

the country's centennial celebrations, Expo brought the world—literally 50 million tourists—to Canada's doorstep. From the diverse exhibitions of the individual provincial pavilions to the stunning architecture of Moshe Safdie's Habitat housing experiment, Expo '67 was one giant birthday party that made the whole country feel good about itself.

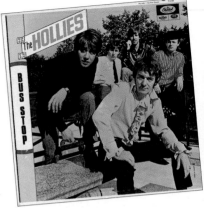

Capitol's executives were smart and held the company's sixth annual convention that summer in Montreal. There, the label's staff was able to bask in the attention given Malka, who performed at Expo, and soak up much of the centennial euphoria. Meanwhile, two other Capitol acts got the royal treatment in Ottawa, as The Staccatos and Quebec's folk group Les Cailloux performed for Queen Elizabeth, who was visiting the nation's capital. The Staccatos, who had just scored a Top 10 hit with "Half Past Midnight," received a five-minute ovation as they ran out before the hometown crowd of 25,000 teenagers and Her Majesty.

Capitol's vice-president, Edward Leetham, was named executive vice-president and general manager in 1967. Leetham's promotion came at an auspicious time for Capitol Canada. Following the convention in Montreal, he presided over the opening of the company's new offices on the newly named American Drive in Mississauga, Ontario (Leetham chose the name in homage to the company's U.S. roots). A 50,000-square-foot space on four acres of land near the Toronto airport, the facility housed both the head offices and a central distribution warehouse (Capitol had begun supplying department stores with records and tapes—known in the industry as rackjobbing—the previous year, to take care of its own distribution needs). There was also plenty of room for expansion—even enough for the manufacturing plant that company executives dreamed of someday opening.

Among the guests who flew in for the official ceremonies were Sir Joseph Lockwood, chairman of the board of EMI in England,

Country artist Gary Buck signs on the dotted line, with Paul White (left) and Ed Leetham

and Lloyd Dunn, vice-president of Capitol U.S. Many at the label agreed that the new head offices represented a turning point in the Canadian company's history. "It really felt like by moving out to American Drive, we became a real record company," recalls Capitol salesman Bill Bannon.

"All the departments were there—A&R, marketing, sales, promotion, legal—all under one roof. The company really seemed to grow up there."

In 1968, Capitol made Leetham the first Canadian-born president in the company's history. With his appointment, Capitol's next convention, held in Toronto, had all the hoopla of a noisy political rally. Clearly inspired by the election of new prime minister Pierre Elliott Trudeau that spring and the accompanying "Trudeaumania" that swept the country, Leetham entered the convention floor preceded by a Dixieland band and a bevy of bikini-clad women carrying large poster blow-ups of all the head office executives. After stopping to shake many of the delegates' hands, Leetham made his way up to the podium to deliver his address. His speech maintained the political-rally theme, as he referred to the company as "the party." Significantly, Capitol's first Canadian president spoke of the need to make domestic artists a major priority:

Before settling on American Drive in Mississauga, Ont. in 1967, Capitol Canada had several downtown Toronto locations

Capitol Canada's H.F. Burr (top), Ed Leetham and Paul White: breaking ground on American Drive

"To keep our party growing," Leetham told the convention, "we plan to aggressively seek out and acquire the best in Canadian talent and create Canadian hits, which hopefully will become hits in the vast U.S. market. The British did it with The Beatles and many other groups. There is absolutely no reason why we at Capitol cannot lead the way to developing a 'Canadian sound.' To do this requires total teamwork and each of us must continually campaign to keep our product constantly before our Canadian voters."

To illustrate Leetham's nationalistic point, the 1968 convention showcased three recently signed Canadian acts. The Brian Browne Trio performed stylish jazz renditions of contemporary pop hits, while Natalie Baron's rock numbers, sung alternately in English and French, brought the delegates to their feet. The showstopper at the convention was easily The Sugar Shoppe, who thrilled the audience with a flawless perfor-

mance of harmony-drenched theatrical pop. The Shoppe sent delegates away buzzing about this Mamas and Papas–style singing group and armed with its just-released single "Skip-a-Long Sam."

Despite the high hopes and the significant breakthrough on radio for a number of

EMI chairman Sir Joseph Lockwood, Ed Leetham, contractor Orey Fidani and Lloyd Dunn, vice president of Capitol Records' international division at the American Drive opening

Capitol's domestic artists, a lot of Canadian music was still falling on deaf ears. The problem was a general lack of widespread support from some radio stations. Many stations, taking cues from U.S.-based consultants, were programming with a heavy bias toward American music. Small wonder that Joni Mitchell, Neil Young, The Band, The Sparrows and David Clayton Thomas had, by 1968, all pulled up stakes and headed south. Something had to change.

There had been attempts to improve the airplay situation for Canadian artists. In an influential series of articles in 1968 titled "Legislated Radio," *RPM Weekly* had begun advocating for government intervention to force

Capitol Canada's new headquarters on American Drive opened with great fanfare in 1967 during the Summer of Love

With Ed Leetham appointed as Capitol Canada's first Canadian-born president, the company's 1968 convention had all the hoopla of a noisy political rally

Leetham with The Sugar Shoppe's Peter Mann, Laurie Hood, Lee Harris and Victor Garber

broadcasters to play Canadian records. *RPM* had also been responsible for establishing the Maple Leaf System, an attempt to coordinate the playing of indigenous discs by 12 major radio stations across the country. However, the member stations eventually disbanded and MLS was shelved due to lack of interest.

Canadian broadcasters, in fact, resisted all record company efforts to influence what they played. Still, the mere threat of legislation helped to boost the Canadian quotient on the airwaves for a while, as stations attempted to put a more patriotic face on their programming. This prompted Capitol to step up its domestic signings, and inspired other major labels in Canada to follow suit. The support was only temporary. When Pierre Juneau, chairman of the Canadian Radio-television and Telecommunications Commission (CRTC), the government's regulatory body for broadcasting, eventually proposed legislation requiring AM stations to play 30 per cent Canadian content, battle lines were drawn right across the Canadian music industry: artists and record companies like Capitol were in favour of the legislation, while broadcasters were vehemently opposed.

Meanwhile, live music was thriving—especially at the outdoor rock festivals that sprang up across Canada in 1969. These festivals, financed by young, risk-taking capitalists, provided memorable communal experiences for music lovers and important showcases for countless bands. Promoters John Brower and Ken Walker were responsible for two of the year's most successful festivals: the Toronto Pop Festival, featuring recent Capitol U.S. signing The Band, and the Toronto Rock 'n' Roll Revival show, which included John Lennon's Plastic Ono Band.

Capitol had already recorded Lennon and his wife Yoko Ono's anti-war anthem "Give Peace a Chance" in Montreal's Queen Elizabeth

Hotel, where the couple staged their famous bed-in for peace. Assisted by Capitol's Quebec A&R director Pierre Dubord and recorded by Andre Perry, the song was released on The Beatles' new Apple label and instantly made the Canadian charts in the late summer of '69.

The winds of change blew through Capitol's doors in 1969. The year started out with American appointee Ronald Plumb taking over the Canadian operation after the sudden resignation of Leetham, who moved on to become a management consultant. Capitol Canada then took a major step into the retail business with the purchase of Sherman Enterprises, Ltd., which included retail outlets in Ontario and Quebec. This, in addition to other acquired chains in the early 1970s, would form a network of stores that in 1987 became HMV Canada.

As the tumultuous peace-and-love decade came to a close and other record companies in Canada were playing catch-up, Capitol was preparing to launch a new wave of Canadian talent. Although an American executive was once again running the company, Plumb would merely help get Capitol Canada's house in order before passing the reins on to his Canadian successor, who would take the company to dramatic new heights. With the arrival of the 1970s, Capitol was about to produce some of Canada's biggest stars.

John Lennon and Yoko Ono at their 1969 Montreal Bed-In: Capitol Canada's Pierre Dubord helped to organize the infamous event

BARRY ALLEN

CAPITOL CANADA
1965

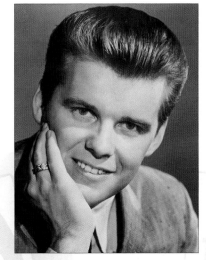

Barry Allen

One of western Canada's first major stars, Barry Allen had everything going for him: talent, good looks and impeccable connections. Aside from musical ability and blond hair and blue eyes, the singer-guitarist got to record in the same place where Buddy Holly made his chart-topping songs in the 1950s—Norman Petty's famed Clovis, New Mexico, studio. Small wonder, then, that Allen became Canada's leading male pop vocalist in the mid-1960s, with several hit songs of his own.

Born in Edmonton in 1945, Allen started out playing in high school

Barry Allen (far right) with (from left) band member Wes Dakus, Capitol Canada's Bud Farquarson, singer Gary Buck, singer Diane Leigh, Capitol Canada's Joe Woodhouse and band member Stu Mitchell, in 1966

bands around town, where he established himself as a hot, young performer. Meanwhile Wes Dakus, the city's top bandleader, was touring with Jimmy Gilmer & the Fireballs, an American group best known for its hit "Sugar Shack." The Fireballs had been working with Petty, and suggested Dakus come to New Mexico to record. That's when Dakus called up Allen. "You've gotta join my band," he told him in 1964. "We're heading south to record with Buddy Holly's producer." Allen, barely 19, didn't hesitate. "Holly was one of my biggest heroes," Allen recalls. "I was studying to become an accountant at the time, but I just said, 'That's it, I quit—I'm going to Clovis.'"

Modelled on vocal-instrumental groups like Gilmer's Fireballs and Holly's Crickets, Wes Dakus & the Rebels impressed Petty with their

playing and tight arrangements. Petty produced a mix of originals and covers (including Manfred Mann's "Do Wah Diddy Diddy") with the group, leading to a deal with Capitol in Canada. *The Wes Dakus Album*, released in September 1965, earned the Rebels an RPM Award for Top Instrumental Group. Petty was equally struck by Allen's singing talent and recorded him separately. Allen's solo debut, *Goin' Places*, came out on Capitol Canada the following March and won Allen his own RPM Award for Most Promising Male Vocalist.

Buoyed by his award and the success of his singles "Easy Come Easy Go" and "It's Alright with Me Now," Capitol rush-released Allen's

second album. When *Lovedrops* came out in June 1966, Canadian music was still largely bound by geography; hits rarely travelled outside the artist's own region and fan base. Allen was already a star in his hometown, and the new album's title track went straight to number one and remained there for over five weeks. But then a buzz about Allen started to spread, as "Lovedrops" began charting from Halifax to Vancouver. In Toronto, the singer was suddenly a "Battle Winner" at the powerful CHUM radio station, with the fastest-rising disc on its hit parade.

Allen, in fact, quickly became one of Canada's first bona fide national pop stars, with a coast-to-coast following. *Lovedrops* went on to sell more than 35,000 copies in Canada and helped to earn Allen another RPM Award—this time for Top Male Vocalist. A succession of singles on Capitol followed, including "Turn Her Down" and "Armful of Teddy Bears." Allen made a number of tours and became a regular guest on such TV shows as CBC's "Music Hop" and CTV's "It's Happening," where he established a reputation as a relaxed and genial performer. Always popular with the girls, he often drew comparisons to Cliff Richard, something that never troubled him. "Along with Holly, Richard was a big influence on me," Allen admits. "I always loved their melodies and the cool sound of their bands."

After his teen-idol years with Capitol, Allen recorded for other labels and producers, including Randy Bachman, who helped to make his "A Wednesday in Your Garden" a minor hit in 1970. Allen was also briefly with the band Painter, which included former members of 49th Parallel, and recorded an album with the group. In 1985, he bought Edmonton's Homestead Studios, where k.d. lang had recorded her debut album, and has since worked regularly as a producer.

Allen says he will always remember his Capitol years, when everything seemed to go his way. "All that travelling was exciting and the concerts and TV shows were great," he recalls. "We had fans who came out to see us and absolutely loved the music. It was unbelievable." So, too, was getting to record in Buddy Holly's fabled studio. "We made at least a dozen trips down there," says Allen. "It's still amazing when I think about it."

THE BAND

The Band: a decidedly down-home, old-timey sound with an undeniably contemporary relevance

The Band came home to Canada in June 1969. As The Hawks, the group had flown Ronnie Hawkins's coop, had become Bob Dylan's backing outfit in 1965 and returned four years later as stars themselves, headlining the Toronto Pop Festival before 50,000 fans at a two-day outdoor event. Although they shared the bill with Chuck Berry, Johnny Winter, Sly and the Family Stone and two other acts from Canada, Steppenwolf and Blood, Sweat & Tears' David Clayton Thomas, many in the crowd had come to see the group whose debut album *Music from Big Pink* had begun to revolutionize rock 'n' roll.

Signed to Capitol in 1967, The Band (as they chose to call themselves) had already supplied songs and musical backing to the recordings that became Dylan's legendary *Basement Tapes*. Now The Band—Canadians Robbie Robertson, Rick Danko, Richard Manuel and Garth Hudson,

The Band's Robbie Robertson (second from left) with Mandala's Domenic Troiano (fourth from left) backstage at 1969's Toronto Pop Festival

along with American-born Levon Helm—was going to get to do its own thing. Only Helm needed convincing. Danko took up the task. "I called Levon," Danko recalled, "and said, 'Levon, we're gonna get ready to record. They're giving us a couple of hundred thousand dollars we'd like to share." Helm's response? "I'll be on the next plane."

Recorded both in New York and Los Angeles, at Capitol's eight-track studio in the Hollywood tower, the sessions produced music that embodied both the past and the present in equal measures. The resulting album, *Music from Big Pink*, came out in the summer of '68. Featuring songs such as "The Weight" and "Chest Fever," it was immediately hailed by critics everywhere. *Life* magazine praised its "clear, cool, country soul that washes the ears with a sound never heard before," while *Rolling Stone* described it as "that good old intangible, can't-put-your-finger-on-it 'White Soul.'"

Big Pink, named for the group's pink aluminum-sided house in Upstate New York, signaled a shift to quieter, acoustic music within rock 'n' roll. Along with Dylan's *John Wesley Harding*, The Byrds' *Sweetheart of the Rodeo* and Ian & Sylvia's *Full Circle*, *Big Pink* was in the vanguard of the emerging country-rock movement. It set the stage

for the group's 1969 album titled simply *The Band*. Musically richer than its predecessor and steeped in Americana, that recording had a decidedly down-home, old-timey feel. Yet no one could deny its contemporary relevance.

The songs on both albums, mostly written by Robertson, perfectly captured the culture of the American South. How could a Canadian write about this world so convincingly? It came from Robertson's trip to Arkansas when, as a 16-year-old, he first ventured south to join Ronnie Hawkins's band. His senses, Robertson later recalled, were working overtime. "There was nothing like it in Toronto," he said. "It smelled different and moved different. The people talked and dressed different. And the air was filled with thick and funky music. I soaked it up like a sponge."

For Robertson and the rest of The Band, their cultural background gave their material its unique perspective. As Canadians (with the exception of Helm), they were outsiders looking in on America, which was, for them, an exotic world. "It was the advantage of having an open eye," Robertson explains. "The people who lived there were accustomed to everyone, so they didn't notice things that I did."

The Band recorded eight albums for Capitol in eight years, including *Stage Fright, Moondog Matinee* and *Northern Lights, Southern Cross*. But the group's first two albums will always be considered The Band's best. When *Time* magazine put them on its cover in January 1970, after the release of *The Band*, it ranked the group at the pinnacle of pop music.

"In the shifting, echoing cacophony of sound and sometimes fury that is the modern rock scene," wrote *Time*'s Jay Cocks, "The Band has now emerged as the one group whose sheer fascination and musical skill may match the excellence—though not the international impact—of The Beatles."

THE ESQUIRES

CAPITOL CANADA
1963

The Esquires enjoy the distinction of being the first Canadian pop group signed to Capitol Records of Canada. Heavily influenced by the pre-Beatles sound of Britain's Cliff Richard & the Shadows, the Ottawa-based band recorded several singles and one album for the label. A "suit group" that could swing with tremolo guitar and a solid backbeat, The Esquires raised the profile of Canadian pop music in the mid-60s, sharing the bill with such British Invasion acts as The Rolling Stones and touring Canada with The Dave Clark Five.

The Esquires' Don Norman, Brian Lewicki (rear), Richard Patterson (front), Gary Comeau and Paul Huot receive their first RPM Award from RPM's Walt Grealis (second from right), backstage at Maple Leaf Gardens

Emulating The Shadows and their guitarist, the ever-bespectacled Hank B. Marvin, The Esquires' first single was a cover of the British band's instrumental "Atlantis." Released in 1963, the song hit number one in the nation's capital, paving the way for the group's next instrumental single, "Man from Adano," which also reached the top spot in Ottawa the following year. Capitol was so impressed with the reception the group received on radio that it rushed The Esquires album out in August 1964.

The Esquires' drummer Richard Patterson (second from left) with The Beach Boys (including erstwhile Beach Boy Glen Campbell at far left) backstage at Toronto's Maple Leaf Gardens, February 21, 1965

Initially, the group—lead guitarist Gary Comeau (bespectacled, like his hero Marvin), rhythm guitarist Paul Huot, bassist Clint Hierlihy and drummer Richard Patterson—featured Bob Harrington on vocals. In 1963, The Esquires became the house band at Ottawa's Pineland Pavilion, a teenage amusement park with go-cart racing outside and a dance club inside. Later that year, after an appearance on a Dick Clark all-star show in Montreal, the group signed with Capitol Records.

Harrington left after recording "I Lost My Girl" and "Gee Whiz It's You," the respective vocal B-sides for the "Atlantis" and "Man from Adano" singles. He was replaced by Don Norman, who sang on all the group's subsequent recordings for Capitol. The group's biggest hit came with the Norman-sung "So Many Other Boys," which eventually peaked at #9 on the *RPM* chart in January 1965. Bob McAdorey, columnist for the *Toronto Telegram*'s "After Four" teen section, reported on the sin-

gle's success with a cheeky dig at the label.

"Capitol Records of Canada has been so busy carrying money to the bank from all the English groups they represent, that last week they were almost apologetic when they asked me to play a record by a Canadian group, The Esquires," wrote McAdorey on November 26, 1964, in a column headlined "Esquires Hit the Big Time." "I really liked it, but the final test is listener reaction, so I played it on the Battle of the New Sounds. Everybody, including Capitol, was absolutely amazed at what happened. The Esquires defeated The Searchers, The Zombies and The Animals to end the week undefeated!"

Paul White, who signed The Esquires to Capitol, is today quick to agree with McAdorey's assessment. "The Beatles made us so much money," admits White, "that it meant for the first time I was able to go out and sign Canadian acts. That was a major fringe benefit. The challenge was to get our salesmen to push the stuff. They'd say 'why do I have to go out and promote The Esquires when all I have to do is walk into Sam's and sell 500 copies of *Beatlemania?*' But eventually, they too saw that Canadian records could sell."

After the release of their self-titled album, featuring "Man from Adano" and a Buddy Holly medley, The Esquires rounded out the year by winning the so-called Top Vocal Instrumental Group prize at the first RPM Awards in 1964. The band went on to open for The Beach Boys at Toronto's Maple Leaf Gardens in 1965 and release two other singles for Capitol, "Cry is All I Do" and "Love's Made a Fool of You," that same year.

The Esquires broke up in 1967. Then, in 1993, a piece of old film footage turned up, featuring the original band in a studio performing "Man from Adano." Considered a music-video prototype and the first of its kind in Canada, it confirmed The Esquires' status as true pioneers of Canadian pop.

DIANE LEIGH

CAPITOL CANADA
1965

Singing at Klondike Days in Edmonton

"Canada's Queen of Country Music." Diane Leigh wore that title like a shining crown throughout much of the 1960s. And deservedly so. The winner of the RPM Award for Top Female Country Singer for five consecutive years, Leigh was a prominent star in Canadian music at a time when, unlike today, few women stood in the spotlight. Her pioneering success helped pave the way for every female country performer in Canada who followed, from Carroll Baker to Shania Twain.

Leigh's rise to stardom began when she was only 15. Born and raised in Toronto, the eldest of five children, Leigh had no dreams of a career in music. In fact, the teenager was working as a typist at the time. A cousin who heard her sing was so struck by her crystal-clear voice that he arranged for her to meet The Sapphires, a local rock-harmony group. After an impromptu audition, Leigh was conscripted and began singing songs by Peggy Lee and Julie London with The Sapphires at teen dances and local music events.

One night, with some friends, an underage Leigh used some fake identification to get into a Toronto bar to hear The Sons of the Saddle, a popular western group. At the time, Leigh professed not to like country music. "I couldn't stand that terrible nasal sound they all used to use," she later recalled. But the group, she discovered, sang country classics in glorious harmony. Emboldened by two beers, Leigh asked if she

Diane Leigh, before signing with Capitol Canada

could sing with them. Although she was turned down, the group invited her back the next day to its rehearsal. Once again, Leigh passed the audition, singing the only country song she knew: "Your Cheating Heart." She went on to perform with Vic Siebert and the Sons at that bar for the better part of a year—and would have sung with them longer had the Women's Christian Temperance Union not discovered that she was underage and forced the club's owner to fire her.

Undeterred, Leigh introduced herself to Jack Starr, owner of Toronto's Horseshoe Tavern, then the city's leading country bar. Using a forged identity, she auditioned and earned herself another singing job. Several days after she started work, three detectives escorted her from the stage after learning she was underage. Realizing club work was out

of the question, Leigh got herself work on Patsy Cline's Canadian tour—as a drummer. When that ended, she headed to the Maritimes with a travelling country show.

Leigh's first major break came when she landed herself a spot on Carl Smith's "Country Music Hall" show on the CTV network. The national profile brought her to the attention of Capitol Records' Paul White, who promptly signed the singer. She and White flew to Nashville, where they recorded several singles and a collection of songs that would eventually make up Leigh's debut album. Around this time, she travelled to Germany to entertain the American armed forces with Graham Townsend, the world-renowned Canadian fiddler, and Jack Kingston (the same country singer who had recorded Capitol Canada's first domestic 78 rpm record in the early 1950s).

Leigh's first single on Capitol, "Won't Be a Lonely Summer," reached the Top 20 at *RPM* in August 1965. When the singer's album, *Shadows of Your Heart*, came out the following summer, it contained a wealth of material written by Canadian songwriters, including Les Pouliot, of "Country Hoedown" and "The Tommy Hunter Show" fame; Lennie Siebert, of The Sons of the Saddle; and Quebec's Douglas Trineer. Capitol released two singles from the album. The title track, written by Canadian country legend Ray Griff, hit #1 on the *RPM* country chart, while "Why Can't He Be You," a Hank Cochran song originally recorded by Patsy Cline, made it to #3.

Leigh released three more singles for Capitol in 1967: "Let's Talk it Over" and two which once again took her to #1 on *RPM*'s country chart, "Mr. Jukebox" and

Performing at Toronto's Horseshoe Tavern with her band, The Shades of Blue

"The Sound that Makes Me Blue." She remained with "Country Music Hall" until 1969, the year she won the last of her five consecutive RPM Awards for Top Female Country Singer. Leigh moved on to record country and gospel albums for a variety of other labels. She continued to make numerous TV appearances on shows such as "Countrytime," "The Tommy Hunter Show" and Harry Hibbs' "At the Caribou" until her retirement from show business in 1976.

JACK LONDON & THE SPARROWS

CAPITOL CANADA

1964

Jack London (centre) with Sparrows (from left) Jerry Edmonton, Dennis Edmonton, Nick St. Nicholas and Art Ayre

With the arrival of the British Invasion in 1964, Canadian record labels were quick to sign any local group that exhibited an English pop sound or mop-top image. Columbia boasted the Merseybeat-like Liverpool Set, while Red Leaf touted the Union Jack–sporting British Modbeats. Few bands were more successful in adopting English affectations than Jack London & the Sparrows.

Formed in Oshawa, east of Toronto, the band was built around the musical talents of singer Dave Marden and two brothers, guitarist Dennis and drummer Jerry McCrohan, whose father owned the local Jubilee ballroom, where they got to see many of the top touring acts of the day. Marden wanted to start a British-style band, but felt that he needed an appropriate image. With Beatlesque bangs, he reinvented himself as Jack London, complete with an English accent. The McCrohans, meanwhile, chose a new surname, Edmonton, because they thought it somehow sounded more English. With the addition of keyboardist Art Ayre and bassist Bruce Palmer, Jack London & the Sparrows (the name Sparrows was itself a homage to Ronnie Hawkins's much-admired band the Hawks) began performing around Oshawa.

The ruse worked almost immediately. No sooner had The Beatles left the country in September of '64 after their first Canadian tour than *RPM Weekly* was trumpeting the local "phenomenon." In a front-page article, Walt Grealis reported that the group "under the guidance of Jack London from England [sic] had them screaming and fainting in Oshawa." Added Grealis, who noted that the band had already received two record contract offers: "This new group have overnight become as big a sensation in Oshawa as The Beatles were initially in Liverpool. I would like to predict [that] they'll make it on talent alone." To underscore his prediction, the magazine named Jack London as the year's Most Promising Male Vocalist three months later in its inaugural RPM Awards.

None of this was lost on Capitol's Geoffrey Racine and Paul White, who had signed the band in September, moved them to Toronto and sent them into the studio with producer Stan Klees. The group's first single, the delightfully Beatle-ish "If You

Don't Want My Love," came out in late '64 and reached #12 at CHUM, while climbing all the way to #3 on the *RPM* chart. The hit single led to TV appearances and some high-profile gigs. Meanwhile, Capitol was flooded with gushing fan tributes, receiving more than a thousand letters a week.

Before completing the album, The Sparrows swapped bass players with another Toronto band with an avian name, The Mynah Birds, led by future punk-funk superstar Rick James. In exchange for Palmer, who eventually found fame in Buffalo Springfield with a later member of The Mynah Birds, Neil Young, The Sparrows got Nick St. Nicholas. The self-titled album *Jack London and the Sparrows* came out in February 1965 and spawned three more singles, including "I'll Be the Boy" (#41 CHUM, #19 *RPM*) and the anguished ballad "Our Love Has Passed," which reached #7 at *RPM*.

But not long after the album's release, in the summer of '65, The Sparrows and Jack London parted ways. The official reason was musical differences: London wanted to keep making pop records; the group's tastes leaned more toward bluesy material. Unofficially, The Sparrows felt that London was more interested in lining his own pockets than looking after the band. According to Jerry Edmonton, the group learned that the contract London signed had all the money going to him. Recalled Edmonton: "He would go in and collect the royalties and we'd see him the next day with a new fur coat, going out to restaurants. I don't ever remember getting a penny."

The Sparrows staged a mutiny and continued without

The pre-Steppenwolf Sparrows, minus London: (from left) St. Nicholas, Jerry Edmonton, Dennis Edmonton, Goldy McJohn and John Kay

London. Now a quartet, the group recorded one more single for Capitol, the feisty punk number "Hard Times with the Law," before teaming up in Toronto's Yorkville district with singer John Kay. That version of The Sparrows (with The Mynah Birds' Goldy McJohn replacing Ayre) eventually flew south to find fame as Steppenwolf.

MALKA & JOSO

CAPITOL CANADA
1964

Malka Marom (left) and Joso Spralja: a beguiling beauty and a pioneering world-music sound

Long before the term "world music" became a popular catch-all for sounds from around the globe, Malka & Joso were singing songs in Spanish, Italian, Hebrew, Creole French, Macedonian and Russian. During the mid-1960s, the handsome folk duo brought a distinctly international flavour to the Canadian folk scene, performing in coffeehouses and concert halls, at folk festivals, and on television with their own weekly CBC program. Malka & Joso's three albums for Capitol were the unlikely hits of the decade, outselling many of the label's English-language albums.

Malka Marom was born in Israel, the daughter of a cantor. Joso Spralja was born in the former Yugoslavia, the son of a fisherman. The two met in Toronto's Yorkville district one night in early 1963, at an after-hours coffeehouse called the 71. It proved a fateful meeting. Recalled Spralja: "Often at 71, I'd stay on to sing until three in the morning for other artists who dropped by. Malka used to come sometimes. One night she offered to teach me a few of the folk songs she knew, and we began to harmonize." Soon after, they began getting steady work together.

That summer, Malka & Joso played the Mariposa Folk Festival in Orillia, Ontario, on a bill with Ian & Sylvia, The Travellers and a duo called The Two Tones that included a young Gordon Lightfoot. By the following year, record retailer Sam Sniderman was an enthusiastic fan and recommended them to Capitol's Paul White. Recalls White: "Sam phoned and told me that I just had to sign this duo. He was always doing that. He said, 'Could you at least meet with them?' I didn't meet with Joso at first, because Malka came in to my office and completely charmed me. She was gorgeous. I think [Capitol president] Geoff Racine melted as well. I went to see what they were like, and she and Joso were absolutely great together. I signed them right away."

In December 1964, Malka & Joso went into Toronto's RCA Studios with guitarists Elie Kastner and Rafael Nuñez and bassist Fred Muscat to begin recording for Capitol. Although the recording session went overtime, it produced enough material for two albums. "This wasn't an expensive undertaking," says White. "If the whole session cost me $1,000, then I was really going crazy."

The first album, *Introducing Malka & Joso*, hit stores in January. Featuring the playful Caribbean standard "Abakaila," Brazilian Dori Caymi's stirring "Curimã" and the rousing Spanish flamenco of "Doce

Cascabeles," it sold well, enjoyed an international release in both England and the United States and garnered rave reviews. Wrote music critic Clyde Gilmour in the *Toronto Telegram*: "In refreshing contrast to many another contemporary balladeer, Malka & Joso do not specialize in suicidal dirges about lynchings, chain gangs, mortgage foreclosures and industrial unrest. They sing about such timeless matters as young love, the serenity of shepherds and the way of a man with a maid."

Malka & Joso's second album, *Mostly Love Songs*, came out in late '65—just as the duo won an RPM Award as the year's Best Folk Group. Then, at Sam Sniderman's suggestion, they proposed an album of songs from Israel to Capitol's Paul White. The label eventually released *Jewish Songs*, which proved to be another best-seller. "I was dubious at first," admits White, "but that album wound up selling 10,000 copies, all through Sam I think."

In the fall of '66, Malka & Joso's "A World of Music" became a replacement for the long-running "Juliette" in the Saturday slot following "Hockey Night in Canada." The weekly CBC series took the duo's cosmopolitan repertoire into the living rooms of the nation. The first program, filmed on location in a Toronto park, featured Brazilian guest Astrud Gilberto walking over a bridge singing "One Note Samba" and Malka, reflected upside down in a pool, reciting "I Will Wait for You." Before they split in 1967, Malka & Joso performed in the United States

Singing about 'young love, the serenity of shepherds and the way of a man with a maid'

and were favourites of "The Tonight Show's" Johnny Carson, who had them on his program an impressive four times.

Canada now boasts a thriving world music scene, with artists who perform everything from Spanish flamenco to Yiddish folk. Malka & Joso were the first on the scene—back in the days when any song not sung in English was considered "exotic."

THE STACCATOS

CAPITOL CANADA
1965

Few Canadian groups experienced a more thrilling ride on rock's roller coaster in the second half of the 1960s than The Staccatos. With a strong work ethic, a loyal fan base and a knack for writing hook-laden pop tunes, the Ottawa band became one of the hottest acts in Canada. After an album and a series of popular singles for Capitol, including the group's best-known, national hit "Half Past Midnight," The Staccatos transformed themselves into Five Man Electrical Band and reached even dizzier heights on the world stage.

"A beat group with a difference" proclaimed *RPM*'s Walt Grealis in the summer of '65. "They have their own sound," Grealis continued, "[but] this sound isn't new. The boys have been on the Ottawa scene a few years as individuals, but it was only after getting together as a group that they really impressed young Ottawa."

Although the boys did develop their own sound, the group—guitarists Vern Craig and Les Emmerson, bassist Brian Rading, drummer Rick Bell and singer and local radio personality Dean Hagopian—initially played immaculate Buddy Holly and Beach Boys covers at teen dances around Ottawa after forming in 1963. As soon as Craig and Emmerson began writing original material, The Staccatos' own sound, a mix of chiming guitars and bell-like harmonies, began to take shape.

The Staccatos' (from left) Les Emmerson, Rick Bell, Brian Rading, Vern Craig and Mike Bell: chiming guitars and bell-like harmonies

With financial backing from the *Ottawa Journal*'s Sandy Gardiner, who also acted as a correspondent for England's *New Musical Express*, the band started recording demo tapes of its songs. The first to catch Capitol Canada's attention was a Craig-Emmerson ballad called "Small Town Girl," which the label released in early '65. The song picked up airplay in a number of regions across Canada and reached #20 on the *RPM* chart. The next single, the hopeful surfer tune "Move to California," primed the market for the group's debut album, *Initially The Staccatos*, recorded in Montreal and released at the end of the year.

Throughout 1966, The Staccatos produced several more singles, including the ballad "It's a Long Way Home" and a peppy cover of Eddie Cochran's "C'mon Everybody." Meanwhile, the group continued to earn a reputation as the hardest-working Canadians in show business. Touring constantly, playing clubs, high schools and arenas from Moncton to Montreal and Hamilton to Hull, the group built a huge following, with one of the biggest fan clubs in the country. By the end of the year, The Staccatos had won two RPM Awards: Top Vocal Instrumental Group, beating out The Guess Who and The Ugly Ducklings, and Best Produced Single for their latest hit "Let's Run Away," which topped "I Symbolize You" by The Last Words and "Brainwashed" by David Clayton Thomas.

The group's biggest hit came in 1967, during Canada's centennial. "Half Past Midnight," a harmony-drenched Cinderella tale written by Emmerson, reached #10 on CHUM and #8 at *RPM*. The single went on to sell over 25,000 copies before getting released in England and the United States, where it piqued the interest of Capitol in Hollywood. After recording a joint album with The Guess Who called *A Wild Pair*, as part of a promotional campaign for Coca-Cola, and winning another RPM Award, Best Produced Single, for "Half Past Midnight," The Staccatos landed themselves a Capitol U.S. deal.

Capitol took them into its studios at the Capitol tower in Los Angeles, where the group recorded a number of Emmerson-penned tracks. Ultimately, label executives there felt the band was "too Beach Boy sounding." After a series of sessions, Capitol did eventually release an album under a new group name, Five Man Electrical Band, which was taken from one of the songs. But the self-titled release was unfocused, featuring country ditties, music-hall numbers and a Beatles cover. Despite the inclusion of "Half Past Midnight," the album made barely a ripple on the U.S. charts.

Emmerson and his cohorts went on to far more success with Five Man Electrical Band on another label. But the group's origins as The Staccatos, especially its tours and numerous hit singles for Capitol, left an indelible mark on the Canadian pop scene.

THE SUGAR SHOPPE

CAPITOL CANADA

1968

The Sugar Shoppe's (from left) Laurie Hood, Peter Mann, Victor Garber and Lee Harris:
glorious four-part harmony

Long before starring on Broadway and playing master ship-builder Thomas Andrews in the blockbuster movie *Titanic*, Victor Garber sang in popular Canadian folk-rock group The Sugar Shoppe. With their lush harmonies and theatrical performances, Garber and bandmates Lee Harris, Laurie Hood and Peter Mann created a stir on both sides of the border in the trippy days after 1967, the Summer of Love. "Talented and amusing," admitted the *Globe and Mail*, while the *Hollywood Reporter* simply gushed, "The Sugar Shoppe is the biggest, hottest, bestest new quartet since The Mamas and the Papas."

The group's genesis arose from an evening in the spring of 1967, when the four sang together and captured the chemistry on a homemade tape recording. Mann, then an arranger and scriptwriter at the CBC, and Harris, with three years of vocal training, were both from Toronto. Garber, an actor at the University of Toronto's Hart House and erstwhile coffeehouse singer, and Hood, a student at U of T's faculty of music, were originally from London, Ontario.

Mann explained to a *Globe* interviewer how The Sugar Shoppe came together. "I brought all the schtick, all the razzmatazz of show business," said Mann. "Vic and Laurie, their roots are real folk; Vic more than Laurie. He turned me on to the whole world of folk arts. Laurie brought in a strong classical influence." He continued: "Lee—she'll hate me for this—is the schoolgirl of the group. She's very much into the drums and pop charts. If something poetic starts to sound too airy and gentle for Lee, she'll say 'Let's put some rhythm under it to state it stronger and give it conviction."

Soon, The Sugar Shoppe was playing six nights a week at Granny's, a popular Toronto nightclub, and recording for Yorkville Records, the successor to Yorktown. The group's upbeat reworking of Bobby Gimby's centennial anthem "Ca-na-da" hit the Top 20 on CHUM and went on to sell 15,000 copies. Capitol's Paul White took notice of the action and arranged for Karl Engemann, head of the American company's A&R division, to fly up. One night at Toronto's Friar's Tavern, where The Sugar Shoppe drew lineups down Yonge Street, turned Engemann's head around. "The place was absolutely packed, " recalls White. "A

number of other labels were there. We could see [Yorkville Records'] Bill Gilliland looking over at us, while we were looking over at someone from Columbia. But Karl just loved the group, and within a month we'd signed them to a U.S. album deal."

Produced by Al De Lory, the man responsible for Glen Campbell's Grammy Award–winning record "By the Time I Get to Phoenix," *The Sugar Shoppe* captured the group's vocal charms in glorious four-part harmony. De Lory brought in top session players, including guitarist Al Viola and drummer Hal Blaine. Excitement quickly spread around Hollywood about the Canadian quartet, which attracted such VIP fans as Bobbi Gentry, Lee Hazelwood, Nancy Wilson and Tiny Tim.

Capitol launched its new signing at the company's American convention in Las Vegas. White remembers that the group was on a bill with Glen Campbell, Woody Allen, Cannonball Adderly and Linda Ronstadt. "It was a real pressure-cooker situation," recalls White. "The Sugar Shoppe had to make a big impression, because the convention was filled with hardened sales guys. The group came out to do their set—I'm sweating at this point. Well, in the end, they had to do an encore. The place went insane for them."

The album spawned three singles in 1968: "Skip-a-Long Sam," "The Attitude" and "Privilege." With appearances on "The Ed Sullivan Show" and "The Tonight Show" with Johnny Carson, The Sugar Shoppe seemed destined for major stardom. Within little over a year, however, the group's members went their separate ways. Mann returned to arranging and producing. Hood undertook session work, while Harris died tragically of complications arising from multiple sclerosis. As for Garber, his talent as a stage and film actor took him far—all the way to the helm of the *Titanic*.

THE SUGAR SHOPPE
SKIP-A-LONG SAM
LET THE TRUTH COME OUT

THE BEACH BOYS

CAPITOL

1962

Brian Wilson was not your typical rock 'n' roll star. Although he was the mastermind of The Beach Boys, the studio genius behind all those perfect aural snapshots of California teenhood, Brian never felt entirely comfortable on stage. Moody and withdrawn, he preferred to leave the spotlight to his brothers Carl and Dennis or his cousin Mike Love. When The Beach Boys hit their commercial peak in the mid-1960s, Brian began finding excuses not to tour—which is why the band's appearances in Canada featured Bruce Johnson (in '65) and Glen Campbell (in '66) in Brian's place.

The three Wilson brothers grew up in the Los Angeles suburb of Hawthorne, just five miles from the ocean (and a dozen from the Capitol tower in Hollywood). Only Dennis actually surfed, but the musically gifted Brian was able to capture the carefree lifestyle of surfing and hot rods in his first songs. Inspired by the harmonies of Capitol recording artists The Four Freshmen, Brian and his brothers began singing and landed their first gig on New Year's Eve 1961.

The Beach Boys' (clockwise from top) Brian Wilson, Carl Wilson, Mike Love, Al Jardine and Dennis Wilson: aural snapshots of California teenhood

Signed to Capitol the following year, The Beach Boys' first single, "Surfin' Safari," became a hit that summer, as did the album of the same name. The group then scored a string of hit singles in 1963, including "Surfin' U.S.A.," "Surfer Girl" and "Little Deuce Coupe." Dressed in slacks and striped short-sleeve shirts, the

Complex harmonies and sophisticated chords gave the group—both on record and in concert—one of the most mellifluous sounds in all of pop music

band members were the epitome of all-American boys when they toured, something they did many times on the West Coast in 1964. CFUN's Red Robinson remembers the group made Vancouver a regular stop in those days. "Our city was just another hop, skip and a jump for them," says Robinson. "They'd come and we'd always interview them, either at the station or in their hotel rooms. They were great to work with and the kids loved them."

After appearing on "The Ed Sullivan Show," The Beach Boys undertook an extensive tour of the East in early 1965. The band performed at the Montreal Forum and Toronto's Maple Leaf Gardens in February, with Ottawa's The Esquires, The Girl Friends and Toronto's The Big Town Boys opening. In a *Toronto Telegram* review of the Gardens show, attended by 8,000 noisy fans, Charles Dennis reported: "America's biggest singing group came to Toronto's scream temple last night." Brian Wilson, Dennis noted, had been replaced by Glen Campbell, "a regular on ABC's Shindig show."

When The Beach Boys returned to the Gardens in September, the

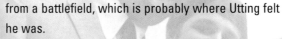

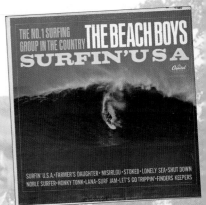

Toronto Star assigned future foreign correspondent Gerald Utting to cover the show. Utting, sitting next to an otherwise normal-looking 15-year-old girl, reported that he found the whole experience "disturbing," from the girl's frenzied screaming to the group's loud and confusing set. "The performance," wrote Utting, "was a cacophonous blend of staccato chords, massed wailing, thundering, meaningless shouts, uniforms of canary yellow shirts and tight, tight pants, semi-erotic gyrations, blinding and ceaseless barrages of flashbulbs, thousands of straining youngsters raising arms high in triumph." Sounds more like a report from a battlefield, which is probably where Utting felt he was.

In fact, the group's complex harmonies and sophisticated chords—both on record and in concert—gave The Beach Boys one of the most mellifluous sounds in all of pop music. With the increasingly reclusive and eccentric Brian at home writing and producing more ambitious material, the group changed with the times. After the mid-60s hits of "Help Me Rhonda," "California Girls" and "Barbara Ann," Brian wrote more spiritual and experimental songs such as "God Only Knows" and "Good Vibrations." The Beach Boys then released *Pet Sounds*, an acclaimed, more experimental album that Paul McCartney later acknowledged was a major source of inspiration for *Sgt. Pepper*. Unfortunately, Capitol didn't know how to market the record to the group's fan base and it sold poorly.

Nevertheless, The Beach Boys enjoyed an incredible run on the Capitol label. Between 1962 and 1969, the group recorded an impressive 13 albums, scored 34 chart records, 26 Top 40 hits, 12 Top 10 singles and three number one singles. In 1964 and '65, The Beach Boys' sales were second only to those of The Beatles at Capitol. In December 1966, they were voted the world's number one group in England's *Melody Maker*, becoming the first to displace The Beatles for the honour. Sadly, for Brian Wilson and his group, they were ultimately eclipsed by McCartney and his band and, in the wake of *Sgt. Pepper*'s success, never regained their artistic footing. Still, during their heyday, no one in pop music could match The Beach Boys for achingly beautiful songs about a more innocent time.

Backstage at Maple Leaf Gardens in 1965, receiving Canadian Danceability Award from Joey Cee (Bruce Johnson is far right): taking 'Toronto's scream temple' by storm

THE BEATLES

PARLOPHONE
1962

On February 22, 1963, Capitol's national promotion manager Paul White did what he did every Friday: he printed the latest issue of his department's newsletter, *The Sizzle Sheet*, and mailed it out to his media contacts across Canada. As usual, the *Sizzle* listed the label's newest singles. Under the title "These are the Next Smash Hits!" were songs by Nat King Cole,

John Lennon, Ringo Starr, George Harrison and Paul McCartney landing for a stopover in Winnipeg, August 20, 1964: Canadian hysteria

It's Beatlemania again!

THE BEATLES NEWEST twist and shout

Frank Ifield, The Chantels, Rolf Harris, Franck Pourcel, Jack Scott, Danny Coughlan and an unknown group from England called The Beatles. Despite White's prediction, none of those singles became hits that year, and only Cole's "Nothing Goes Up" made CHUM's Top 50, peaking at #47.

As Beatleologists know, it would take more than a year for the Fab Four's first Capitol single, "Love Me Do," to make the Canadian charts (when it also made the U.S. *Billboard* charts as an import). But that didn't stop White from pushing. On March 1, he stated hopefully (and rather vaguely) that "'Love Me Do' by The Beatles is starting to gain sales attention." By the third week, a still-determined White was listing the single as a "Choice Up-and-Coming Sure Shot." White continued missing the mark at radio with The Beatles for most of '63. "Please Please Me" and the next single, "From Me to You," both failed to show up on the radar screen.

It wasn't until after Capitol Canada issued "She Loves You" in September that things started slowly heating up. "Please give this

record the VIP treatment it deserves," wrote White in the September 20 issue of the *Sizzle*, reminding readers that "She Loves You" had sold half a million copies within two weeks of its British release. The following week, White credited Oshawa, Ontario's CKLB with being the first station in Canada to chart the single. In early October, he wrote that "She Loves You" has "started off at a much slower rate than we expected, but we're not going to give up yet." True to his word, White told stations to dig out their copy and "give it another try." He added: "If you've lost your sample, write us and we'll send another one!"

Then, in November, the *Sizzle* reported: "We contacted EMI Records in England at 11 a.m. Monday. Received permission to release The Beatles' new album (advance orders 280,000 in England) by 1 p.m. At the time of writing, the jacket is ready, the LP is being pressed for release Friday (November 22). How's that for action!!" Capitol Canada promptly issued the album, titled *Beatlemania! With the Beatles*, and included media quotes on the cover, including the *Ottawa Journal*'s Sandy Gardiner. Both the title and the cover design immediately distinguished it from other versions of the album released around the world.

An early source of full-fledged Beatle fanaticism could be traced that year to London, Ontario. There, Eddie Colero, then a salesman for Columbia Records and now EMI Canada's Director of Special

Landing in Vancouver on August 19, 1964 for the Empire Stadium concert: the city's chief of police had to send M.C. Red Robinson out to quell the crowd—midway through the show

Markets, went into a record store called the Disc Shop and got the shock of his life. "The whole store was wallpapered with album covers of this long-haired group," recalls Colero, who was then trying to sell the *My Fair Lady* soundtrack. "I said to the kid running the store, 'What is this garbage? Get it off the walls. It'll never sell.' Turned out the kid had been to England, had seen The Beatles and brought back all their recordings. There was nothing else in his store but Beatle product. He wound up selling a ton of Beatle imports." That kid, Colero adds with a chuckle, was Richard Bibby, the future president of MCA Records, in both Canada and the United States.

By January 1964, the *Sizzle* reported that Beatlemania was "spreading like wildfire!" It added: "To say that everyone at Canadian-Capitol HQ are 'Beatles Mad' is a slight understatement! The Beatles this week held down No. 1 and 2 positions with singles and their Beatlemania album. This is the only time in Toronto's history that an artist or group has had the top two singles and top album at the same time." White reported that the CHUM chart capitalized on the Beatle craze in Toronto with a front-page photo of the group and a back-page spread of four CHUM deejays "complete with wild Beatle wigs painted on by the CHUM artist."

During the week of The Beatles' February 9 appearance on "The Ed Sullivan Show," Capitol Canada issued the group's second album, *Twist and Shout*, featuring "She Loves You." Already, combined shipments of the group's first six singles had passed the 400,000 mark and their two albums had shipped over 350,000. (A third album, another exclusively Canadian release titled *Long Tall Sally*, came out that spring.) "The albums are moving out like singles and are now listed on Top 40 single surveys," reported the *Sizzle*. Meanwhile, the Ontario chapter of the Canadian Beatle Fan Club had received applications from 10,000 teenagers in just one week.

With The Beatles scheduled to perform at New York's Carnegie Hall, Capitol Canada's Paul White, along with salesmen Joe Woodhouse and Maurice

Zurba, flew down to take in the show. White described the experience in the *Sizzle*:

"Our hectic and exciting day started when we joined reps from *Cashbox*, *Billboard* and Swan Records (they have 'She Loves You' in the States and were due to present The Beatles with a Gold Record) at The Beatles' hideaway, the Plaza Hotel. It so happens that Wednesday was Lincoln's birthday so every kid in New York was off school... Anyway, when we arrived at the Plaza, we discovered 2,000 teenagers waiting outside—inside—all around the block for their heroes to show up. Seems the boys were due at the Hotel from Grand Central Station and the fans had been waiting for two hours. We stationed ourselves at a side door (along with 500 others and waited)... suddenly ear-splitting shrieks broke out among the waiting kids—The Beatles had arrived!! A flying wedge of six cops hustled the boys through the lobby—hundreds of fans in hot pursuit. We stood back and watched as Ringo, Paul, George and John fought their way into an elevator—even then they couldn't escape their fans.

Meeting the press in the Hot Stove Lounge at Toronto's Maple Leaf Gardens, August 17, 1966: witty banter and endearing flippancy

ROW SEAT
LL 12
FLOOR
Retain Stub — Good Only
SERIES **C**
MON. SEPT. 7th
Davis Printing Limited
THE "BEATLES"
2.30 P.M.   PRICE: $5.50
ADMIT ONE. Entrance by Main
Door or by Church Street Door.
M~ple Leaf G~

1964

SEC. ROW SEAT
68 L 16
WEST
Retain Stub — Good Only
SERIES 57
TUES. AUG. 17th
Davis Printing Limited
THE "BEATLES"
4.00 P.M.   PRICE $5.00
ADMIT ONE. Entrance by Main
Door or by West Door, Carlton St.

1965

SEC. ROW SEAT
71 J 6
EAST
Retain Stub — Good Only
SERIES R1
WED. AUG. 17th
Davis Printing Limited
THE "BEATLES"
4.00 P.M.   PRICE $5.00
ADMIT ONE. Entrance by Main
Door or by Church Street Door.
Maple Leaf Gardens
LIMITED
CONDITION OF SALE: Upon refund-
~se price the man-

1966

But can she sing harmony? Miss Canada, Carol Ann Balmer, meets the Fab Four in Toronto, September 7, 1964

ROW SEAT
KK 42
FLOOR
Retain Stub — Good Only
SERIES **B**
MON. SEPT. 7th
Davis Printing Limited
THE "BEATLES"
8.30 P.M.   PRICE: $5.50
ADMIT ONE. Entrance by Main
Door or by Church Street Door.
Maple Leaf Gardens
LIMITED
CONDITION~
ing~

1964

ROW SEAT
AA 1
FLOOR
SERIES 58
TUES. AUG. 17th
Retain Stub — Good Only
Davis Printing Limited
THE "BEATLES"
8.30 P.M.

1965

SEC. ROW SEAT
51 J 8
EAST
Retain Stub — Good Only
SERIES R2
WED. AUG. 17th
Davis Printing Limited
THE "BEATLES"
8.30 P.M.   PRICE $5.50
ADMIT ONE. Entrance by Main
Door or by Church Street Door.
Maple Leaf Gardens
LIMITED
CONDITION OF SALE: Upon refund-

1966

Six girls squeezed in and were taken up to the Beatles floor before being turned away.

"We eventually took an elevator to the 12th floor—proved we were legal and were admitted to The Beatles' suite. Their rooms were littered with news stories of their trip from all over the States and Canada. As we moved into their room their afternoon mail arrived—five sacks of it!! The presentation and picture session was soon over and we dived in to say 'hello' to The Beatles. Incidentally, we presented them with copies of the charts we had received here last week representing Canadian stations coast-to-coast. We found The Beatles courteous, friendly and eager to see how their records were doing here. They already knew how popular they are here but we sat down and look over the surveys. Afterwards, they asked us to thank everyone in Canada for giving so much time to their records and said they really hoped they could play here later in '64."

By March, six of the Top 10 positions on the CHUM chart were filled by Beatle singles (another two were taken by other Capitol acts). By April, tickets for a Labour Day concert at Toronto's Maple Leaf Gardens had sold out within an hour and fifteen minutes, after 6,000 Beatle fans had lined up—including a few dozen who'd camped out for several days. Similar scenes took place in Montreal and Vancouver. The Beatle ticket fuss in Toronto made bigger news than the Stanley Cup finals, in which the Toronto Maple Leafs played host to the Detroit Red Wings. "You won't believe this," said Leaf assistant general manager King Clancy, "but we've had people offering to trade their Stanley Cup tickets—for Beatle tickets. It wouldn't be right," added Clancy, a man of Celtic descent, "even if the Beatles were Irish."

That summer, The Beatles' movie debut *A Hard Day's Night* only served to fuel interest in the group. By the time The Beatles arrived in Canada in August for their Vancouver concert, followed by two in each of Toronto and Montreal, the excitement had reached levels of full-blown hysteria. At the Vancouver show at Empire Stadium, the Beatles' manager, Brian Epstein, and the city's chief of police sent disc jockey Red Robinson, who was hosting, out to quell the crowd—midway through the band's performance. "The chief of police said, 'If they don't back away from the stage, somebody is going to get hurt,'" Robinson recalls. "Then Brian Epstein said to me, 'Red, go up there at the end of this song and break in on The Beatles.' I said 'Okay.' Can you imagine my position?" Robinson got up his nerve and did it, but not before getting an expletive uttered at him by an indignant John Lennon.

John, George, Paul and Ringo receive Diamond Award on September 7, 1964, for total Canadian sales of one million, from Capitol Canada's Paul White, Geoffrey Racine, Taylor Campbell and Edward Leetham

The Beatles' Toronto appearance was equally eventful. Radio stations CHUM and CKEY set up remote operations in a parking lot opposite the Gardens. During the course of the day, they gave away 5,000 copies of Beatle dictionaries (with definitions for English expressions like "take a butcher's," meaning "have a look") that Capitol Canada had specially printed. Between the two concerts, Capitol arranged a gold-record presentation for *Beatlemania!* to the group on the Gardens' stage. White, president Geoffrey Racine, vice-president Edward Leetham and sales manager Taylor Campbell all posed with the four famous mop-tops for a photograph during the presentation. "We gave The Beatles a copy of the original pressing," recalls White, "one of the ones we called 'mother.' It wasn't an especially classy-looking thing, but it at least marked the occasion."

Capitol salesman Bill Bannon remembers a variety of Beatle promotional items, aside from Beatle dictionaries, that the label made available—items that would now fetch hundreds of dollars on the collectors' market. "We had Beatle wigs and those Beatle bobble heads made out of ceramic," says Bannon. "Fans would mail in requests to our Queen Street office. We used to send out photos like crazy. We could never keep up with the demand. It was just insane."

It's difficult to convey now the extent to which Beatlemania swept Canada. "Everything," recalls Maurice Zurba, "was Beatle this and Beatle that. For a while, it seemed like that was the only thing selling or that anyone talked about." Zurba, like many Capitol employees at the time, can still remember the catalogue numbers for the top-selling Beatle singles and albums. Fans, meanwhile, eagerly awaited each record and rushed out to buy it on the day of release. Radio responded by treating each release as a major event, worthy of special all-day features.

After two more North American tours, where Toronto was the only Canadian stop, the mania was mostly over, but the group's influence and record sales continued to escalate. Every time a Beatle opened his mouth or donned a particular piece of clothing, it was widely reported and often imitated. Who can forget the controversy surrounding John Lennon's "we're bigger than Jesus" comment, or the group's iridescent Carnaby Street attire? Countless Beatle-inspired records came out, "Ringo, I Love You" by Bobby Jo Mason,

'I'll show you how it's done.' Paul takes a turn on the skins prior to the band's September 7, 1964 appearance at Maple Leaf Gardens, with a dubious George, Ringo and John looking on (note curious cops, lower left)

Police escort as The Beatles as the group leaves Toronto for the last time, August 18, 1966

Montreal DJ Michel Desrochers, of radio station CJMS, meets Paul McCartney backstage at the Forum, September 8, 1964

Over 3,000 Beatlemaniacs greeted their idols upon their arrival at Montreal's international airport

who became better known as Cher. Capitol released a few of their own: The Four Preps' "A Letter to The Beatles," Peter Sellers' singing "A Hard Day's Night" as Laurence Olivier and "Ringo Deer" by CHUM disc jockey Garry Ferrier, which reached #7 on his station's chart.

Most people can still remember where they were the first time they heard *Sgt. Pepper's Lonely Hearts Club Band*. In Canada, the album played like a summer soundtrack during the centennial celebrations of Expo '67. Just as The Beatles had, as personalities, transformed the western world, so too did their recording revolutionize the music world. Musicians began viewing albums as an organic whole, rather than a collection of commercial singles and "filler." For disc jockeys like CFUN's Red Robinson in Vancouver, The Beatles' landmark album gave birth to a new medium. "It changed radio after that," says Robinson. "The subculture was now where it was all coming from—and this new thing called FM radio where they could talk forever and play 10-minute cuts. It was albums like *Sgt. Pepper* and what came after it that gave FM its start."

Onstage at the Forum: the group had to struggle to hear itself over the deafening din of screaming Montreal fans

In May 1967, EMI announced that total sales of The Beatles' records topped the 200-million mark worldwide. The group's success gave them the clout to establish their own label, Apple Records, which they announced after returning from their spiritual sojourn to India in 1968. Distributed by Capitol, Apple became the first group-run label to release recordings other than its own. When Apple was launched in Canada, Capitol organized a lavish party at Toronto's Sutton Place Hotel, featuring the label's first four singles: Jackie Lomax's "Sour Milk Sea," The Black Dyke Mills Brass Band's "Thingumybob," Mary Hopkin's "Those Were the Days" and The Beatles' own "Hey Jude," which immediately shot to number one across Canada. A new era was born.

Increasingly, each member of The Beatles was moving in his own direction. The group's subsequent albums, *The Beatles*, *Abbey Road* and *Let It Be*, represented either brilliant studio creations with mostly solo vocals or else half-hearted group efforts to "get back."

The Beatles officially broke up in 1970, but they left a legacy that, in artistic, financial and cultural terms, is immeasurable. During their seven-year stint as a working band, The Beatles broke every record and earned every accolade they received. Over the course of 18 albums released between 1964 and 1970, the group made Capitol millions and gave the world enough memories to last for many lifetimes to come.

THE BEAT GOES ON

For a while, it really did seem like North America was under attack. English bands began storming our shores in early 1964 with The Beatles, followed in quick succession by The Dave Clark Five, The Swinging Blue Jeans, Billy J. Kramer & the Dakotas, Gerry & the Pacemakers and Peter & Gordon. All were released on Capitol in Canada. And each established a beachhead in Canada first, displacing American acts like Bobby Vinton, Gene Pitney and even Elvis Presley in the process. Then they took over the U.S. airwaves. By the fall of '64, their landing parties had arrived and captured the concert circuit as well. North American teenagers seemed happy to capitulate.

The advance guard had actually come a couple of years earlier, with the first singles by British vocalists Helen Shapiro and Cliff Richard. Shapiro and, especially, Richard scored a series of hit singles in Canada. Shapiro's "I Don't Care" was among Capitol's top five sellers in 1962, while Richard held four of the label's top ten selling singles in '63. Although Shapiro and Richard were soon eclipsed by the beat-driven bands from Liverpool and London, their pop songs primed the market for what was to follow.

The Beatles played in front of millions of Canadians on the night of February 9, 1964, with the group's TV appearance on "The Ed Sullivan Show." But Gerry & the Pacemakers were the first British Invasion group to tour Canada. Immediately following their own guest spot on Sullivan's "rilly beeg shew" in May, the band performed in Toronto and Montreal while its song "I'm the One" was riding high in the charts. Capitol's

Singer Helen Shapiro: her topselling pop songs primed the Canadian market for what was to follow

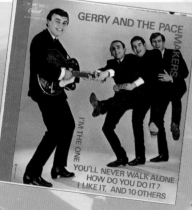

Paul White, who'd pushed his company to release the British bands on Capitol Canada after his success with Shapiro and Richard, remembers being completely unprepared for the greeting Gerry and his group received at Toronto's Eaton Auditorium on College Street.

"My assistant, Corinne Peterson, and I went to the auditorium in the afternoon to put Gerry & the Pacemakers posters up," recalls White. "When we came back later, they were all gone. The place, which usually held piano recitals, was packed with 1,250 teenage girls. The man who ran the auditorium was totally horrified. The girls sat dutifully through openers Shirley Matthews and Robbie Lane & the Disciples fronted by a bearded Ronnie Hawkins. But when Gerry and his group came out, they started screaming louder and louder. It was absolutely deafening. We should've realized then that the British Invasion was coming. But none of us had a clue what was just around the corner."

This was White's first experience with mass hysteria and he admits that he found it frightening. "The crowd surged forward to the stage and the girls started grabbing at Gerry and the group," says White, "tearing at their clothing—like they wanted a piece of them. Even CHUM's Jungle Jay Nelson, who was hosting, had his suit ripped." Added White: "I remember Ronnie Hawkins came back out and started chucking people off them. We were all acting as bouncers. Eventually, we got everyone calmed down and Gerry did his set. But you couldn't hear him over the screaming." The *Toronto Telegram*, which described the show as "pandemonium," proclaimed: "The Eaton Auditorium will never be the same."

In the wake of The Beatles' first Canadian dates in August and September 1964, a seemingly endless parade of their compatriots followed. The Dave Clark Five, The Beatles' London-based rivals, landed

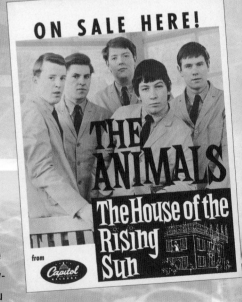

Manfred Mann performing in 1965 on the British TV show Thank Your Lucky Stars

in October to kick off their North American tour at the Montreal Forum. Stepping off a Martin 404 Exec chartered plane (renamed a DC-5 for its occupants), the group was greeted by a thousand screaming fans. Capitol staff were also on hand, including president Geoffrey Racine, for a press conference and a presentation to the group of a silver record honouring the band's sales in Canada. Things, however, didn't quite go as planned.

To begin with, everything got delayed as fans chased the group through the airport. Four members of the band were scrambling around on the third floor of the terminal building, while guitarist Rick Huxley was trapped down on the second floor, where the media was awaiting the band's arrival. Eventually, Mounties rescued Huxley, and the press conference was able to begin. The whole thing was then cut short due to police concerns about a noisy teenage mob downstairs and their own inadequate numbers to deal with them. Still, that night at the Forum, the DC5 thrilled their fans with all their hits, including "Glad All Over," "Bits and Pieces" and "Do You Love Me." A number of Canadian acts opened the show,

including Pierre Lalonde and Capitol recording artists The Esquires.

That month, Gerry & the Pacemakers were back in Canada, this time with Billy J. Kramer & the Dakotas, kicking off their tour in Vancouver. Gerry Marsden was enjoying a new Canadian hit, "I Like It," while Billy J. Kramer had scored with "Bad to Me" and "From a Window," both written by The Beatles' John Lennon and Paul McCartney. This was in no way surprising since Kramer, like Marsden, were managed by The Beatles' Brian Epstein.

Throughout the rest of 1964 and into '65, other British bands on Capitol crowded the Top 10. Among the leading contenders were Freddie & the Dreamers ("I'm Telling You Now") and Manfred Mann ("Do Wah Diddy Diddy"). The label also had The Yardbirds ("Heart Full of Soul") and the initial hits by The Animals ("House of the Rising Sun") and Herman's Hermits ("I'm Into Something Good"). In 1966, The Hollies became a Top 10 phenomenon for Capitol with such irresistible songs as "Bus Stop," "Stop Stop Stop" and "On a Carousel."

"Capitol was the main player in Canada through the 1960s," confirms Vancouver deejay Red Robinson, an inductee in the Rock and Roll Hall of Fame in Cleveland. "I don't care what anybody says, because I was there. Paul White was the driving force. Without him, his vision and his ear—the man had an incredible ear for music—we wouldn't have been able to enjoy all those great sounds of the British Invasion the way we did and when we did. That's what put Capitol on top."

The Hollies, with a beardless Graham Nash (far left) long before teaming up with Crosby, Stills and Young

CLIFF RICHARD

EMI
1958

A singing talent and boyish good looks. Britain's Cliff Richard shared both those qualities with his American counterpart Elvis Presley. And like Presley, Richard exploited them to his advantage through the medium of film. Beginning in the late 1950s and through the '60s, Richard appeared in more than half a dozen movies. Each of them featured a soundtrack, with Richard backed by his band The Shadows. And each of them produced at least one Top 10 hit. By the time The Beatles arrived in Canada in 1964, Richard was already a major star whose top-selling records primed the market for English pop.

Born Harry Webb in Lucknow, India, Richard got his start in music playing guitar and singing with "skiffle" groups (acoustic bands that performed a mix of folk, blues and jazz) in England after his family moved there in 1948. At a Soho coffee bar in London called the 2i's, he met up with a group of musicians led by guitarist Hank Marvin who called themselves The Drifters. Signed by EMI in 1958, Richard scored with his first recording, "Move It," which reached #2 on the British charts. After a wildly successful U.K. tour, movie offers poured in, and in 1959 he starred in the film *Serious Charge*, which featured "Living Doll," Richard's first number one hit in the U.K.

The following year, Richard and his band visited North America in advance of the release of his next movie, *Expresso Bongo*. Packaged on a tour advertised as "The Biggest Stars of 1960," they performed in January at Toronto's Maple Leaf Gardens and the Memorial Auditorium in Kitchener, Ontario, on a bill with such acts as Bobby Rydell and The Isley Brothers.

A pattern was set. Long before the advent of music videos, Richard began maximizing his music's exposure by singing in his movies. The release of his next film, *Wonderful to Be Young*, brought the singer and his band to North America for a promotional tour in October 1962. After appearing on "The Ed Sullivan Show," Richard and the group, now renamed The Shadows, performed "The Young Ones" at the movie's premiere at Toronto's Imperial cinema. Afterwards, Richard spoke of the importance of the Sullivan show, which showcased his ballad style and dancing ability. "That TV appearance was one chance in a million," Richard told the *Toronto Telegram*. "Sixty million people saw me do something different—I wasn't typecast. If they come to the movie, they'll get me doing rock 'n' roll."

As the singer appeared in the movie Expresso Bongo *in 1960, when he and his band toured Canada*

By the time of Richard's next Canadian movie release in early '63, Capitol had licensed his recordings in Canada. Paul White wasted no time cashing in on the promotional possibilities of *Summer Holiday*, which opened at Canadian drive-ins over the Easter weekend. He promptly released the soundtrack and began running radio contests for movie passes and record giveaways. By July, Ottawa fan Ron Dennison had written to Britain's *New Musical Express*, saying, "Cliff Richard has at last broken through in Canada! 'Bachelor Boy' was number one in most Canadian cities, and currently Summer Holiday is the best-selling LP in the country…In fact, he is now so popular over here that several groups are modelling themselves on Cliff and the Shadows."

Richard's breakthrough also prompted White to make a point about Canadian radio: "Cliff has proven that a good record does not have to appear on the *American Cashbox* and *Billboard* charts before it is played, and becomes a hit, in Canada," White stated in *Sizzle Sheet*. "At the time of writing (May 1963), neither "Bachelor Boy" nor "Summer Holiday" has been released in the States. But, in Canada, with at least 10 stations, both discs are in first and second place, and on the remaining charts one or both are in the Top Ten. A good record can make the big time in Canada without the aid of the trade papers."

After Richard scored yet another number one hit in Canada in late '63 with "It's All in the Game," his movie *Wonderful Life* provided White with further promotional opportunities. The film featured two more songs, "On the Beach" and "A Matter of Moments," that did well on the charts. By this time, however, The Beatles and the rest of the British Invasion had hit and Richard's chance at superstardom in North American had passed.

Richard may have been hamstrung by his early billing as "Britain's answer to Elvis Presley." Richard never shook the comparison. And that may explain why he and manager Peter Gormley were reluctant to tour in the U.S. Says White: "I think they were always a little intimidated by America, which is too bad because they could've used Canada as their launch pad. Cliff Richard was huge here."

Canadian Affiliate Labels

HAWK

Owned by Ronnie Hawkins, considered by many to be the godfather of Canadian music, Hawk Records provided Capitol Canada with several hits in the mid-1960s. Hawkins' "Bluebirds Over the Mountain" reached #2 on *RPM*'s Top 10 chart in the winter of '65, while his "Goin' to the River" hit #1 on the Top 40 that spring. But the Toronto-based Hawk was also home to another local hitmaker.

Hawkins had started the label shortly after his backing group left his stable at Toronto's Le Coq D'Or tavern to become better known as Capitol recording artists The Band. He quickly hired Robbie Lane & the Disciples as their replacements. That group recorded two hits on Hawk Records, including "Fannie Mae" and "Ain't Love a Funny Thing," which hit #6 on *RPM*'s Top 40 chart.

Oddly enough, Lane and his guitarist with the Disciples, Domenic Troiano, both later became Capitol recording artists.

ROMAN

Through a distribution deal with Toronto-based Roman Records, formed by Toronto radio disc jockey Duff Roman, Capitol played a role in the early careers of such pioneering Canadian rock acts as The Paupers, David Clayton Thomas and his band, The Shays.

In 1965, Roman Records released two singles by Clayton Thomas ("Take Me Back" and "Out of the Sunshine") and one each by The Paupers ("For What I Am") and The Shays ("This Hour Has Seven Days"). Although only "Out of the Sunshine" received any airplay outside the Toronto area, the label scored one of the biggest Canadian hits of the decade with Clayton Thomas's "Brainwashed."

Released in the summer of '66, "Brainwashed" was three and a half minutes of raging protest. With Clayton Thomas's frenzied vocals criticizing the U.S. presence in Vietnam over a pulsing bass, slashing guitar and some fleet-fingered piano work from jazz genius Tony Collacott, the song shook up the Canadian music scene in the summer of '66. It went to #5 on *RPM*'s Top 40 and topped Toronto's CHUM chart, where it dislodged even The Beatles and The Rolling Stones.

YORKTOWN

Capitol also enjoyed an association with one of Canada's most critically acclaimed garage rock bands, thanks to a deal with Toronto's Yorktown Records. The label, owned by Bill Gilliland and Fred White, was home to The Ugly Ducklings, who were one of the most popular groups playing in Toronto's Yorkville district. With Capitol behind the Ducklings' first singles, the band quickly gained national attention.

Yorktown's first release was a keeper: a snarling piece of punk by the Ducks called "Nothin'." When the song was entered in the weekly "battle of the bands" contest at Toronto's CHUM radio station, it won 13 consecutive times. That success led the Ducklings directly to the gig of their dreams—opening for their heroes, The Rolling Stones, at Toronto's Maple Leaf Gardens in the summer of '66.

Yorktown and Capitol issued two more hits by The Ugly Ducklings, including "She Ain't No Use to Me" and "Just in Case You Wonder." All of those singles have been reissued on CDs in the '90s, as the Ducks remain one of the cult favourites of Canadian rock.

NOVELTIES

Honky the Christmas Goose

Johnny Bower, the all-star goalie with the Toronto Maple Leafs, enjoyed a brief but memorable career as a Capitol recording artist. Although the Vezina Trophy winner was more used to blocking shots than scoring hits, he netted a big one in the winter of 1965 with his recording of "Honky the Christmas Goose."

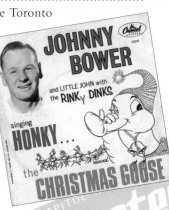

Recorded with a group of session musicians under the name Little John and the Rinky Dinks, the song hit #1 on the influential CHUM chart. The single, released with a picture sleeve featuring a photo of Bower and a cartoon of Honky, remains a much sought-after item among record collectors and a curiosity piece for hockey fans with fond memories of Bower as a formidable puck stopper.

Like a Dribbling Fram

One of Capitol Canada's biggest hits in the mid-1960s was a bizarre Bob Dylan parody called "Like a Dribbling Fram." Recorded by Race Marbles, the song caused a stir when it was released in late 1965. Although Race Marbles was unknown at the time, radio programmers and music critics embraced the singer's wacky Dylan send-up.

In Canada, the song hit #3 on *RPM*'s Top 10 chart. In the United States, where it was

"HOW IS YOUR BIRD...?"
Introducing the Sensational
RACE MARBLES

"LIKE A DRIBBLING FRAM"

ON SALE HERE FROM *Capitol* RECORDS

released on the Tower label, the single was "picked" by both *Billboard* and *Cashbox*. *Billboard*'s "Pop Spotlight" column described it as a "wild novelty debut of hilarious material that covers all the tunes and expressions of the day," adding the prediction that it "could be a monster."

After the hoopla died down, Race Marble's true identity was revealed. It turned out to be CHUM disc jockey Garry Ferrier, who had earlier made the charts for Capitol with his Beatle novelty song "Ringo Deer."

Scrooge and the Stars

Ottawa's Rich Little became one of America's favourite comedians in the 1960s with his celebrity impersonations. Before he moved on to Las Vegas and a successful career with his own TV specials, Little recorded two popular comedy albums for Capitol in Canada.

The first release, 1963's *My Fellow Canadians*, saw Little in the role of Prime Minister John Diefenbaker. For the follow-up recording, Little ambitiously supplied 22 well-known voices as he offered his twisted rendition of Charles Dickens's *A Christmas Carol*. With Jack Benny as Scrooge and Ed Sullivan, Lloyd Bridges and Walter Brennan as the Three Spirits, Little's *Scrooge and the Stars* became an instant comedy classic.

Canada Observed

Released in 1967 as Capitol's contribution to Canada's centennial celebrations, *Canada Observed* could well have been called "Canada Absurd." Devised and produced by TV writer Chris Beard and Capitol's Paul White, the album was an unusual telling of the story of Canada, performed by the cast of CBC's satirical TV show "Nightcap."

Billy Van and Bonnie Brooks played the characters of Lumberjack and Indian Maiden, respectively, while Al Hamel (later host of several U.S. game shows) took on the role of Mountie. The story also featured such historical figures as Leif Eriksson (Beard) and Laura Secord (Vanda King). Music was provided by a stellar group of Canadian musicians led by trumpeter Guido Basso, clarinetist Moe Koffman and guitarist Ed Bickert. The album reached its absurdist zenith with an eyewitness account of Laura Secord's frustrations at Customs as she tries to warn of the American invasion, and "ABC's Wide World of Wars," a play-by-play analysis of the Battle of the Plains of Abraham.

Sounds Canadian:

1970 - 1979

SOUNDS CANADIAN

CHAPTER THREE

SOUNDS CANADIAN:
1970 - 1979

Change was in the air. It was early 1970 and the CRTC's proposed Canadian content regulations for broadcast (given the sobriquet CanCon) were being hotly debated in Ottawa. There were some who said that Capitol knew which way the wind was blowing when it launched "Sounds Canadian," a lavish spring campaign to promote the label's domestic talent. In fact, Capitol had already made a commitment to seek out and sign local artists two years earlier, at its national convention. Sounds Canadian was simply a natural umbrella under which the company could market all those signings.

The campaign kicked off with a four-page ad in *RPM Weekly*, which read: "With so many Canadian artists today making it big in the States, we figured it was about time someone here gave them a chance to be heard. Canadian musicians, performers, and singers are every bit as talented and professional as their counterparts south of the border. Do they have to cause a stir in the States before we'll listen? Or is it just that we never seem to notice what's right here in our own backyard? We at Capitol lean very strongly towards the latter. Sounds Canadian has been designed to fill the void."

Capitol Canada's reception on American Drive in the early 1970s: a chance for domestic talent to be heard

The first recordings released under the Sounds Canadian banner included albums by Edward Bear, Gary Buck, Gene MacLellan, Mother Tucker's Yellow Duck, Pierre Lalonde and Anne Murray. All began garnering airplay across the country that year. Those who experienced the greatest mainstream success were Edward Bear and Anne Murray. The Bear's fortunes took a dramatic turn upward when its marimba-flavoured "You, Me and Mexico" shot to #3 on the Canadian charts in May. The song also opened doors for the Toronto band south of the border. Murray's breakthrough came with her recording of "Snowbird," a song by

"Musicians, performers and singers every bit as talented and professional as their counterparts south of the border"

fellow Maritimer Gene MacLellan. The wistful tune became a huge hit in both Canada and the United States in late summer. Murray, in fact, would soon become Capitol's premier Canadian artist and the benchmark for its entire domestic roster.

The success of Murray and Edward Bear could not have come at a better time. For too long, Capitol worldwide had been coasting on the consistently strong sales of The Beatles. Maurice Zurba, then Ontario sales representative, puts it this way: "The marvellous thing with The Beatles was that we had so much success. The terrible thing was that we had too much." Added Zurba, now retired and living like a snowbird himself, spending his winters in Florida: "Sometimes, when you have that level of success, you rest on your laurels. I think that was happening with our company to a degree. It had all become too easy."

The news in April 1970 that The Beatles were breaking up cast a pall over Capitol's operations everywhere. Although the year had started out

Mother Tucker's Yellow Duck: one of the new breed of bands out of western Canada

with the group's latest classic, *Abbey Road*, at the top of the charts, it was clear that the company could no longer expect to be carried by its best-selling act. Capitol would have to work for its hits just like every other label. At Capitol Canada's national convention, held in June in Vancouver, Capitol U.S. president Stanley Gortikov spoke about a new beginning. "Tomorrow is the first day of the rest of your life," he told the gathering, borrowing a popular expression of

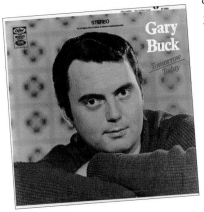

the day. "So it is for you, as you newly appraise who you are, and where you are going."

Sales manager Zurba, who acted as master of ceremonies for the gala evening, gave an indication of where the company was heading when he introduced Anne Murray to Capitol's staff and assembled guests. "This was the first time Anne had ever sung to one of our conventions," recalls Zurba. "She came out barefoot, with her guitar slung across her chest, and sang 'Snowbird.' The audience went crazy. It was incredibly moving. You could tell right then and there that she was going to be huge."

With a budding star on its roster and the challenges of the post-Beatles era looming, Capitol needed new leadership. Right after the convention, the parent company, Capitol U.S., announced that Arnold Gosewich would take over from Ron Plumb, who was returning to the label's Los Angeles offices. Gosewich had already proven himself an asset two years earlier, when Capitol acquired his former employer, the Ottawa-based retail and racking business, Alex Sherman Enterprises, and appointed him vice-president, group marketing. That acquisition, involving a network of Ontario and Quebec record stores known as Sherman Music Centres, enabled Capitol Canada to expand into the retail trade, and mirrored a move the parent company made south of the border with the Tower chain.

As executive vice-president and general manager, Gosewich sized up the Canadian operation and found it wanting. "Frankly, we were losing money," admits Gosewich. "The American company, the traditional provider of new artists for Capitol

Sherman Music Centres: the network of Ontario and Quebec record stores enabled Capitol Canada to expand into retail

in Canada, wasn't doing well either [it lost over $8 million after taxes during the 1970–71 fiscal year]. To use a retailer's term, we simply didn't have the inventory." Something had to be done.

Anne Murray at Capitol Canada's 1970 convention: "she came out barefoot, sang Snowbird and the audience went crazy"

Help initially came in the form of Frank Davies, a savvy young Brit who had just started a label in Toronto called Daffodil Records. (Oddly enough, Davies had worked for EMI in London before moving to Canada at the encouragement of Ronnie Hawkins, who'd raved to him about all the Canadian talent just waiting to be developed.) Already, Daffodil had two Canadian acts in its stable: blues singer–harmonica player Richard Newell, a.k.a. King Biscuit Boy, and Crowbar, a raucous bar band that had served its apprenticeship with Hawkins. Capitol signed a distribution deal with Daffodil and the first single, a collaborative effort between both acts called "Corrina Corrina," made *RPM*'s Top 30 that fall.

Buoyed by the single's success and with Capitol's help, Daffodil issued *Official Music*, King Biscuit Boy's blues-soaked debut album with Crowbar. Packaged in flour sacks imported from Arkansas, in homage to Newell's hero Sonny Boy Williamson, the album immediately signalled a shift toward more adventurous releases. Says Larry LeBlanc, then a young music reporter, now Canadian editor of *Billboard*: "Frank Davies was a unique, inspirational character on the scene at the time, a long-haired, urbane Englishman who wore immaculately tailored suits. He was internationally minded right from the start and taught Capitol in Canada to think big."

On January 18, 1971, the Canadian content regulations became law, requiring that radio broadcasters feature a minimum of 30 per cent

Canadian music in its programming. That same day, Capitol released Daffodil's next single, "Oh What a Feeling" by Crowbar. And what a rush it was. A rock 'n' roll boogie with an infectious party atmosphere, the song became an instant CanCon anthem and shot straight to the top of the *RPM* charts. Crowbar rode that single right into the United States, where the group's debut album, *Bad Manors*, was received with open arms. *Rolling Stone* called it "one of the happiest, raunchiest, freshest emanations of a life energy to pin the grid in many moons."

While Crowbar was basking in the glow of CanCon, others were not so enamoured of the new regulations. Radio programmers complained about a lack of Canadian material to fill their 30 per cent quotas. Capitol came to their rescue with a double-album set featuring artists from its domestic roster and international Capitol acts performing Canadian compositions. Although its title read like a dry, government policy paper, *Capitol Records Guide to Canadian Content Programming* was nonetheless an inventive solution, featuring tracks by such domestic artists as Anne Murray and The Band, and American acts like Glen Campbell performing Joni Mitchell's "Both Sides Now." Gosewich, who in March was appointed Capitol's president, instilled a sense of patriotic pride at the label. "We began promoting Canadian music more aggressively," he recalls, "and it started to make a difference."

Among the many Canadian acts launched by the label during 1971 were newcomers Aarons & Ackley, The Pepper Tree and Fergus Hambleton, later the leader of the award-winning reggae band The Sattalites. Capitol also signed two veteran artists that year: former bobbysoxer Bobby Curtola and Tommy Graham, who had recorded for Capitol in the 1960s with his band The Big Town Boys. All of them began showing up on radio playlists across the country.

WAYNE DION PROMOTIONS
presents
The Grimsby Rock & Blues
REVIVAL
FEATURING: KING BISCUIT BOY
AND: CROWBAR
WITH: VEDAS
DAVE CHARLES — EMCEE — CKOC
Sat., August 22 – 8 p.m.
GRIMSBY ARENA
TICKETS — $2.25
Available At:
Joe Spratt Sports, Grimsby Plaza
Grimsby Arena
Melody Lane Record Shop, Hamilton
Sherman's Record Centre, Hamilton
CKOC Radio Station, Hamilton

Capitol keeps on building with solid hits by Canada's top artists.

Capitol's biggest hits that year, however, were transatlantic. Collectively, The Beatles were no more, but, as individuals, they remained an artistic and commercial force with releases on their own, Capitol-distributed

Apple label. Beginning with Ringo Starr's "It Don't Come Easy" and followed by Paul McCartney's "Uncle Albert/Admiral Halsey" and John Lennon's "Imagine," each of them reached #1 on the *RPM* chart. George Harrison's *The Concert for Bangla Desh* was a critically acclaimed benefit

Daffodil recording artists Crowbar, presenting Prime Minister Pierre Trudeau with his own Crowbar pendant in Perth, Ontario in 1971

album that won Album of the Year honours at the 1972 Grammy Awards.

Increasingly, however, the Canadian music industry was becoming focused on its own. Discussions at the 1972 Juno Awards, reported Richard Flohil in *The Canadian Composer*, were devoted almost entirely to domestic talent. "Canadiana—Top 40, bubblegum, rock 'n' roll—is on everyone's lips this year," wrote Flohil. "The talk is about Crowbar, Fergus, Lighthouse, Anne Murray, Gordon Lightfoot, Brave Belt, The Guess Who and The Stampeders." He added: "Donny Osmond, Three Dog Night, Led Zeppelin and all the other international names who sell millions of records all over the world, are just passed over."

Once again, Anne Murray won the Juno for Female Vocalist of the Year, while her *Talk It Over in the Morning* release was honoured as the year's best-produced album. The singer scored her second major Canadian hit that spring when her recording of Lightfoot's "Cotton Jenny" topped the *RPM* charts. And Murray's success was followed by Edward Bear, whose "Masquerade" went Top 10. Other

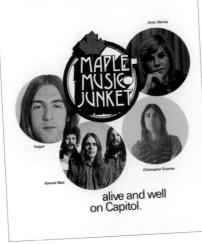

Canadian music lives.

MAPLE MUSIC JUNKET

alive and well on Capitol.

Capitol artists who scored hits in '72 included Flying Circus, one of a number of new signings along with Shirley Eikhard, Christopher Kearney, New Potatoes and Bob McBride, former lead singer with

Country star Gary Buck at the Maple Music Junket, 1972

Lighthouse who came through a licensing deal with the Toronto label H.P. & Bell. Meanwhile, A Foot in Coldwater became Daffodil's next success when the group's single "(Make Me Do) Anything You Want" made the charts.

Showing Capitol's commitment to indigenous sounds, Gosewich joined journalist Ritchie Yorke in spearheading 1972's Maple Music Junket. An unprecedented promotional project to develop markets in Europe for Canadian recordings, the Junket flew 80 leading European writers, editors, broadcasters, producers and filmmakers to Montreal and Toronto for a one-week crash course in CanCon. Gosewich helped to raise $70,000 from the Canadian music industry and another $30,000 from the federal government to cover the costs of the chartered Canadian Pacific flight and concerts to be staged in both cities. Among the Capitol artists who performed at sold-out concerts at Montreal's Place des Arts and Toronto's Massey Hall were Anne Murray, Gary Buck, Fergus Hambleton, Christopher Kearney, Crowbar, Edward Bear and The Pepper Tree.

The Maple Music Junket was an unqualified success. "An awareness of things Canadian is happening," confirmed Andy Gray, of England's *New Musical Express*, following the event.

Singer Christopher Kearney at the 1972 Junket

"Vive Canada!" he added in a gush of enthusiasm. For Gosewich, the Junket was a necessary step on the part of Canadian record companies to raise their artists' profiles. "It was our job to promote the fact that these performers existed," says Gosewich. "We couldn't count on radio to do that. It had to be part of an overall marketing strategy coming from us."

For his pioneering efforts and leadership within the industry, Gosewich received *Billboard*'s Trendsetter of the Year award.

Capitol's president was also honoured at the 1973 Juno Awards as Industry Man of the Year. The label, which won the award for Canadian Content Company of the Year, made a strong showing right across the board at the Junos that March. Shirley Eikhard won for Female Country Singer of the Year. And while Anne Murray and Edward Bear were up accepting two awards each, their latest singles, "Danny's Song" and "Last Song," respectively, were both Top 10 at *RPM* and *Billboard*. Meanwhile, Bob McBride's "Pretty City Lady" was Top 20 at *RPM* and "Wildflower" by Skylark, a West Coast Capitol act featuring Canadians David Foster and B. J. Cook, hit the *Billboard* Top 10. By September, *Billboard* magazine reported: "The majority of majors have commendably expended large sums in Canadian talent investment, [but] only one—Capitol Canada—has been able to make Canadian production profitable."

Gosewich points to teamwork as the reason for the company's improved showing. "We were like a football squad and I was lucky enough to be the quarterback at the

time," he says. "Like any good quarterback, you can't call good plays unless you've got a good team to execute them. I had a terrific team of guys who reported to me [Dave Evans in marketing, Paul White in A&R, Malcolm Perlman in finance, John Macleod in business affairs, Brian Josling in retail and Glen Lane in personnel] and we developed a refreshing level of candor with each other. We became more productive because we were learning to accept criticism in a constructive way and eliminate the politics that typically exist within a corporation."

In the summer of '73, Gosewich had a giant cardboard thermometer installed in the warehouse. As sales figures rose, so did the "temperature" in the plant. It was, he now admits, a little hokey, but it helped to involve employees— from the salesman to the shipper—in the quest for higher production. "I thought it was important to let everyone know how we were doing," he explains, "in the hope that

people would work hard and pull together. I'm happy to say that it was successful."

Along with Canadian hits, numerous artists from Capitol's international roster topped the charts that year, including singles by McCartney, Starr, Helen Reddy and Grand Funk Railroad. England's Pink Floyd scored a breakthrough with "Money," which reached #18 at *RPM* that summer. Al Andruchow, then a West Coast

Vice-president of marketing, Dave Evans: pushing Capitol Canada to the forefront

salesman for Capitol, now vice-president of sales, remembers Floyd playing to a small crowd in Vancouver in 1973. "The concert was at the old Forum at Exhibition Place," recalls Andruchow. "There were maybe 2,500 people there, tops. The band wasn't very big at all yet, although it was a lot bigger in Canada than the States—and bigger in Quebec than anywhere else. Of course, *Dark Side of the Moon* eventually went on to become one of the best-selling albums of all time."

Pink Floyd's *Dark Side of the Moon* came via Capitol's Harvest subsidiary in England. Harvest enjoyed another Canadian breakthrough with the British progressive rock band Babe Ruth, which played to large audiences in Canada in the early 1970s. With its strong fan base in the Great White North, the group saw its 1972 debut album *First Base* reach gold-level sales of 50,000 copies in Canada. A Canadian-only CD collection, *The Best of Babe Ruth*, was released in 1991.

Anne Murray enjoyed another banner year in 1974. By the time Capitol U.S. held its board of directors meeting in Toronto in June—the first time such a meeting was conducted outside of the United States—there was much to celebrate. Murray had once again dominated the Juno Awards, winning Top Female Vocalist and Best Pop Album honours. And the singer had placed two songs in or near the Top 10 at both *RPM* and *Billboard*, "Love Song" and a surprisingly gritty rendition of The Beatles' "You Won't See Me." None of this was lost on the international company's top executives, including Bhaskar Menon, from Los Angeles, and Sir John Read, of the London office, both of whom attended the Toronto meeting.

Following the 1974 meeting, the Canadian operation received a new corporate name: Capitol Records–EMI of Canada, or Capitol-EMI. The change was designed to reflect the Canadian company's membership in the worldwide EMI group of record companies.

Although the '70s would soon become known as the decade of disco (and of pet rocks and eight-track tapes, which Capitol Canada began manufacturing in 1970 along with cassettes), there was still plenty of pop and rock 'n' roll around in 1974. Some of it came directly from Capitol U.S. acts like Grand Funk Railroad, Bob Seger and The Steve Miller Band, whose song "The Joker" topped the charts that year. Some hits came from ex-Beatles on the Apple label. Starr's "You're Sixteen" reached #2 at *RPM*, while McCartney's "Band on the Run" hit the number one spot. Other rocking sounds were the work of Capitol Canada's affiliated labels, including Daffodil, which signed Toronto band Fludd and enjoyed a best-selling single with "Cousin Mary."

Capitol-EMI also struck up a licensing and distribution deal with the New York–based Bell Records, soon to become Arista, which would eventually provide the label with a wealth of hits. One Bell/Arista artist who created quite a stir in '74 was Suzi Quatro. A rebellious rocker who dressed in tight leather jumpsuits, Quatro made an in-store appearance in Calgary during the summer that Andruchow recalls turned into a mini-riot. "Over 700 kids, mostly boys, came

Arista Records' Clive Davis (centre) signs a licensing deal with Capitol Canada's Arnold Gosewich, Dave Evans, Paul White and an unidentified Arista executive, 1972, bringing a flood of topselling artists into Capitol's fold, including Barry Manilow, Al Stewart, The Alan Parsons Project and Bay City Rollers

Barry Manilow (second from right) with Capitol Canada's Eddie Colero, Dave Evans and Bob Rowe

Bay City Rollers with Capitol Canada's Brian Carson (rear left) and sales representative John Toews (rear right) with his family

to see her at Kelly's department store," says Andruchow, "and they wrecked all the racks in the record department. The guys in hardware downstairs were freaking out. In the end, they had to close the store."

Although it didn't spark riots, Beau Dommage did attract a devoted following among francophone Canadians in the mid-70s. The premier act signed by Capitol-EMI, Beau Dommage actually became the best-selling domestic act on the entire label when its debut album sold an astonishing 350,000 copies in 1974. Suzanne Stevens, another Quebec signing, won a Juno Award in early '75 as Most Promising Female Vocalist. Later that year, Stevens also scored a major hit with the disco-pop sound of "Make Me Your Baby." Singer Pierre Lalonde, Raoul Dugay, Christine Chartrand and Lise Thoin rounded out an impressive roster of Quebec talent.

Meanwhile, Capitol-EMI continued to be inspired by the success of Anne Murray. Along with two more Junos, Murray won her first Grammy Award in 1975 for Best Female Country Vocal for "Love Song." The label, in fact, maintained a strong country profile on both sides of the border that year. While the American company had artists such as Merle Haggard, Buck Owens and Glen Campbell, whose "Rhinestone Cowboy" topped the charts, Capitol's Canadian side had Murray, Colleen Peterson and Sylvia Tyson, formerly of the legendary folk duo Ian & Sylvia.

Rollermania came to Capitol (and Canada) in 1976 with the arrival of Scotland's Bay City Rollers. A young pop group signed to Arista, the Rollers were touted as the "new Beatles" when they arrived in Toronto in June to record an album with producer Jimmy Ienner and to hold their first North American press conference. With their tartan uniforms and knicker-length pants, the boys attracted a fanatical, mostly female following and scored a series of hits that year, including "Saturday Night" and "Money Honey," both of which topped the *RPM* chart.

Also crossing the Atlantic that year was Paul McCartney, who

Morse Code: the Quebec band, like its provincial counterparts Maneige and Beau Dommage, helped to develop the label's strong presence in French Canada

brought his first tour, Wings Over America, while his latest release, "Silly Love Songs," dominated the airwaves. The timing was highly calculated. McCartney had waited until he had proven he could still create top-selling radio hits in the post-Beatles era. The tour thrilled old and new fans alike because McCartney chose to include a liberal dose of Beatle material, including "Lady Madonna," "I've Just Seen a Face" and "Yesterday," along with his own solo work.

The successful careers of Anne Murray and Mssrs. McCartney, Lennon, Harrison and Starr had something to do with it. Clearly, there were other

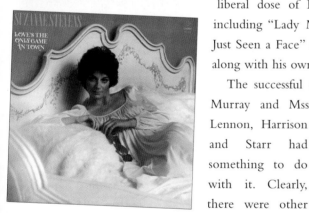

reasons why in June 1976, Capitol-EMI was able to report that it had just concluded the most successful fiscal year in its history. For one thing, sales from the affiliated labels, Arista, H.P. & Bell and now Chrysalis and United Artists, were bringing substantial revenues into the coffers. "We were no longer relying on simply what the American company was giving us," confirms Gosewich. "We were expanding and that growth started paying dividends."

Part of that expansion and profit came from retail. In 1973, the company had acquired two more chains,

A pinstriped Colleen Peterson accepts her Juno Award for best new female vocalist in 1977, with RPM's Walt Grealis and Stan Klees looking on

Mister Sound in Ontario and Scotty's in Alberta. Two years later, all the stores were renamed Mister Sound, with the exception of those in Quebec, which continued to carry the name Sherman Music Centre. At the same time, the company's rackjobbing business, Kensington Distributors, and its publishing division, Beechwood Music, were doing well.

Meanwhile, the A&R department led by Paul White continued to discover and develop new talent in the mid-70s, including Morse Code, Maneige, Deja Vu and Bill Amesbury. Chrysalis, for its part, signed Vancouver's Nick Gilder, ex-vocalist with Sweeney Todd. Opportunities for Canadian acts improved considerably when Capitol U.S. announced a corporate restructuring that saw the A&R departments of Canada and the United States combined into one. Paul White, Canada's vice-president of A&R, began working directly with Rupert Perry, the vice-president of A&R in Hollywood. Suddenly several Canadian signings, including Colleen Peterson and Domenic Troiano, were offered simultaneous release in both Canada and the United States. A new era was underway.

One of the most eventful years in Capitol-EMI's history, 1977 seemed to be one long series of breakthroughs and achievements for the company. In March,

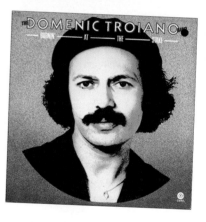

Colleen Peterson made headlines as the Peterborough, Ontario, native won the Juno Award for Best New Female Vocalist. That same month, Deane Cameron started work in the label's A&R department. The young man was no stranger to the company. He had actually started working for Capitol in its warehouse seven years earlier. After learning the ropes in the stockroom, Cameron talked his way into a "jack-of-all-trades" job with Daffodil Records, which then had

Anne Murray's future was so bright, she had to wear shades—even in the pressing plant, which she often graced with her presence

office space on Capitol's premises. When Daffodil moved its distribution to A&M (named for owners Herb Alpert and Jerry Moss) and then GRT (General Recording Tape) for a brief time, Cameron went with it, but now he was back at Capitol and impressing everyone with his high energy and enthusiasm.

On June 15, Capitol-EMI officially opened its own pressing plant. A $2 million, 40,000-square-foot facility built on land adjacent to the American Drive building, the plant was proof that the company had grown so much that it could afford to do its own manufacturing. Previously, all record pressing had been contracted out to either RCA or CBS. The plant had actually begun operation in 1976. (The first run had been a single by Suzanne Stevens, titled "Knowing How, Knowing When." A limited

Max Webster (Mike Tilka, Gary McCracken, Kim Mitchell and Terry Watkinson), one of Canrock's most outrageous and original acts, came via Anthem Records

edition of the first single was pressed with a special commemorative label reading, "Born to A. Gosewich, President of Capitol Canada, the first Canadian Capitol pressing plant, June 7, 1976. Produced with great care by a good mother." The special jacket was autographed by members of the plant staff.) June 15, 1977 marked the day when it reached full capacity, with seventeen 12-inch presses (for LPs) and seven 7-inches (45s) capable of handling orders for up to 10 million records a year.

A giant striped tent was set up in the Capitol-EMI parking lot for a garden party–style event. Gosewich and his staff welcomed such official guests as Ontario treasurer Darcy McKeough, EMI chairman Sir John Read and Capitol Industries president Bhaskar Menon, who were joined by other EMI representatives who had flown in from England, France and Switzerland. The champagne flowed as artists, from Americans Glen Campbell and Al Martino to Canadians Bill Amesbury,

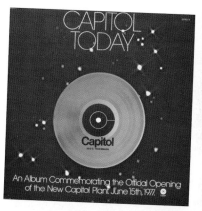

Gene MacLellan and Domenic Troiano, arrived to take part in the festivities. It was a proud day for everyone on Capitol's staff.

Not long after the plant was up and running, Gosewich shocked the music world by announcing that he was leaving the company. The man who had shown an admirable commitment to Canadian talent, boosted the company's revenues through licensing deals and overseen the expansion into retail and manufacturing said it was simply time to move on. Some Capitol staff members felt betrayed when they learned Gosewich was moving over to run CBS Records, but industry observers like Walt Grealis, editor of *RPM Weekly*, said his contribution both to the company and

to Canadian music was enormous. "Arnold was a leader," says Grealis. "Some people didn't like him because he was aggressive. But he was a mover and a shaker and got things done. He was one of the most prominent Capitol presidents up to that time and left a fine legacy."

Dave Evans, the company's vice-president of marketing, took over from Gosewich. Little did Evans know, but 1978 was going to be every bit as eventful as the previous year. First, the game of musical chairs within the company continued. In April, Paul White announced that he, too, was leaving Capitol, after working for the company for over 20 years and contributing greatly to its success. White's assistant, Deane Cameron, was

Hugh Wiets, the company's future vice-president of manufacturing and distribution, presides over the plant's state-of-the-art taping equipment

Plant employee Brenda Odell: by 1977, the company was producing recordings in 8-track, cassette and both seven- and twelve-inch vinyl configurations

Plant employee Doris Philon, at the gauss high speed duplicating bin

Plant employee Shirley Atkinson, moving 8-track cartridges

Plant employee Christine Corbin, at the 8-track winding machine

Supervisors Hans Klopfer (left, bending) and Percy Temple inspect one of the plant's 7-inch record presses with mechanic Paul Mulvenna

Plant employee Renate Geske, doing quality control

The record pressing plant, a $2 million, 40,000-square-foot facility, officially opened to great fanfare on June 15, 1977

an obvious choice for the job of Canadian A&R director. After flying down to Chicago for an interview with Rupert Perry, Cameron was promoted. The young Toronto native proved himself a most capable candidate. In fact, almost right away, he began making his mark on the A&R landscape.

One of the first things Cameron did was bring in distribution deals with two more Canadian independents: Toronto-based Anthem Records, formed by Ray Danniels, that featured rock groups Rush and Max Webster, and Montreal-based Aquarius Records, started by Terry Flood and the home of April Wine, then one of Canada's most successful rock bands. Recalls Cameron: "I called Ray and Terry out of the blue and told them they should be here for distribution. Anthem was with PolyGram at the time and Aquarius was with London. I told them Capitol was where it was happening." There was, however, a catch: in return, both Danniels and Flood wanted U.S. releases for their acts. A tall order. To everyone's surprise, Cameron succeeded in landing the required deals. "Max Webster and April Wine," he now says proudly, "were my first signings worldwide."

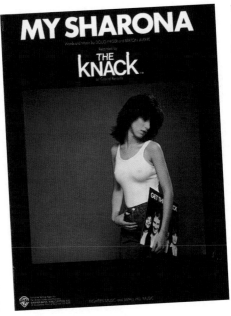

Among the top-selling acts that year were Arista's Al Stewart and The Alan Parsons Project and United Artists' Gerry Rafferty, whose "Baker Street" was a number one hit. Nick Gilder also reached the top spot with his "Hot Child in the City," which became the first Chrysalis single to go gold.

No success was sweeter for Capitol-EMI than that enjoyed by Anne Murray. Her next single, a tender ballad by Randy Goodrum called "You Needed Me," shot straight to

Blondie's Deborah Harry gives a toss at Toronto's El Mocambo, 1978

the top of both the *RPM* and *Billboard* charts that fall. Murray never looked back. The following March, she swept the Junos again and took her second Grammy Award, this time in the Female Pop Vocal category. Murray, who once worried that she'd be a one-hit wonder with "Snowbird," proved she was here to stay.

As the decade came to a close, disco was virtually dead, 8-tracks were going the way of the wax cylinder and pet rocks had given way to punk rock. EMI in England had, in fact, already been immortalized in an unflattering song by punk pioneers The Sex Pistols. Although the label never did recover from that insult in time to land another punk act, it did successfully catch the subsequent new wave movement. New York's Blondie had a number one on the Chrysalis label with "Heart of Glass," while the Los Angeles band The Knack did the same thing for Capitol with "My Sharona."

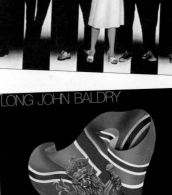

Under Cameron's direction in '79, Capitol-EMI's A&R activity almost tripled from the previous year. Canadian signings included Red Rider, Private Eye, Surrender and legendary blues singer Long John Baldry. A new policy emanating from Los Angeles, and effective at the beginning of February, stated that in future there would be one Canadian release each month, and all promotional and marketing efforts would focus on that artist. Meanwhile, each Canadian Capitol release would also be released internationally.

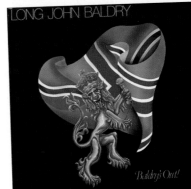

By the middle of the year, president Dave Evans told *RPM Weekly* that Capitol-EMI's sales figures for the last ten months were up 38 per cent over the last fiscal year. He cited April Wine's *Greatest Hits* and Long John Baldry's *Baldry's Out* as gold album releases. And he pointed out that Domenic Troiano's "We All Need Love" had become a Top 40 hit, while Anne Murray's "I Just Fall in Love Again" was yet another number one single. At the end of the interview, Evans thanked Arista, Anthem, Aquarius, Daffodil and United Artists "for their contribution to a successful year and an exciting future."

BEAU DOMMAGE

CAPITOL CANADA
1974

Group members (back row) Pierre Bertrand, Marie-Michele Desrosiers, Michel Hinton, Pierre Huet, Robert Léger and (front row) manager Yves Savard with members Réal Desrosiers and Michel Rivard enjoying triple platinum success: "the first flowering of an original sound from Montreal"

Montreal in the mid-70s. Beau Dommage captured that time and place so perfectly that, for many people, they are synonymous. Riding a wave of cultural nationalism in Quebec, the group became Canada's most successful band, in 1974 selling more than 350,000 copies of its first Capitol album (mostly in Quebec), while its follow-up was the first Canadian recording to ship platinum. Although Beau Dommage broke up in 1978, the longevity of its influence was already assured. Many of the group's best songs became anthems. As Ray Conlogue, the *Globe and Mail*'s Montreal correspondent, noted: "Countless singers reprised its hits…and a new generation, which wasn't even born in 1974, knows the big songs by heart."

Formed at the University of Quebec in Montreal in 1972, the group was initially made up of guitarist Michel Rivard, bassist Pierre Bertrand and keyboardist Robert Léger, who all came from either musical or theatrical backgrounds. At first, they performed as La Quenouille Bleue. But after singer Marie-Michèle Desrosiers and drummer Réal Desrosiers (no relation) joined, they renamed themselves Beau Dommage, an old Quebec expression meaning "of course" or "sure as hell."

Before long, the band was appearing regularly at various CEGEPS, *boites à chansons* (coffeehouses) and concert halls. Pierre Dubord, Capitol's A&R man in Quebec, remembers the first time he heard them: "I received their tape from a promo rep and wanted to see them live. Then I caught them at a rehearsal in a basement club and was immediately taken with their presence, their music and what they were saying in their songs. They were singing about Montreal, the streets, the mountain and different areas. Right away, I knew they were different and I signed them on the spot."

The group's sound, captured on its 1974 self-titled debut album, was deceptively laid-back; although gentle and largely acoustic, it packed a rhythmic and harmonic wallop. Aside from stirring hometown tributes such as "Montréal" and "Chinatown," the album's best song was "La complainte du phoque en Alaska" ("Lament of the Alaska Seal"). Using the metaphor of a seal who joins the circus to express the importance of maintaining one's roots, the song, written by Rivard, was quickly embraced by the Quebec nationalist movement. Explained Bertrand: "Somehow, Michel's poetic unconscious tapped into the collective unconscious. Pretty soon, people were singing the song as an allegory of why you should be faithful to your identity as a

francophone, why you shouldn't let yourself be assimilated."

Beau Dommage received the stamp of approval for the song when legendary Quebec singer Félix Leclerc recorded his own version of "Complainte du phoque." As Léger told *The Canadian Composer* in 1975: "To know that the grandfather of Quebec *chanson* listens to our album and finds a song that he's prepared to take on means that he sees himself in it, and that means that Quebec *chanson* is in good health, that it's not a bunch of fragments that have nothing in common, that it isn't just a series of little trips or fads; there's a continuity to it."

On its second album, *Où est passée la noce?*, the group added electric, brass and string instrumentation and took a more experimental approach to its material. One track, "Un incident à Bois-des-Filion," ran 20 minutes and 30 seconds in length. Once again, the messages of the songs struck a resonant chord. The album's most popular track was "Le blues d'la métropole." Set to a slow blues beat, the song seemed to reflect the history of Quebec youth since

Singer Marie-Michele Desrosiers: the group's sound was a cross between Quebec's chansonniers and The Beatles

Expo '67. Rivard told the *Globe and Mail*: "In spite of the rock-pop format, we're really closer to the *chansonniers*, a cross between them and the Beatles generation." He added: "We resemble Quebec. Like [the province], our music is a melting pot of French and American influences."

After two more albums on Capitol, Beau Dommage broke up in 1978, citing "fatigue" as a factor. Rivard went on to a successful solo career before the group reunited, first in 1984, then again in 1992. In 1991, EMI reissued the band's Capitol albums in a four-CD box set, which promptly sold more than 50,000 copies. Concludes Dubord: "Beau Dommage are unique in the history of Canadian music. They represented the end of an era of copycat groups and the first flowering of an original sound. They sang about their own town, in their own Montreal dialect and accent. It was a very special time."

EDWARD BEAR

CAPITOL CANADA
1969

A hit song can do strange and wonderful things to a rock group. Take Edward Bear's "You, Me and Mexico." When the three-piece band recorded the sunny pop tune, it was the oddball track among a collection of darker, blues-based jams on *Bearings*, the group's debut album. Sweetened by arranger Doug Riley to include marimba and mariachi-style horns by jazz trumpeter Guido Basso, the song's Mexican flavour caught on at AM radio, where it reached #3 on the *RPM* chart. The song's success painted Edward Bear as a pop group, which it wasn't at the time.

Named after A. A. Milne's Winnie the Pooh character, Edward Bear grew out of the last vestiges of Toronto's Yorkville scene. Originally a five-piece outfit, the group auditioned 15 drummers before arriving at Larry Evoy. Good thing, too, because Evoy became the band's lead singer and chief songwriter. With keyboardist Paul Weldon and guitarist Danny Marks, Evoy found a receptive ear at Capitol, which signed the trio to a recording deal. *Bearings* cost $15,000 to produce (a significant amount in those days) and Capitol conducted an ambitious publicity campaign with posters, buttons, bumper stickers and special displays.

The album's "You, Me and Mexico" scored almost instantly on AM radio in the spring of 1970. Evoy told *The Canadian Composer* that he felt the single was helped by the move toward Canadian content legislation. "[The song] came just before the CRTC regulations happened," said Evoy. "It got a great deal of airplay, in part because the radio stations were playing it in an effort to tell the CRTC that they really didn't need the regulations—we certainly gained from that."

The group, according to Marks, was "much heavier" than the song made them appear. "We'd play these long, extended jams with really menacing sounding solos," recalls Marks. "And after we opened for the Paul Butterfield Blues Band and Led Zeppelin in Toronto, which we did twice, a lot of local musicians told us that we inspired them with those shows. It was frustrating that many people didn't know that about us."

Edward Bear decided to go for a tougher sound on its second album, *Eclipse*, and, for its next single, chose Marks's bluesy "You Can't Deny It." According to Weldon, "Capitol wanted us to stick with

Larry Evoy, Danny Marks and Paul Weldon: rugged blues beginnings, sunny-pop reputation

the pop sound, because they said that's what the listeners will expect," he says. "But we wanted to show our other side. As it turned out, neither Danny's song nor the album did very well, which proved Capitol's point. So we moved more toward the pop stuff Larry was writing."

At the same time, Edward Bear was learning to take care of business, setting up a corporation to oversee the group's affairs. Drawing weekly salaries from Canada Bear Ltd., Marks did the group's bookings; Weldon, who worked for an architectural firm, designed all Edward Bear's artwork and marketing campaigns; and Evoy, with help from his bookkeeping mother, was responsible for taking care of the trio's business side. By the fall of 1970, with the group performing at festivals and in concert halls across the country, Canada Bear Ltd. was a going concern.

The Bear's evolution took an unusual turn when Evoy joined the Church of Scientology, a move which, along with the group's pop direction, caused Marks to leave (he was replaced by Roger Ellis). Evoy's "Fly Across the Sea" and "Masquerade," from the group's third, self-titled album, were both hit singles that re-established the Bear's patented pop sound. Then Weldon became a father and split (replaced by Bob Kendall), sold his shares in Canada Bear Ltd. for enough for a sizable down payment on a house, and watched as the next release put the band right over the top.

Number one in Canada, number three in the United States, where it sold 1.2 million copies, the breezy "Last Song" was Evoy's greatest moment in the sun. The band won a Juno Award for Outstanding Performance of the Year in 1972 and continued touring into the mid-70s, backed by New Potatoes, a band with its own Capitol recording contract. How did Evoy come up with his million seller? "By listening to AM radio," he told *The Globe and Mail* in 1973. "I really love it. I'm like a consumer as well as a supplier. I supply the kind of songs I like to hear."

PIERRE LALONDE

CAPITOL CANADA
1969

Lalonde: prime, French-to-English crossover material and a pioneer who paved the way for Quebec acts like Suzanne Stevens and Beau Dommage

Smooth, suave, sophisticated. No wonder Quebec's Pierre Lalonde was once dubbed a "young Perry Como." With his easygoing vocal style and middle-of-the-road repertoire, covering pop hits by Paul Anka, Neil Diamond and James Taylor, Lalonde was prime, French-to-English "crossover" material when Capitol signed him in the late 1960s. Already a veteran of Quebec's pop market with his own television show, the handsome singer was perfectly suited to a bilingual career, having lived in the United States during his teens and mastered the English language.

Born in Montreal in 1941, the son of 1940s vocalist Jean Lalonde, Pierre made his singing debut at the age of four on CKAC radio. He later acted in CBC Radio drama series before moving with his family to New York. Not long after returning to Quebec in 1960, Lalonde worked in radio and began recording his own singles. Two years later he was made host of CFTM-TV's "Jeunesse d'aujourd'hui," a weekly program that featured the pop hits of the day, and remained with the program for the rest of the decade. In 1967, he achieved the bilingual ultimate: hosting both "Jeunesse" and a weekly TV show in New York, using the stage name Peter Martin. "It was fun," admitted Lalonde, "except that I was killing myself. I lived in a suitcase. I had to choose and I'd rather make a comfortable living here than make a million in New York. I hate New York. Nobody's personal."

When Capitol became aware of Lalonde, he was still signed to the Montreal-based Trans-Canada label. That didn't stop Capitol's A&R department from approaching the singer and expressing an interest. "Lalonde was already hugely successful," recalls Pierre Dubord, the company's A&R man in Quebec. "He was making singles and promoting them through his TV shows. His singles automatically sold upwards of 30,000 copies—he was that big. And women loved him. We made an offer and signed him as soon as his contract with Trans-Canada ran out."

His appeal was immediately noted by the *Globe and Mail*, which described Lalonde as having "a face that's boyishly handsome, a

manner that's quiet and assured, and a clean-cut look that endears him to mothers as much as daughters." The newspaper added: "At 28, he's a busy bachelor who swings only moderately. He spends his money on his 33-acre retreat in the Laurentians."

One of the first singles Capitol recorded with Lalonde was a French version of Anka's "Put Your Head on My Shoulder." Lalonde's major hit came with his version of Neil Diamond's "Caroline," which sold more than 50,000 copies, making it at that point the biggest-selling Canadian-artist single in Capitol's history. The label ultimately recorded five French albums and three in English. One of them, a self-titled album released in 1971, featured James Taylor's "Something's Wrong" and "Brighten Your Night with My Day." Backed by such fine session players as bassist Dennis Pendrith and keyboardist Pat Godfrey, and singers Diane Brooks and Steve Kennedy, the album included covers of songs by Tom Paxton, Tim Hardin, John Sebastian and Carole King.

Lalonde was not the only Quebecker who turned to English. French radio stations do not hesitate to program songs in English, he told the *Globe* in the late 1960s. But he added that he did not know of a single English-Canadian performer who made a significant effort to appeal to the Quebec market by singing in French. "We have an edge here in Quebec," Lalonde told the newspaper. "The language barrier restricts the competition. The only Canadian recording industry is the French-Canadian recording industry and it's because Quebec had wanted things in French. There won't be an English-Canadian recording industry until the CRTC requires Canadian content in radio."

Although Lalonde's English recordings never matched the sales of his French hits, his signing to Capitol gave the label a significant presence in Quebec and signalled to other artists in the province that the label was interested in French-Canadian talent. Ultimately, the smooth crooner paved the way for Suzanne Stevens and Beau Dommage, two acts that went on to even greater success. As such, Lalonde ranks as one of Capitol's pioneer artists.

Presenting Anne Murray with an award for "Snowbird" at the 1970 Capitol Canada sales convention in Vancouver: a smooth crooner

ANNE MURRAY

CAPITOL CANADA
1969

When Canadians tuned in to CBC's popular "Singalong Jubilee" during the summers of 1966 and '67, they found themselves drawn to a blond-haired singer from Springhill, Nova Scotia, who seemed to evoke the very essence of youthful purity. Although Anne Murray would grow to chafe under the restrictive stereotype, her girl-next-door image was instantly etched in the national psyche. As *Maclean's* later put it: "People loved her for the goodness she projected. She became our permanent high-school sweetheart. In some ways, she became part of the Canadian nationalism movement."

While Murray's star was born in the warm glow of Canada's centennial celebrations, it began to shine most brightly after the singer signed with Capitol and the label released "Snowbird" in the summer of 1970. From that point onward, Murray has remained with Capitol and become one of Canada's preeminent cultural exports: worldwide album sales in excess of 30 million copies, multi-platinum sales in North America and Australia and silver status in the United Kingdom. Meanwhile, the music industry has recognized her achievements with numerous awards, including four Grammys, three American Music Awards, three Country Music Association Awards, three Canadian Country Music Association Awards and 24 Juno Awards—more than any other single artist. In 1993, Murray was inducted into the Juno Hall of Fame. When she received her star on the Hollywood Walk of Fame in 1980, Mounties attended the ceremony. She is, in short, a Canadian icon and the brightest jewel in Capitol's crown.

The only daughter among five sons born to James Murray, a doctor and Marion Murray, a nurse, Anne focused on music studies, including six years of piano and three of vocal lessons begun at the age of 15. Although trained as a soprano, Murray's warm, rich tones were more suited to a lower register. Italian arias and French and German art songs were part of her studies, while at home she listened to Patti Page and Capitol recording artists Les Paul and

Murray: a Canadian icon and the brightest jewel in Capitol's crown

Mary Ford. When she made her debut on a local television show in 1962 with an all-female choral group, she sang the popular ballad "Moon River."

After her second year at the University of New Brunswick, where she was working on a degree in physical education, Murray auditioned for "Singalong Jubilee." With a baritone ukelele in hand, she sang the folk standard "Mary Don't You Weep." Murray didn't pass the audition in 1964 because the show already had more than enough altos, but she made enough of an impression that producer-host Bill Langstroth called her back two years later.

She made her debut on the show on her 21st birthday and appeared as a regular through the summer of '66. After a year as a gym teacher in Prince Edward Island, Murray moved to Halifax and became a featured soloist on "Jubilee." There, she came to know people who would be instrumental in her career—the legendary Maritime mafia—including her first manager, Langstroth; her first record producer, Brian Ahern; and musicians and songwriters such as Ken Tobias, Steve Rhymer, Robbie MacNeill and Gene MacLellan.

In the summer of '68 Murray heard from Ahern, who had moved to Toronto and was working for Arc Records. Come down to the Big Smoke, he told her, and make an album with me. Recorded for a paltry $3,000, *What About Me* came out that year featuring covers of songs by such Canadian composers as Ken Tobias, Joni Mitchell, Alan MacRae and David Wiffen. The album sold moderately well on the strength of the buoyant title track and Murray's high profile through her appearances on "Jubilee" and the CBC teen series "Let's Go." Most importantly, the experience gave the singer a taste of the recording studio, an environment where she would soon perfect her craft.

Around this time, Murray's "Jubilee" appearances had caught the attention of Capitol's Paul White, who asked the label's Maritimes salesman, Alex Clark, to find out about "that barefoot girl with the extraordinary voice." Clark gave White the bad news that she was

At Toronto's O'Keefe Centre, 1974: "God's gift to the male race," wrote gonzo U.S. rock critic Lester Bangs

already signed to Arc, with her first album out. White contacted Ahern anyway and set up a meeting. It was the summer of '69, the Woodstock era and the Age of Aquarius. In the sunny boardroom of Capitol's American Drive headquarters, a bearded White and the label's legal counsel, John Macleod, sat opposite Murray and Ahern and talked about their dreams of recording a well-financed album. An agreement was reached (after the Arc contract became null and void) and, by August, the Maritimers were in a Toronto studio making *This Way is My Way*.

Although Murray's Capitol debut included "Snowbird," the ballad wasn't the album's first single. Instead, the label released Murray's rendition of "Thirsty Boots," by folksinger Eric Anderson, in the fall of 1969. It was, White recalls, "a complete flop." Even the next single, another MacLellan song called "Bidin' My Time," failed to click. White had, by

now, signed MacLellan as an artist and Capitol's publishing division, Beechwood, had picked him up as a songwriter. After Murray's recording of "Bidin' My Time" failed in the United States, Beechwood's Happy Wilson started hounding radio stations to give the flipside, "Snowbird," a try. When several U.S. radio stations began playing it, Capitol's promotional staff started pushing the song. Suddenly, "Snowbird" snowballed and Murray's career took off.

With "Snowbird" sitting near the top of the pop and country charts in Canada and the United States, Murray was a star of a magnitude her native country had rarely known. TV appearances on "The Glen Campbell Goodtime

Hour" and "The Merv Griffin Show" and an engagement at the Imperial Room in Toronto's Royal York Hotel quickly followed. By 1971, her dizzying schedule forced her to move to Toronto. There, Capitol provided her with a 22nd-floor midtown apartment on Balloil Street, filled with yellow and orange leather furniture. The label hardly needed to have bothered; she was rarely there. Riding on the back of the million-selling "Snowbird," Murray was busy flying to Lake Tahoe to duet with Glen Campbell at Harrah's, Vancouver to perform at The Cave, and Los Angeles, where she sang on the Grammy Awards, and was nominated in two categories.

The huge success of her first record proved a tough act to follow. "All I could think about was that I was a one-hit wonder," Murray told *Maclean's* in 1974. But Capitol remained committed and Murray bounced back with two ballads by Kenny Loggins, "Danny's Song" and

With Gene MacLellan, writer of "Snowbird" and other Murray hits, winter 1972: strong Maritime connections

"Love Song," and a remake of The Beatles' "You Won't See Me." That track, like her early version of James Taylor's "Night Owl," showed she could rock with the best of them. Along with country hits "He Thinks I Don't Care" and "Son of a Rotten Gambler," Murray established herself as a triple-format threat on pop, country and easy-listening charts. The

With singer George Hamilton IV, his wife and The Stampeders' Ronnie King at the 1970 RPM Gold Leaf Awards: "a classy lady"

singer, meanwhile, made no such distinctions in her music. "As soon as you put on steel guitar, it's country," she told an interviewer in 1974. "As soon as you take it off, it's not. It's so stupid."

Murray had proven that "Snowbird" was no fluke. She even had a Grammy Award, for Best Country Vocal Performance, to prove it. Now her business partners, including Langstroth, Ahern and manager Leonard Rambeau, had their sights set on taking Murray to greater heights in the American market. Working from the singer's new house in Toronto's posh Forest Hill district, they teamed up with U.S.-based managers Allan Strale and Shep Gordon, the man responsible for launching shock rocker Alice Cooper's career, to reshape Murray's image from Canadian sweetheart to worldly superstar. Together with Capitol, they threw a party for her at Hollywood's trendy Troubadour club on American Thanksgiving. After emerging from a giant wooden turkey and singing for the gathering, Murray joined such celebrity guests as John Lennon, Harry Nilsson, ex-Monkee Mickey Dolenz and Cooper himself for a now-famous group photo. Such associations, along with the infamously laudatory (and libidinous) review by gonzo U.S. rock critic Lester Bangs, who called her "God's gift to the male race," only served to raise her growing cool quotient. Wrote Bangs: "You many think she's middling milquetoast marianne school teacher parchesi player… but I wanna coo sweet nuttins in her well-formed Canadian ear."

With Capitol Canada president Arnold Gosewich and Paul White, 1970: more awards than any other Canadian artist

By 1976, it was time for a break. Having quietly married Langstroth in 1975, Murray went into semi-retirement to have their first child, William. Always guarded about her privacy, she told *Maclean's* that she needed time off "for peace of mind." Within two years, Murray was revitalized and ready to take on new challenges. After moving into a new house in the Toronto suburb of Thornhill, she was back out on the world stage in 1978 with a new album titled *Let's Keep it That Way*. For all her soaring, mid-70s success, Murray was about to hit the pop stratosphere. A single from the album, a tender, heartfelt rendition of a Randy Goodrum ballad, was just the ticket. By November, "You Needed Me" had shot to #1 on the *Billboard* and *RPM* charts. From then on, Murray's status as a superstar was assured. The following March, she beat out Donna Summer and even Barbra Streisand for her second Grammy Award, this time for Best Female Pop Vocal.

Deane Cameron, then Paul White's young assistant, now president

With Capitol Canada's A&R assistant Deane Cameron, Kenny Friesen, Murray's manager Leonard Rambeau, Paul White, Jim Ed Norman and hockey convert Rupert Perry, head of A&R Capitol USA: Queen Anne

of EMI Music Canada, remembers the day "You Needed Me" was recorded. "It was a Thursday afternoon," Cameron recalls, "and Paul took me over to Eastern Sound studios in Toronto, just as they were putting the strings on. I stood there and shivered as I listened to that track. Anne's voice was so moving and the whole production was absolutely brilliant." Added Cameron: "Anne has a tremendous ability to pick material that not only suits her voice but that really represents who she is. That's part of her talent. And she's been pretty good at picking out which tracks will make the best singles as well, the way she did with that one."

Along with songs by Kenny Rogers, Johnny Nash and Jackie De Shannon, *Let's Keep it That Way* also featured Canadian composer Brent Titcomb's "I Still Wish the Very Best for You," the sixth Titcomb song Murray had recorded. Throughout her career, Murray has remained supportive of such Canadian songwriters as Gene MacLellan, Robbie MacNeill, Bruce Cockburn, Shirley Eikhard and Colleen Peterson. But when asked how she goes about choosing a song, Murray admits she has no particular formula. "I listen to it, I like it, and I do it," she says matter-of-factly.

That no-nonsense, cocky attitude has coloured Murray's entire

"Our permanent high-school sweetheart," people loved the goodness she projected

career. What you see is, pretty much, what you get. As manager Leonard Rambeau told *Maclean's* in 1980: "With Anne, you've basically got the talent and the voice, and you can't go out and gimmick her." He added: "You have to present her as she is. What I've tried to do—and we've both tried to do together—is treat her as a classy lady." Which she is.

Almost every

At the Juno podium (again): "a tremendous ability to pick material that suits her voice"

employee at Capitol Canada during the 1970s has a story about Anne Murray, about her genuine sincerity, humour and relaxed, down-to-earth ways in dealing with everyone from pressing-plant workers to the company president. Bill Bannon, then the label's national promotion manager, now director of marketing services for Sony Music Canada, recalls the high standards Murray brought to everything she did. "Anne

was really into what she did," says Bannon. "She'd drop by the Capitol offices on American Drive from time to time and always made a point of going around and saying hi to everyone." He added: "She really believed in her craft as well. I never saw Anne do a bad show— and I saw a lot of her shows. She was flying really high in those days."

Through the 1980s, the hits continued, although now confined to the country charts. "A Little Good News," "Nobody Loves Me Like You Do," "Just Another Woman in Love" and "Now and Forever (You and Me)" all went straight to number one. Murray, meanwhile, won two more Grammy Awards for Best Female Country Vocal Performance. In 1989, the Anne Murray Centre opened in Springhill, Nova Scotia, and became a major tourist attraction. In 1993, she was inducted into the Canadian Music Hall of Fame at a ceremony attended by Gordon Lightfoot, Glen Campbell, Gene MacLellan, k.d. lang, Rita MacNeil and Céline Dion. In her acceptance speech, Murray saved her last thank-you for Leonard Rambeau, "my number-one man, my manager and right arm, for a list of things too long to recite."

After Rambeau's tragic death from cancer in 1995, Murray overcame grief to record her 30th album, titled simply *Anne Murray*. Featuring duets with Bryan Adams and Aaron Neville, as well as background vocals by Jann Arden and Murray's daughter, Dawn Langstroth, the album signalled a new chapter in a long and brilliant career.

With Gordon Lightfoot at a post-Juno reception at Toronto's Royal York Hotel in 1977: etched in the national psyche

In its review of the record, the *Halifax Daily News* stated: "It's a tribute to a classy talent who has defied trends and confounded the pundits, while dealing with the music industry consistently on her own terms."

COLLEEN PETERSON

CAPITOL CANADA
1976

"Souvenirs, they stay with you forever"

Peterson: a gifted country singer-songwriter with "an edge of soul"

Her songs were a lot like souvenirs. And fortunately, before she died in 1996, Canada's Colleen Peterson left a good many of them behind for her fans to savour. Jazz-tinged tunes written on piano. Country-flavoured material crafted on a big Gibson guitar she once found under her uncle's bed. Equally fluent in folk and blues, Peterson was a quintessential roots artist who refused to follow musical trends. As poet Judith Fitzgerald put it, in a tribute written for the *Globe and Mail*: "Colleen Peterson simply could not play by unwritten industry rules, could not dance to its sell-your-soul tune, could never compromise what she considered a God-given gift."

When she signed with Capitol Records in 1976, at the age of 26, Peterson was already a veteran of the music business. Born in Peterborough, Ontario in 1950, the blond-haired daughter of a financial executive bought her first guitar at 13 with Lucky Green stamps and taught herself to play. She fell in love with the music of Aretha Franklin while gravitating to the folk music of the coffeehouse circuit. So, at 16, Peterson pursued both interests, singing with David Wiffen and Bruce Cockburn as a member of the Ottawa-based folk group Three's a Crowd and performing rhythm-and-blues material on CTV's teen show "It's Happening." She also sang with such Ottawa bands as The Five-D and recorded an album in New York with the rock group Takin' Care of Business. By 1967, her talent won her an *RPM* award for Most Promising Female Vocalist.

Peterson's resumé grew increasingly diverse. In 1970, she joined the Toronto cast of the controversial musical *Hair*. Then she teamed up with singer Mark Haines, in a folk duo called Spriggs and Bringle, and toured North America for several years. "By 1974," Peterson later told the *Toronto Star*, "I was pretty sure I was going to be a country singer. But," she added, "I'm not a country girl, I'm a suburban girl, so what I sing has to have an edge of soul to it."

True to her word, Peterson's 1976 Capitol debut was brimming with soulfulness. Recorded in Nashville, *Beginning to Feel Like Home* even featured a hit single, the upbeat country twang of Rusty Wier's "Don't It Make You Wanna Dance." But Peterson's wide range of material gave the album an appealing, timeless quality. Besides her own graceful "Souvenirs" and swinging "You're Not the Only One," she covered songs by writers as diverse as Willie Nelson, Mississippi John Hurt, Jesse Winchester and Willie P. Bennett.

In a quirky twist of fate, the album won another music industry award—a Juno this time—again for Most Promising Female Vocalist. Bemused, Peterson forged ahead and recorded two more elegant albums for Capitol: *Colleen* (1977) and *Takin' My Boots Off* (1978). In the meantime, others discovered her songs, including labelmate Anne Murray, who recorded her "Carolina Sun." But Peterson's own recording career wasn't clicking—the industry deemed that she was too "pop" for Nashville and too "country" for pop radio.

Frustrated, Peterson joined Charlie Daniels's rockaboogie band as a backup singer in 1982 and toured with them for several years. "I oohed and aahed my way through the U.S.A.," she admitted in an interview with the *Globe and Mail*. "When I was offered the job, it was very easy work. I just put my own career on the backburner." After honing her craft in Nashville, singing demos and writing—always writing, Peterson returned to her hometown of Peterborough.

Then, just as she was settling into a quiet rural existence, a "new country" radio station started playing a noncommercial recording she'd once made of Willie Nelson's "Crazy," a song made famous by Patsy Cline in the 1950s. Slowly but surely, it became a hit. No one was more surprised than Peterson. "The irony is that I got out of country music nearly 10 years ago," she told the *Toronto Star* in 1993. "I never wanted to be pigeonholed, and since then I've been all over the musical map singing and playing and writing what I like."

That summer, Peterson found a new outlet for her all-over-the-map material: Quartette, the a cappella group she formed with Sylvia Tyson, Cindy Church and Caitlin Hanford. Among the gems she wrote and performed with Quartette before she died in 1996 was "The Best is Yet to Come," a country-swing tune of unbridled hope.

SUZANNE STEVENS

CAPITOL CANADA
1973

"The Cinderella of Song." That's how *Billboard* described Suzanne Stevens in April 1975. "The fairy-tale career of Canada's newest bright star took a dramatic upswing at the March 24 Juno Awards show," the magazine reported, "when Suzanne Stevens was named this year's Most Promising New Artist in front of a nationwide television audience."

The fairy-tale analogy was perfectly apt. Stevens had been working as a receptionist just two years earlier, with no real ambitions beyond entering a few talent shows. Then, in March 1973, Quebec's Channel 10 named Stevens the station's discovery of the year and rewarded her with a 13-week prime-time summer TV series. Lightning struck twice:

Canada's first bilingual star and a forerunner to Céline Dion

ten days later, the province's largest broadcast chain, Radio Mutuel, picked Stevens as their discovery of the year. That led to a major concert appearance opening for Renée Claude at Montreal's Salle Claude Champagne and brought Stevens to the attention of Capitol Records.

Like Céline Dion, Stevens was the youngest born to a large Quebec family. Her mother was French, her father English. Suzanne and her 11 brothers and sisters were brought up to speak both languages fluently. Despite seven years of piano lessons and work with an amateur theatre

group, Stevens saw no professional future in the arts. And she had to pinch herself when the talent contest and subsequent slot opening for Renée Claude led to a recording contract with Capitol.

Blessed with an exquisite voice, with plenty of emotion and control, Stevens recorded her first single, "Le soleil," in the spring of '73. By midsummer, the song was #1 on most Quebec charts. By the start of the following year, Stevens had her first introduction to the rest of Canada, with an appearance on CBC's "Juliette and Friends" television show. After two more charted singles in Quebec to her credit, she began recording her debut album. *En route* appeared in 1974, with a lavish record-launch party for journalists aboard a champagne-fuelled Quebecair flight over the Laurentians. That album was followed in '75 by *Moi, de la t'te aux pieds*.

An English-language single was the next logical step and Capitol released two: "Mother of Us All" and "House Full of Women." When Stevens won the Juno Award for Most Promising Female Artist in the spring of '75, it was a big year for Quebec artists. Her male counterpart in the winning circle was Gino Vannelli.

It wasn't until the release of her English-language debut album in 1975 that Stevens fully broke through. *Love's the Only Game in Town*, a mix of disco-pop, romantic ballads and torch songs, produced the danceable hit single "Make Me Your Baby," which reached #6 on *RPM*'s Top 40 chart. The album also included songs written by fellow Capitol recording artists Sylvia Tyson, Gene MacLellan and Yves Lapierre, of the folk group Les Cailloux.

The singer's crossover drew mixed reactions from the media. "Some critics think it's great," Stevens told the *Globe and Mail*, "but some of them are on the negative side. They ask, 'Aren't you satisfied with the success you're having in Quebec?'" She continued: "I wanted to record in English from the start, because that way I can reach more people. The more people you reach, the more you feel secure and that you're doing something worthwhile."

Stevens recorded her next two English albums, *Crystal Carriage* and *Stardust Lady*, in Los Angeles. One more French album on Capitol followed, *Les nuits sont trop longues*, in 1979. Her recordings were released in Canada, the United States, England and in France on the Pathé–EMI label. Remembered for a quality voice that stood out among so many disco screamers—a "diamond in a sea of broken glass," as the *Toronto Star*'s Bruce Kirkland put it—Stevens was Canada's first major bilingual star, a forerunner to Céline Dion.

DOMENIC TROIANO

CAPITOL CANADA
1976

His Capitol albums run the gamut from gospel-tinged numbers and rapid-fire funk workouts to jazz fusion and Band-like countryish material

Canadian Music Hall of Fame member Domenic Troiano has long been regarded as a musician's musician, a brilliant lead guitarist whose work has graced recordings by artists such as Joe Cocker, Diana Ross, Donald Fagen, Etta James, Ronnie Hawkins, James Cotton and David Clayton Thomas. Troiano served as the ideal sideman to groups like The James Gang and The Guess Who, and was an integral member of a triumvirate of revered Canadian bands: The Five Rogues, Mandala and Bush. But from 1976–79, the legendary guitarist also led his own band and made three acclaimed albums for Capitol Records. "They were," Troiano recalls, "some of the most creative and exciting times of my life."

Born in Modugno, Italy in 1946, Troiano moved to Toronto with his parents at the age of three. When he was 12, he saw his first rock group, a band called Johnny Rhythm and the Suedes that included guitarist Robbie Robertson. It was a defining moment. Mesmerized, Troiano soaked up every lick that afternoon. Soon, he was playing guitar himself and became a quick study at home on the instrument. When Robertson joined Ronnie Hawkins's group, The Hawks, Troiano followed him around to every gig. Then, Troiano actually replaced Robertson as a member of Hawkins's next backing band, Robbie Lane & the Disciples. And he hadn't even finished high school.

...iano: a Canadian guitar god with one of rock's most ...ressive resumes

In 1964, Troiano left Hawkins to join The Five Rogues, the house band at a Yonge Street rhythm-and-blues club called The Bluenote. There, he backed local singers like Diane Brooks, Eric Mercury, Shawne Jackson and David Clayton Thomas and such visiting r&b artists as Stevie Wonder, The Supremes, Edwin Starr and The Righteous Brothers. By 1966, The Rogues had transformed into Mandala, whose "soul crusade" won them a strong following across North America. Bluesman Bo Diddley was impressed enough to recommend the Toronto musicians to his label, Chess Records, which promptly signed the band. Mandala recorded the Troiano-penned classic "Opportunity" in 1967, followed by an album on Atlantic, featuring another hit, "Love-itis."

By the summer of '69, Mandala had evolved into Bush, a California-based rock band with funk overtones. After one album and such

distinctive songs as "I Can Hear You Calling," Bush disbanded. Troiano remained in Los Angeles and became a much in-demand session player while recording his solo debut album for Mercury Records. He toured and recorded two albums with The James Gang, filling in for the departed Joe Walsh. Then, after recording another album for Mercury, he got a call in 1974 from Burton Cummings, who was looking for a new guitarist for The Guess Who. Troiano recorded a pair of albums with the Winnipeg band before it broke up the following year.

Back in Toronto after living in Los Angeles for six years, Troiano assembled a band he described as a cross between Sly and the Family Stone and the rock-oriented Mahavishnu Orchestra. Featuring keyboardists Dave Tyson and Fred Mandel, bassist Keith Jones, drummer Jim Norman and percussionist Wayne St. John, the group represented a turning point in Troiano's career. "This band is really the first I could ever call my own," he told the *Toronto Star*'s Peter Goddard in 1976. And he added that he planned to put his group through its paces. "The big-name bands spend eight hours a day flying from city to city, running around in limousines. They never practice. Their music stays the same. That's not going to happen to this band."

Troiano's three Capitol albums proved his point. *Burnin' at the Stake* (1977) boasted gospel-tinged numbers and rapid-fire funk workouts, while *The Joke's On Me* (1978) featured jazz fusion and Band-like countryish tunes. *Fret Fever* (1979) took Troiano's eclecticism even further, adding soulful r&b, blues-based jams and crunching rock anthems, including the dance hit "We All Need Love" (#34, *RPM*). On all the albums, Troiano's guitar playing remained consistently lyrical, intelligent and fluid enough to suit any musical style. EMI Music Canada has since reissued the best of those recordings on the CD *Troiano Triple Play: 1976–1980*.

In the 1980s, Troiano began a new phase in his career: scoring for TV and film, earning credits for such television series as "Night Heat," "Diamonds," "Top Cops" and "True Blue" and films like *Gunfighters* and *Swordsman*. In 1996, he was inducted into the Canadian Music Hall of Fame. Troiano remains involved with contemporary music, producing hot new talents like dance-pop diva Patria. "I like to keep doing different things," he says simply. Songwriter, TV and film scorer, producer and guitarist extraordinaire, Domenic Troiano has proven he can do it all.

SYLVIA TYSON

CAPITOL CANADA
1974

Tyson: a pivotal role in the birth of popular Canadian music

A s one half of Ian & Sylvia, Canada's first
international folk stars, Sylvia Tyson
played a pivotal role in the birth of popular
Canadian music. Her success with her partner in the 1960s—sold-out shows at Carnegie
Hall, headline appearances at the Newport
and Mariposa festivals and hit songs such as Ian's "Four Strong
Winds" and Sylvia's "You Were On My Mind"—opened doors for
Canadian singer-songwriters, including Gordon Lightfoot, Joni Mitchell
and Neil Young. And Sylvia's ability to balance family and career, while
asserting herself creatively, inspired many female performers who followed. By the time she signed with Capitol Records in the mid-70s,
Sylvia had come into her own.

A church organist's daughter, Sylvia Fricker grew up in Chatham,
Ontario, a small farming town east of Windsor. With a $25 guitar her
parents bought her from the Eaton's mail-order catalogue, she taught
herself to play old English folk songs from books she borrowed at the
local library. By 1958, the 18-year-old Fricker had already performed at
the community centre and craved bigger challenges.

Sylvia made the first of what she called "field trips" to Toronto by
train to see what the city had to offer. On one of her first trips, Fricker
met a handsome cowboy from British Columbia named Ian Tyson and
the two began singing together in Toronto's Yorkville district. Almost
immediately, the magical blend of their voices—Tyson's warm and
smooth as leather, Fricker's cool as the night air—set them apart from
the dozens of other folk acts playing on the coffeehouse circuit. The
pair's song selection was equally striking. They were the first on the
scene to perform traditional Canadian songs, ballads like "Mary Anne"
and "Un Canadien Errant."

Ian & Sylvia encountered Bob Dylan in New York's Greenwich Village
in 1963 and were immediately struck by this scruffy young folksinger's
songs, especially "Blowin' in the Wind." If this "raggedy-ass kid" could
write his own songs, Tyson thought, so could he. The next morning,
Tyson penned his first composition, the now Canadian classic "Four
Strong Winds." A short time after that, Fricker wrote her first song. A
massive hit for Australia's We Five in the summer of '65, "You Were On
My Mind" earned substantial royalties for Fricker.

Over the course of seven acclaimed albums for Vanguard, two each
for MGM and Columbia and one for the Ampex label, Ian & Sylvia's
sound evolved from folk to country-rock. By the mid-70s the couple, who
had married in 1964 to have a child, were
moving apart. While Sylvia devoted herself to
raising their son, Clay, Ian
hosted his own show,
"Nashville North," on the
CTV network. In 1974,
Sylvia's own solo career started taking off. First, she
became the host of her own weekly radio show on
CBC, "Touch the Earth," which featured interviews
with and performances by an eclectic range of musicians. Then she signed with Capitol and began recording her debut solo album.

Released during International Women's Year in 1975,
Woman's World was clearly a statement of female independence.
Although it was produced by Ian, all ten songs on the album were written by Sylvia. At the record's launch at Twenty-One McGill, an exclusive women's club in downtown Toronto, she performed half a dozen of
them, including "Patience is a Solitary
Game," which she told the audience "has
to do with marriage, which is sometimes
easy, sometimes hard, but something to be
worked at, I think." The album went on to
sell 35,000 copies in Canada. Both it and
the single "Sleep on My Shoulder" earned
Sylvia a Juno nomination, but, strangely,
in the Best New Female category. The single also won her an *RPM*-sponsored Big
Country Award for Outstanding
Performance by a Female Country Singer.

Following Sylvia's performance at a
Gordon Lightfoot-organized Olympic benefit concert at Maple Leaf
Gardens, Capitol released her second album, *Cool Wind from the North*,
in the fall of '76. Once again produced by Ian, the album placed even
greater emphasis on Sylvia's characteristic country-warbling vibrato.
Its fiddle-drenched single "River Road," later a hit for Crystal Gayle,
seemed to indicate a deepening commitment to country music. But as
she demonstrated on her independently released albums in the 1980s
and with the fine women's vocal group Quartette in the 1990s, her
music has always touched on other styles, including jazz and blues.
"Any music that's really good," she told *RPM*, "has roots and tradition."

With Ian Tyson (sunglasses), flanked by Capitol Canada's Arnold Gosewich
and Paul White, outside the label's A&R office in Toronto's Yorkville district

THE BEATLES (SOLO)

APPLE
1970

JOHN LENNON

By 1969, The Beatles as a band was effectively a bust. Lennon, by then married to Yoko Ono, was already pursuing individual projects. In late May, he and Ono checked into Montreal's Queen Elizabeth Hotel and announced, at the height of the Vietnam War, their "bed-in" for peace. Pierre Dubord, Capitol's A&R director for Quebec, will never forget the day he got a phone call from head office, telling him to prepare for a recording with John Lennon. Recalls Dubord: "I said, 'Does he want me to line him up a studio in Montreal?' And I was told, 'No, Mr. Lennon wants to record in his hotel room.' I knew right then it was going to be an experience."

There was no such thing as remote recording trucks in those days, so Dubord and local producer Andre Perry brought in some rented equipment. There, in Suite 1742, the two set up a makeshift recording studio for the famous Beatle and his wife. Surrounded by reporters from around the world and an entourage that included LSD guru Timothy Leary, comedians Tommy Smothers and Dick Gregory, deejay Murray the K, singer Petula Clark, Toronto rabbi Abraham Feinberg and the Canadian chapter of Radha Krishna Temple, Dubord watched as a bearded Lennon practiced a new song he had written for a group of Montreal teenagers who'd asked him for a "message." Backed by Smothers on guitar and a chorus that included Hare Krishna members, Leary and Dubord himself, John and Yoko recorded "Give Peace a Chance." Recalls Dubord: "John and Yoko took the tape back to Apple and mixed it. We got the record back a month later and Capitol released it in July. It went Top 10 on *Billboard* within a month." An instant anthem.

Lennon performed the song when he returned to Canada in September to headline the Rock 'n' Roll Revival Concert at Toronto's Varsity Stadium. The concert also featured such rock legends as Little Richard, Chuck Berry, Jerry Lee Lewis, Fats Domino, Bo Diddley, Gene Vincent, as well as contemporary acts like The Doors, Alice Cooper and Canadian blues band Whiskey Howl. Backed by the newly formed

Lennon and Ono at Toronto's Rock 'n' Roll Revival concert at Varsity Stadium, September 15, 1969: "All we are saying...."

Lennon with Pierre Dubord, Capitol's A&R director for Quebec, in Suite 1742 of Montreal's Queen Elizabeth Hotel, May 1969: a bed-in for peace and an instant anthem

Plastic Ono Band, a group that included guitarist Eric Clapton, Lennon sang the words to "Give Peace a Chance" accompanied by most of the audience of 27,000, who flashed the two-fingered V-for-peace sign. Although his performance was at times ragged (and marred, many felt, by Yoko's screeching-inside-a-giant-bag routine), it conveyed a rowdy, infectious spirit, later captured on the album *Live Peace in Toronto*.

Lennon and Ono returned to Canada in December of that year. "The press in Canada gives us a chance," Lennon said at the time. "They treat us as human beings, which is a pleasant change. It seems that we get more smiles and genuine help from Canada than anywhere else—that's why we're here." Lennon and his wife came back to plan a massive peace festival that was to be held at Mosport, a car-racing track east of Toronto. Giant billboards proclaiming "War is Over! If You Want It" were erected in downtown Toronto. Using the home of Ronnie Hawkins as a base, the couple held a press conference at the Ontario Science Centre, and met

Hanging out with Prime Minister Trudeau in the nation's capital: meeting of the minds

with media guru Marshall McLuhan and Prime Minister Pierre Trudeau. After the hour-long meeting with Trudeau in Ottawa, Lennon pronounced: "If all politicians were like Mr. Trudeau, there would be world peace. You don't know how lucky you are in Canada."

With Mounties in 1969: "we get more smiles and genuine help from Canada," said Lennon at the time, "than anywhere else"

While still planning the peace festival, Lennon came up with his first Top 10 single in March 1970. Produced by Phil Spector and featuring George Harrison, "Instant Karma" was an instant hit (#2 *RPM*, #3 *Billboard*). Although the festival never materialized, Lennon had already done much for the cause of world peace with several anthems.

His next album, *Plastic Ono Band*, drew praise for its deeply personal songs, including "Mother" and "Working Class Hero." Lennon's first number one single as a solo artist came with "Imagine" (#1 *RPM*, #3

Billboard), the idealistic gem of a title track from his 1971 album of the same name.

After the 1972 double album, *Some Time in New York City*, Lennon recorded *Mind Games*. Although it reached the Top 10 in 1973, the album was soon eclipsed by releases by the other former Beatles. Lennon's commercial breakthrough came the following year with *Walls and Bridges*, which produced his first number one hit in the United States with the uptempo "Whatever Gets You Through the Night," on which he was joined by Elton John. Lennon released two other albums in the mid-70s: the Phil Spector–produced oldies collection *Rock 'n' Roll* and *Shaved Fish*, a greatest-hits collection that included such earlier singles as "Cold Turkey" and "Happy Xmas (War is Over)."

On December 8, 1980, Lennon was assassinated outside the Dakota apartment that he shared with Ono on New York City's Upper West

McCartney onstage in Vancouver, 1976: Wings over Canada

Side. Capitol-EMI paid tribute to the work of one of the twentieth century's greatest artists with the release of several albums, including *Live in New York City*, *Menlove Avenue* and *Imagine: John Lennon*, the soundtrack from the 1988 film documentary. The company also released two collections: 1990's four-CD, 73-track set titled simply *Lennon*, and 1999's all-encompassing *Ultimate Box Set*. Meanwhile, EMI continues to be associated with the Lennon legacy through Sean Ono Lennon whose debut album, *Into the Sun* (on The Beastie Boys' Grand Royal imprint), was distributed by the label.

PAUL McCARTNEY

When Wings landed in Canada during the spring of '76, it was Paul McCartney's first North American tour in a decade. Although it had been six years since his previous band's official breakup, McCartney's sold-out appearance at Toronto's Maple Leaf Gardens sparked a scene eerily reminiscent of Beatlemania. Rumours that John, George and Ringo would be in town for a reunion with Paul created the pandemonium. Scalpers had a field day, netting as much as $300 for a pair of $9.50 tickets, several girls fainted and more than 5,000 disappointed fans were locked out of the arena. Meanwhile, a reinforced squad of 60 police were dispatched to the area as traffic was brought to a standstill. Confirmed Stan Obodiac, publicity director at the Gardens: "These are the most incredible scenes since The Beatles last played here."

The reunion, of course, never did materialize. But McCartney performed "Yesterday," "Lady Madonna" and several other Beatles songs, along with material from his *Band on the Run*, *Venus and Mars* and *Wings at the Speed of Sound* albums. That seemed to be enough for many of the 18,000 people in attendance. "McCartney and Wings re-created the essence of an old Beatles show," wrote the *Toronto Star*'s Peter Goddard in his review of the show, "this time with a first-rate sound system and for an audience willing to listen more than scream."

In some respects, The Beatles had never really gone away. More than 50 per cent of the group's sales up to that point (9 million albums in Canada alone, about 100 million in North America) had come after the breakup. And in early 1976, some 23 Beatles songs were among the top 100–selling singles in Britain, with "Yesterday" on its way to number one. Sensing a trend, that year, Capitol-EMI released a double-album collection of old Beatles rockers called *Rock 'n' Roll Music.*

The simultaneous success of solo albums by each of the former Beatles created an unexpected double bonanza for the company. Although Lennon, Harrison and Starr all enjoyed top-selling records throughout the 1970s, none matched McCartney's commercial heights. Beginning with his self-titled solo debut, which reached number one

With Wings, receiving Platinum from Capitol Canada's president Arnold Gosewich, backstage at Toronto's Maple Leaf Gardens, 1976: "the most incredible scene since The Beatles last played here," said the Gardens' Stan Obodiac

without the benefit of a single, McCartney went from strength to strength. His second album, *Ram*, featured the chart-topping single "Uncle Albert/Admiral Halsey," while the weaker *Wings Wildlife* still managed to make the Top 10. After he scored with "Hi Hi Hi" (#5 *RPM*, #10 *Billboard*), McCartney never really looked back. His next two singles, "My Love" and the James Bond theme "Live and Let Die" both topped the charts, paving the way for his next album.

Recorded at EMI's studios in Lagos, Nigeria, *Band on the Run* was the breakthrough McCartney needed. A double Grammy Award winner and a critical favourite, the album was a miracle born out of adversity. Just before flying to Lagos, half of Wings quit, leaving only Paul, his wife, Linda, and guitarist Denny Laine to make the trip. Shortly after arriving at a half-completed recording studio, McCartney was robbed of the cassettes of all the new songs for the album. Rather than pack it in and take the next flight home, McCartney buckled down and produced what is almost universally regarded as the best post-Beatles album.

Featuring the symphonic title track, the rocking "Jet," the lyrical "Bluebird" and the bristling "Let Me Roll It" —songs "as good as anything else in pop music, including Beatles songs," as *Mojo* magazine concluded in its five-star review of the album's 25th anniversary edition, *Band on the Run* stands as an artistic triumph. It didn't do too badly commercially either: its international sales stand at six million copies and counting.

Throughout the rest of the '70s, McCartney continued to have a huge impact as a recording artist, with such hit singles as "Listen to What the Man Said," "Silly Love Songs" and "With a Little Luck," which all reached #1 at both *RPM* and *Billboard.* Although McCartney left Capitol in 1979, he returned six years later and produced a formidable comeback album with *Flowers in the Dirt* in 1989, featuring collaborations with Elvis Costello and such pop gems as "My Brave Face" and "This One." After releasing his first classical recording, *Liverpool Oratorio*, McCartney returned to pop music, collaborating with Costello again on 1993's *Off the Ground.* In 1999, McCartney was inducted into the Rock and Roll Hall of Fame for his post-Beatles contributions to pop music.

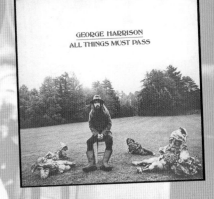

GEORGE HARRISON

The so-called "quiet one" within The Beatles, George Harrison found his voice after the breakup of the group. With the release of *All Things Must Pass* in 1970, Harrison proved that, while he always played "second fiddle" in songwriting to Lennon and McCartney, he too could be

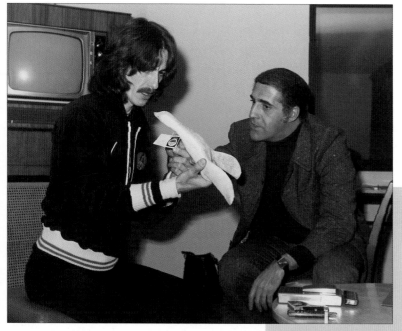

Does this thing fly? Harrison puzzles over a piece of Inuit art presented by Capitol Canada's president Arnold Gosewich, December 1974

Peak-a-boo: among the solo Beatles, Ringo was the toppermost of the poppermost, after McCartney

prolific. The three-record Apple set spawned three hits, including "My Sweet Lord" (#1 at *RPM* and *Billboard*), "Isn't It a Pity" and "What is Life" (#1 *RPM*, #3 *Billboard*).

In late summer 1971, Harrison sponsored and hosted two benefit concerts at New York's Madison Square Garden for Bangladesh. Featuring a stellar cast of guests, including Bob Dylan, Ringo Starr, Eric Clapton and Leon Russell, the concerts resulted in a documentary film and another three record set, which won a Grammy Award. Meanwhile, Harrison's issue-oriented song "Bangla Desh" went Top 20 in Canada and Top 30 in the United States. Harrison bounced

Starr assuming a regal pose: it don't come easy

back in 1973 with "Give Me Love (Give Me Peace on Earth)," which reached #1 at *Billboard* and #9 at *RPM*. Taken from his *Living in the Material World* album, the hit song sent the former Beatle out on the road with a show that included organist Billy Preston and sitarist Ravi Shankar, with whom Harrison had studied. When the tour pulled into Canada in December 1974, Capitol-EMI hosted a reception for Harrison at Toronto's Inn on the Park hotel. There, he was presented with a platinum award and an *RPM* Gold Leaf Award for past record sales in Canada.

Two more Apple albums followed: *Dark Horse* (which became the name of Harrison's own record label) and *Extra Texture (Read All About It)*. In 1976, Capitol-EMI released *The Best of George Harrison*, which matched Harrison's solo work with some of his best-known Beatles songs, including "Something," "Here Comes the Sun" and "While My Guitar Gently Weeps."

RINGO STARR

After McCartney, Ringo Starr was the most commercially successful solo act from The Beatles. His 1973 album, titled simply *Ringo*, was also the closest thing to a full-fledged Beatles album after the breakup, including as it did contributions from all four members. Featuring such chart-topping hits as "Photograph" and "You're Sixteen," it paved the way for Starr's final two Apple/Capitol albums, *Goodnight Vienna* and *Blast From Your Past*.

Previously, Starr recorded a collection of Tin Pan Alley standards (*Sentimental Journey*) and a Nashville-recorded country session (*Beaucoups of Blues*). His first major chart success in Canada began in 1971 with "It Don't Come Easy" (#1 *RPM*) and continued the following year with "Back Off Boogaloo" (#2). His last number one for Apple/Capitol came with the Apple released single "No No Song," a cover of a Hoyt Axton song.

GLEN CAMPBELL

CAPITOL
1962

For many Canadians, Glen Campbell will be forever linked with Anne Murray. In the early 1970s, Canada's Snowbird became a regular guest on "The Glen Campbell Goodtime Hour" TV show. During duets, their voices blended so well and there was such a strong chemistry that further collaborations seemed inevitable, given that both singers were Capitol artists and, for a brief while, shared the same manager, Nick Savano. In 1971, Murray and Campbell teamed up on Murray's fifth Capitol album. Featuring a medley of "I Say a Little Prayer" and "By the Time I Get to Phoenix," as well as a string-laden version of the romantic nugget "Canadian Sunset," the album made the best-seller lists and led to a North American tour of the two artists.

Like Murray, Campbell was never entirely comfortable with his role as a country star. "I'm not a country singer," he has often insisted. "I'm a country boy who sings." In fact, Campbell

A flagship Capitol artist, former Beach Boy and one of pop's finest interpreters

enjoyed success in both the pop and country fields. And long before he topped the charts in 1975 with "Rhinestone Cowboy," a song which permanently sealed the image, Campbell was actually a guitarist-for-hire for many pop artists, including Frank Sinatra, Elvis Presley, Rick Nelson and The Mamas and the Papas. His first performance in Canada was with The Beach Boys in 1965, as a stand-in for Brian Wilson at Toronto's Maple Leaf Gardens.

Campbell, the Rhinestone Cowboy

The youngest of 12 children born to a poor rural family in Delight, Arkansas, Campbell decided to seek greener pastures at an early age. With guitar in hand, the handsome singer with the dimpled chin headed to Los Angeles and landed a job playing with The Champs, who'd recently scored a hit with "Tequila" (also in the lineup were Jimmy Seals and Dash Crofts). After a short stint as a demo artist and songwriter for American Music Publishing, Campbell was signed to Capitol as a solo artist. Most of his income, however, came from studio work; in 1963 alone he made 586 studio appearances and earned $40,000.

Following his role as an erstwhile Beach Boy, Campbell became a

session musician on TV's "Shindig," where the British singer Donovan introduced him to "Universal Soldier." Campbell recorded the protest song by Canadian singer (and future EMI Music Canada recording artist) Buffy Sainte-Marie and it became his first Top 50 hit. Although he also recorded one of his own compositions, the spiritually themed "Less of Me," "Universal Soldier" launched Campbell's career as an adept interpreter of others' songs. Wisely, from then on Capitol allowed him to choose his own material and producers.

Campbell's choices paid off. For the next several years he scored a succession of hits with John Hartford's "Gentle on My Mind" and three songs by Jimmy Webb: "By the Time I Get to Phoenix" (#9 *RPM*, 1967), "Wichita Lineman" (#1 *RPM*, 1968) and "Galveston" (#2 *RPM*, 1969). Meanwhile, his appearances on "Summer Brothers Smothers Show" led to his own TV variety program on which he eventually met Murray. Campbell also made his movie debut in the John Wayne western *True Grit*.

The hits dried up until "Rhinestone Cowboy" struck paydirt in the spring of '75, reaching #1 at both *RPM* and *Billboard*. The song, about a young rural musician struggling to make a decent living in the big, bad city, seemed to sum up the life of Campbell, who battled alcoholism, drugs and a series of broken marriages. It was a theme he revisited in his next hit, "Country Boy (You've Got Your Feet in L.A.)." Campbell's last major chart success came with Allen Toussaint's "Southern Nights," a number one song for him in 1977.

Life in the fast lane had taken its toll by the early 1980s. "Understandably, it all became too much and Campbell surrendered to Christianity and gospel records," wrote *Mojo* magazine's John Aizelwood, in his review of *Glen Campbell: The Capitol Years '65/'77*. "But for a time, he demonstrated that greats don't have to write their own songs." Campbell—with and without Anne Murray—will be remembered as a flagship Capitol artist and one of pop music's finest interpreters.

THE STEVE MILLER BAND

CAPITOL
1967

Miller in Vancouver, 1977: the city had a special affinity for the Space Cowboy

Some called him the Space Cowboy, others dubbed him the Gangster of Love. "A picker, a grinner, a lover and a sinner," Steve Miller professed to be all these things and more, including "a joker, a smoker and a midnight toker." But with his psychedelic, blues-based rock sound, Miller was actually just a damn good rock 'n' roller—one of the definitive rockers, in fact, of the 1970s. Many of his songs became staples of Top 40 radio, while classics such as "The Joker" and "Fly Like an Eagle" topped the charts in both Canada and the United States. Miller's impact remains strong to this day: his 1978 *Greatest Hits* package can often still be found at the number one position of the catalogue albums chart.

In many ways, Miller was the quintessential Capitol artist. The singer-guitarist recorded nearly 20 albums over the course of three decades for the label, beginning in 1968. And Miller's Capitol roots run even deeper. His music-loving parents, a Dallas doctor and his wife, a singer in her own right, often brought home guests like Charles Mingus and T-Bone Walker. One night, they introduced their son to Capitol recording artists Les Paul and Mary Ford. It proved to be a turning point: the four-year-old Steve was shown some guitar chords and was later allowed to sit in on some of the couple's recording sessions. Miller could hardly have found a better role model than guitarist Les Paul.

Miller formed his first band at age 12, with another budding singer-guitarist, William Royce "Boz" Scaggs. After playing together in another group at the University of Wisconsin, Miller and Scaggs briefly went their separate ways. After spending time in Chicago, soaking up the blues, Miller moved to San Francisco. There, he joined a scene that included The Grateful Dead, The Jefferson Airplane and Quicksilver Messenger Service. Reunited with Scaggs, Miller landed an enviable, five-album contract with Capitol that paid unusually high royalties and gave Miller complete artistic control and ownership of publishing. Yet it proved to be one of the best deals Capitol ever made.

The unpretentiously named The Steve Miller Band recorded two albums, *Children of the Future* and *Sailor*, before Scaggs left to pursue a solo career. From 1969–72, the band made a series of albums with tracks that enjoyed heavy exposure on FM radio, including Brave New World's "My Dark Hour," featuring Paul McCartney on bass (credited under his pseudonym Phil Ramon).

It wasn't until 1973, after recovering from hepatitis and a broken neck from a car accident, that Miller scored his first hit single. With a bouncy rhythm and a vocal sound that *Village Voice* critic Robert Christgau

aptly described as "woozy," "The Joker" took Miller straight to the top (#1 *Billboard*, #2 *RPM*) and went gold in the States, while the album of the same name went platinum with sales of one million. Suddenly, The Steve Miller Band was in demand everywhere as a concert attraction. As road warriors on the run, the group had little time to return to the studio. When they did, three years later, Miller and his mates made an album that further boosted their mainstream success. *Fly Like an Eagle* produced three hit singles, including the title track, "Rock 'n' Me" and "Take the Money and Run."

When The Steve Miller Band pulled into Vancouver in January 1977, it was one of the biggest concert draws of the year. But it was a mark of Miller's down-to-earth attitude that he and the group arrived without a road manager. "They

Into overdrive with Randy Bachman (left) and Elvin Bishop (centre) at Vancouver's The Cave, 1977: a damn good rock 'n' roller

came to town in two rented station wagons," recalls Al Andruchow, then Capitol-EMI's western region manager. "Steve had the credit card and they checked into the Plaza, where we had an office in those days. He was a really laid-back kind of guy. You'd never know he was a major rock star."

Before the show, Capitol-EMI president Arnold Gosewich, who had flown out from Toronto, presented Miller and the group with a platinum award for the *Fly Like an Eagle* album, for sales of 100,000 copies in Canada. After performing before a sold-out crowd of 14,000, Miller and his band piled into their rented station wagons and headed for the next stop. "Steve wasn't much for hanging around," says Andruchow, now EMI Music Canada's vice-president of sales. "He was the kind of guy who liked to play his show and move on."

PINK FLOYD

EMI
1967

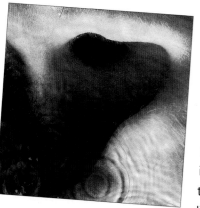

When England's Pink Floyd toured North America in March 1967 1973, the group was only a moderately successful art-rock band with no previous commercial success. As rock reporter Wilder Penfield III, a former publicist for Capitol Records, put it in the *Toronto Star* that month: "Except for FM radio stations, the media in North America have all but ignored them. Never have they had a hit single record here. Of their three movie sound-tracks, only Michelangelo Antonioni's commercial failure *Zabriskie Point* has had anything approaching mass distribution."

Yet the band's Toronto debut at Maple Leaf Gardens was virtually sold out. "This," con-cluded Penfield, "is astonishing."

As Floyd aficionados know, that tour coin-cided with the release of the group's seminal album *Dark Side of the Moon*. A collection of songs that eschewed conventional pop for-mats, *Dark Side* went on to become the biggest-sell-ing album in Capitol Records' history—bigger even than any Beatles LP—with sales of more than 12 mil-lion copies in the United States alone. The album remained on the *Billboard* chart for an unprecedented 741 weeks, and catapulted the formerly underground Pink Floyd way out into the com-mercial pop stratosphere. The album was also a source of inspiration for progressive-rock fans and musicians everywhere.

Like many English groups, Pink Floyd has its roots in the blues and began playing American r&b material at school dances in the mid-60s.

By 1967, members Syd Barrett, Richard Wright, Nick Mason and Roger Waters had developed a more psy-chedelic sound and added slide and light shows to their gigs at places like London's UFO Club. The bril-liant but erratic Barrett exited the following year, replaced by David Gilmour, and the group began pro-ducing longer, more experimental epics. With the release in 1970 of *Atom Heart Mother*, the band topped the British charts, but North American suc-cess still eluded them.

Pink Floyd toured Canada for the first time that year, playing Vancouver, Calgary, Edmonton, Saskatoon, Regina and Winnipeg in October (a brave undertaking for any underground band at that time). In fact, Floyd played Vancouver for the next two consecutive

Pink Floyd, 1967 (clockwise from top) Roger Waters, Rick Wright, Syd Barrett and Nick Mason

years and always attracted an audience of the psychedelically inclined in that western city.

Pink Floyd's Vancouver following was nothing compared to the devoted fans the band attracted in Montreal. According to Bill Rotari, then Capitol-EMI's Quebec regional manager, *La belle province* had a history of breaking English progres-sive-rock groups before any other part of Canada. "Groups like Jethro Tull, Genesis and especially Pink Floyd were always greeted with open arms in Quebec," says Rotari. "When Pink Floyd came through in 1972, touring their *Meddle* album, they drew huge crowds in Montreal and Quebec City. It's the European influence here that made their sound so acceptable."

Writing in the *Montreal Gazette*, critic Bill Mann described the scene at Pink Floyd's March 1973 sold-out concert at the Montreal Forum. "Kids have hitchhiked in from Quebec City and further environs to see what is probably the last legitimate underground band in exis-tence," wrote Mann. "People are going bananas everywhere," he added, in response to the group's quadrophonic sound-and-light show, which he described as "the most stunning visual show in entertainment today." Mann concluded his review with this endorsement: "You wouldn't believe how big Pink Floyd is in this province. They could have easily sold out two shows here."

When the *Dark Side of the Moon* tour hit Toronto's Maple Leaf Gardens, *Toronto Star* critic Peter Goddard wrote that Pink Floyd's 20,000 pounds of sound and lighting equipment stole the show. "It was rock based in technology," wrote Goddard, "rock that owed more to H. G. Wells and *The War of the Worlds*, rock where the visual gave extra meaning to the aural, rock taken to the point where it has to change into something else."

Despite *Dark Side*'s bleak themes of alienation, paranoia and schizo-phrenia and sterile soundscape of recorded heartbeats and ringing cash registers, it produced a hit single in "Money" and went on to become one of the most influential rock albums of all time.

BOB SEGER

CAPITOL
1969

Seger: working on his night moves

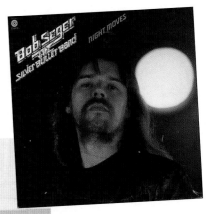

Straddling the Motor City musical traditions of hard rock and soul, Bob Seger became a hometown hero in Detroit during the early 1970s. Seger might have remained a local phenomenon were it not for his talent and the support shown by several individuals, including two Canadians. As music director at Windsor, Ontario's CKLW, a powerful border station that beamed its signal into the American Midwest, Rosalie Trombley put Seger's records in heavy rotation and helped to establish a national audience for his soaring, hard-driving sound. And Toronto-based record producer Jack Richardson, best known for his work with The Guess Who, produced the singer's breakthrough hit, "Night Moves," from the album of the same name. After that song pushed album sales past the five million mark, Seger never looked back.

Seger's beginnings were humble in the extreme. His father, an alcoholic and failed musician, left when Seger was 12, forcing he and his mother and brother to live in near poverty. Yet Bob was drawn to music himself, soaking up the r&b sounds of the street and listening to James Brown on his transistor radio. After taking up the guitar, he formed a string of garage bands with names like The Decibels, The Town Criers and The Omens. One of Seger's first songs, "East Side Story," was covered by The Underdogs, a band that included Michael and Suzi Quatro, and Glenn Frey, who later went on to success with The Eagles. Seger's own recording of the song became a local hit in 1966.

By 1969, after he had scored several other radio successes in the Detroit area, Seger was signed to Capitol. Almost immediately, he had a national hit on his hands with "Rambling Gambling Man" (#18 *RPM*, #17 *Billboard*), taken from the Capitol album of the same name. Then Seger abruptly quit music to go to college. When he returned in 1972, he recorded briefly on his own label, Palladium. Rosalie Trombley, who had already helped to break Seger nationally, remembers this as Seger's transitional period. "Bob's manager, Punch Andrews, played me a demo tape of some of Bob's latest songs and asked me what I thought," Trombley recalls. "I told him, 'Not too much.' Frankly, I thought Bob was going off on a tangent at the time, influenced by underground artists like Frank Zappa."

At this point, Trombley had still not met Seger. Imagine her surprise then, when she heard his next album, *Back in '72*, and discovered a song named after her. Although some stations were already playing "Rosalie," Trombley blocked it at CKLW because she felt it would be too self-serving. It was only after Seger re-signed with Capitol and had recorded his *Beautiful Loser*, *Live Bullet* and *Night Moves* albums that she finally met the man. It was backstage at Seger's first headline appearance at Detroit's Cobo Hall in 1977. About a year later, over lunch in Windsor, Seger told Trombley why he'd written a song about her. He was reacting to her rejection of his demo tape. Recalls Trombley: "He told me he was really pissed off at me at the time. Knowing that, the song then took on a new meaning, when it goes 'Rosalie, she knows music/I know music/Good old teen queen Rosalie.'"

Seger and Trombley remained on good terms from then on. He even accompanied Trombley and her daughter, Diane, to see Paul McCartney at the Detroit Olympia in 1976 for the *Wings Over America* tour. And when Seger played in London, Ontario, two years later, Trombley and CKLW staff members drove up with Capitol-EMI promotion man Ron Douglas in a rented motorhome and surprised Seger backstage after the show. Says Trombley: "I was always attracted to his music. He wrote about everyday things and people could easily identify with the stories he told in his songs."

Seger went on to huge success through the late 1970s, the '80s and into the early '90s with Capitol albums like *Stranger in Town*, *Against the Wind*, *Like a Rock* and *The Fire Inside*. Although he scored with uptempo rockers like "Old Time Rock & Roll," his biggest hits have been ballads. And none was bigger than "Night Moves." Recorded at Toronto's Nimbus Nine Studios, the song took on a powerful edge when Jack Richardson brought in Canadian keyboard genius Doug Riley and three talented backup singers, Sharon Lee Williams, Rhonda Silver and Laurel Ward, who added gospel-like accompaniment to Seger's soulful vocals. The song remains one of rock's all-time classics.

With CKLW's DJ "good old teen queen" Rosalie Trombley and station program director Les Garland

Canadian Affiliate Labels

DAFFODIL

In the wild and woolly days of the early '70s, when trying to break a new band in Canada still required an act of courage, Daffodil Records displayed an abundance of bravery, imagination and good taste. Owned by Frank Davies, who migrated from England in 1970, Daffodil, together with Capitol, developed some of the earliest stars of the CanCon era, including Crowbar, King Biscuit Boy, A Foot in Coldwater, Fludd and Tom Cochrane. Indeed, Crowbar's "Oh What a Feeling," which Davies also produced, was the first ever CanCon single to be released and to top the charts after the regulations came into effect in January 1971. Its significance was recognized by CARAS when the song was chosen as the theme for the 25th anniversary telecast of the 1996 Juno Awards, as well as the title of an accompanying book on the history of Canadian pop music and best-selling CD box set.

Davies, who ran his Love Productions company and Daffodil label initially out of his Toronto apartment, struck up a distribution deal with Capitol's president Arnold Gosewich. One of his first hirings was Deane Cameron, Cochrane's drummer, who later joined Capitol himself and moved through the ranks to become president of EMI Music Canada. Besides Crowbar and King Biscuit Boy's "Corrina Corrina" (#5 on *RPM*'s Top 40), Daffodil's biggest hits with Capitol included A Foot in Coldwater's "(Make Me Do) Anything You Want" (#3) and Fludd's "Cousin Mary" (#11). All remain timeless Canadian rock classics.

After a four-year absence, Daffodil returned to Capitol in 1978 and brought back its entire catalogue, including albums by Toronto's Klaatu, who earlier had gained notoriety when a U.S. rock critic speculated that the then–mystery group might be The Beatles incognito. Keeping it in the family, Davies took

Foot in Coldwater: timeless Canadian rock classics like '(Make Me Do) Anything You Want' were among the Daffodil label's contributions

Klaatu to Capitol (U.S.) for the rest of the world. Davies, now a successful Canadian music publisher, credits Capitol with having helped his label break into the United States in those early years, where it landed a deal for Crowbar and King Biscuit Boy with Paramount Records. "The

amazing thing historically was that the first four albums, two each by Biscuit and Crowbar, all charted in the U.S.," says Davies. "Through their marketing and promotion efforts in Canada, Capitol helped us to translate our success south of the border as they did later for a Foot in Cold Water when I signed them to Island in the U.K. and Elektra in the U.S."

The Daffodil catalogue continued to be distributed by Capitol in Canada well into the mid-80s.

H.P. & BELL

H.P. & Bell began in 1971 as a management company, formed by keyboardist Paul Hoffert, drummer Skip Prokop and manager Bruce Bell of Lighthouse, Canada's popular jazz-rock big band of the early '70s. But its representation of artists evolved into production work, and the company soon began issuing recordings the following year—thanks to a licensing deal with Capitol-EMI of Canada.

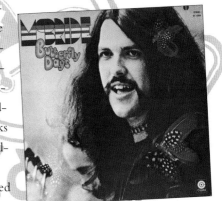

The first album released through that deal was *Gypsy Road*, the Canadian debut by Flying Circus, an Australian band that migrated to Canada in 1972. The group enjoyed two hit singles: "Maple Lady" and "Old Enough (To Break My Heart)," which reached #9 on the *RPM* Top 40. The Flying Circus album was quickly followed by *Butterfly Days*, the solo debut by Lighthouse singer Bob McBride, which spawned the hit single "Pretty City Lady" and landed McBride a Juno Award in March 1973 for Outstanding Male Performance of the Year.

A third artist produced by H.P. & Bell and released on Capitol was Bill

King. An American keyboardist who had worked with Janis Joplin, Chuck Berry and Linda Ronstadt, King left the U.S. army in the early '70s and fled to Canada, where he worked on the campaign to have Washington grant amnesty to conscientious objectors to the Vietnam War. Not long after crossing the border, he formed his own band. King's 1973 debut, *Goodbye Superdad*, earned him critical acclaim and led to a follow-up album, *Blue Skies*. With Capitol-EMI's muscle behind it, H.P. & Bell became a successful independent label—and a formidable launching pad for new Canadian talent.

Novelties

Cantata Canada

"A rock musical about the people, places and times of Canada." That's what producer Don Hutton had in mind when he conceived *Cantata Canada*. Hutton commissioned some of the country's leading composers to write songs about Canadian themes selected by a team of historians. Toronto's Marc Jordan handled the plight of farm workers, while Edmonton's Bob Ruzicka tackled the

opening of the Canadian North, and Graeme Card, of the prairie band Humphrey and the Dumptrucks, put the Battle of the Plains of Abraham to song. Then, with the material performed and recorded by the Calgary rock band Privilege, backed by members of the Vancouver Symphony Orchestra, it became first a stage show and then—thanks to enthusiastic support from Capitol-EMI—an album. It seemed like the project couldn't miss.

Unfortunately, it did. The album was launched in 1973, with Capitol-EMI supplying a major marketing push. "Capitol Canada has become personally involved through its president Arnold Gosewich," reported *RPM*. "It is through Gosewich that Capitol has mustered all its nationalistic feelings into backing this project with the greatest financial and promotional muscle in the company's history." But, despite a promotional budget rumoured to have exceeded $100,000, the album stiffed. More than 50,000 copies of the record were left sitting in Capitol-EMI's warehouse and the album became known around the industry as "Arnold's folly." As ambitious and admirable as the project was, it seemed that Canadians were not interested in hearing their history set to a rock beat.

Goon Again

One of the greatest radio programs of all time, "The Goon Show" ruled the airwaves from 1952 to 1960. A BBC production featuring the brilliant comedy troupe of Peter Sellers, Spike Milligan, Harry Secombe and friends, the Goons reached millions of listeners around the world through widespread syndication. Hugely influential, with fans ranging from The Beatles and Prince Charles to many of

the world's top comedians, the Goons enjoyed an especially devoted following in Canada, where the program was heard on the CBC. In the 1970s, Capitol-EMI helped to launch a Canadian Goon revival by issuing several recordings of the most popular shows.

The program's appeal lay in its zany humour and such memorable characters as Ned Seagoon (Secombe), Henry Crun, Major Dennis Bloodnok and Hercules Gryptype-Thynne (all Sellers) and Eccles, Miss Minnie Bannister and Count Moriarty (all Milligan). Sellers and Milligan, both of whom had lived in India, also regularly lapsed into Hindi accents as (interchangeably) Lalkaka, Banerjee, and Singiz Thingh. Among the recordings released by Capitol-EMI, following a Goon reunion held in 1972, were *First Men on the Moon* and *Goon Again*.

Goon Again featured "The China Story" which, along with "Dishonoured" and "The Man Who Never Was," ranked among the most popular sketches of the series. In "The China Story," "Blitish Ablassador" Neddie Seagoon is inveigled into blowing up the fiendish headquarters of fiendish General Kash Mai Chek. Ultimately, the show's sheer wackiness took its toll on the cast, with Milligan suffering a nervous breakdown and a broken marriage and announcer Andrew Timothy leaving the program claiming that he feared for his sanity. Still, that lunacy will be fondly remembered by anyone touched by the madcap world of Sellers and company. Goon but not forgotten.

CHAPTER FOUR

THE NEW WAVE:

1980 - 1989

THE NEW WAVE:
1980 - 1989

In the 1980s, the music industry saw the advent of a new technology and a new medium: the compact disc and the music video. Both helped the record industry to pull itself out of the economic slump that it found itself in at the dawn of the decade. CDs, which Capitol-EMI began issuing early in 1984, piqued con-sumer interest because they offered a durable source of music and an easi-er way of accessing it. Videos proved to be the ultimate promotional tool. With the 1981 launch of the U.S. MTV network, the musical land-scape in North America was forever changed. *The New Music*, syndicated out of Toronto by Citytv, had begun showing clips as early as 1979. Canadian cries of "I want my MTV" were answered five years later with the arrival of MuchMusic, "the nation's music station."

It's true that "video killed the radio star," as The Buggles sang so prophetically in early 1980. But it also made stars out of a whole generation of pop musicians who were other-wise ignored by radio. The first artists to take advantage of the new medium

Video-savvy rockers Duran Duran, posing with sales awards from Capitol-EMI staff members, enjoyed an enthusiastic reception in Canada on Citytv's The New Music and later on MuchMusic

Talk Talk were part of the "New British Invasion" that landed on Canadian shores in the early 1980s (left to right: Paul Webb, Lee Harris, Mark Hollis)

came from Britain, where a long history of pop music on television provided a market for videos way ahead of anything seen in the United States. America had The Knack, which became a top-selling act from Capitol. But this was the British new wave, and it helped to bring an excitement back to music—something not seen since the 1960s. Capitol-EMI had a good chunk of it, including Duran Duran, Billy Idol, Thomas Dolby and Talk Talk. When the company launched a promotional campaign for those acts in the summer of '82, it quite rightly headed the ads "The New British Invasion."

On the domestic front, the Canadian label was still enjoying Anne Murray's perennial success. Murray remained a leader, not just for Capitol-EMI but for the whole Canadian music industry. At the 1980 and '81 Junos, the veteran pop performer won awards

Blinded with sales awards, England's Thomas Dolby (third from right) tries not to look too smug as he rubs elbows with Capitol-EMI staffers

in both the best album and single categories, as well as taking the best female and best country female vocalist honours. Although Murray held on in '82 to win both vocalist awards, she lost the best album and single titles to Loverboy, a band that Capitol-EMI president Dave Evans and his A&R man, Deane Cameron, had tried to sign. "I was incredibly influenced by the whole punk, new wave and power pop trend," recalls

Cameron. "But I was just one vote on Capitol's A&R committee for North America. I lost Teenage Head and Loverboy because we couldn't give them U.S. commitment."

Still, Cameron did sign some impressive new wave, rock and pop acts in the early '80s. They included Prism, Streetheart, Luba, Sherry Kean, The Deserters, Strange Advance, David Wilcox, Lisa Dal Bello and Long John Baldry. Add to that Anne Murray and Red Rider, Anthem's Rush and Aquarius's April Wine, and it was a formidable list. Some of the acts were signed to Capitol, others to EMI America, a newly created label that became the home for Kenny Rogers, Kim Carnes and such respected British acts as David Bowie and Kate Bush. Cameron was jubilant: "There was one point when,

between EMI America and Capitol, we had ten Canadian acts on the U.S. rosters. That's a pretty sizable contingent for the early '80s."

Capitol-EMI remained first in the Canadian repertoire business. And under Evans's leadership, it was also in the forefront of technological change, which vastly improved the company's manufacturing capa-

Toronto singer Lisa Dal Bello underwent a "profound personal metamorphosis" in the early 1980s, transforming herself from a dance-pop performer into an eclectic new wave artist on Capitol-EMI known as simply Dalbello

bility. By 1982, 8-track tapes had been phased out and the production of cassettes, the format made popular through home and car stereos and portable tape players, was in high gear. That year, the company's

Throughout the entire decade, Capitol-EMI distributed the powerhouse sounds of Anthem recording artists and Canrock giants Rush (from left, Geddy Lee, Alex Lifeson and Neil Peart)

equipment four years later, boosted production to 120 units a minute, or upwards of an astonishing 60,000 units a day. By 1991, the tape plant produced an unprecedented number—in excess of 10 million units—including cassettes for a major competitor.

Meanwhile, vinyl production, which reached its peak in 1982 with the pressing of seven million LPs and three million 45s, was already in decline the following year. Each decade, it seemed, had its predominant recording medium: in the 1950s, it was the 45; in the '60s, the LP; in the '70s, the cassette. The '80s would soon see the arrival of its own unique format, but that was still a couple of years away.

engineers made a series of research breakthroughs that set the production standard for the entire industry. Led by Dan Middleton, the resident "audio scientist," the engineers created SDR (super dynamic range) technology for cassette tape duplication, a quality control principle quickly adopted by U.S. manufacturers. Says Hugh Wiets, the company's vice-president of manufacturing and distribution: "Dan invented the tone burst system, the incremental tone you hear at the head of the tape, which makes it possible to check audio quality. He's a good guy to have. A number of his inventions, including that one, were picked up by EMI worldwide."

By the spring of 1983, there was much to celebrate on the sales front. The label took out a two-page colour ad listing its latest certifications in *The Record*, a new Canadian music industry trade journal launched two years earlier by David Farrell. Among them were double platinum

Aquarius recording artists April Wine (from left Jerry Mercer, Steve Lang, Gary Moffet and Myles Goodwyn): part of a formidable list

awards for Bob Seger and The Stray Cats, platinum for Iron Maiden, Billy Squier, Pat Benatar, Duran Duran and Kenny Rogers, and gold for Little River Band, J. Geils Band and Canadian signings Frank Mills, Strange Advance, Streetheart and Red Rider. In fact, with management from Vancouver's Bruce Allen, Red Rider had begun making huge gains in the United States, opening tours for The Kinks, The Beach Boys and Jefferson Starship, and scoring major FM hits like "Lunatic Fringe."

Not surprisingly, with such technically superior cassettes on the market, Capitol-EMI saw a rise in tape sales (it also saw its competitors, A&M, MCA, PolyGram and WEA, follow suit with their own tape upgrading in

'83). Under Wiets's direction, production at the company's tape plant increased dramatically. By 1985, while the company was still assembling cassettes by hand, 25,000 tapes a day were being produced. Automation the following year, along with further expansion and state-of-the-art

In April 1983, Capitol-EMI reported that the first three months of the year represented the second best first quarter in the company's history. Evans told *The*

Easy-listening hits came courtesy of Canada's Frank Mills

Silver-haired crooner Kenny Rogers hit platinum sales in early 1983

Record that new music contributed immensely to the first-quarter bonanza. Specifically, he credited the "New British Invasion" campaign and the company's SDR cassettes, which had far exceeded the initial sales forecasts. Evans noted that it was an extraordinary rebound after an abnormally soft year earlier for the company. At one point that spring, the label held down the top three album sales positions, with David Bowie's EMI debut *Let's Dance*, Duran Duran's *Rio* and Thomas Dolby's *Blinded Me with Science*.

After a busy summer in which Bowie continued to dominate with *Let's Dance* and a North American tour, Evans announced that Capitol-EMI expected to release 30 new albums before Christmas. To help oversee the increased activity, in the fall he appointed two new vice-presidents: Cameron, for talent acquisition, and David Munns, for marketing.

Bolstered executive ranks couldn't have come at a better time. The year 1984 was one of Capitol-EMI's busiest ever. It began with the company issuing its first CDs in January. The initial batch comprised eight classical and ten pop recordings. By June, the label announced that it was phasing out its vinyl pressing operation at American Drive. Evans cited increasing costs, deteriorating record volumes, a weak economy and home taping as the nails in vinyl's coffin. The company's tape-duplicating operation, he added, would remain open. But the digital age had clearly arrived. Within two years, the label, like all record companies, would be rapidly stepping up CD production, as the mirror-like little discs became de rigueur with consumers.

The summer of '84 saw new releases from Red Rider and Lisa Dal Bello, who began a new artistic incarnation as simply Dalbello with *Whomanfoursays*, a powerful album that *Maclean's* magazine termed a "profound personal metamorphosis" for the artist. There were also full-length releases from Luba, Sherry Kean and other domestic acts. In August, amid Canada's best Olympic showing at the Los Angeles summer games, David Munns took out a timely ad in

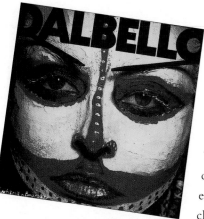

The Record. Headed "Olym-picks," it featured the names of Dalbello, Helix, Luba, Red Rider and Zappacosta inside the five-ring symbol of the games.

August 1984 was the month that MuchMusic went on the air. The brainchild of Citytv broad-caster Moses Znaimer and produc-er John Martin, the pay-TV music channel immediately became a major player in Canadian music, as "veejays" J.D. Roberts, Jeanie Beker, Daniel Richler and Christopher Ward began putting videos by such Capitol-EMI acts as Duran Duran, Thomas Dolby, Strange Advance and Sherry Kean into heavy rotation. Videos added as much as 20 per cent to the production costs of an album. But, as *RPM* editor Walt Grealis told *Saturday Night* magazine at the time of MuchMusic's launch, "It's hard to break a new artist without one."

One of the brightest new faces in Canadian pop, Corey Hart made his debut on MuchMusic that summer. The Montreal singer, signed to Aquarius and thus distrib-uted by Capitol-EMI, enjoyed an instant high profile thanks to his video for "Sunglasses at Night," the single from his *First Offense* album. And although hardly a new artist, Tina Turner also enjoyed major mid-year attention with *Private Dancer*. Featuring the hit single "What's Love Got to Do With It?," the album rejuvenated the career of the 46-year-old singer and quickly became one of Capitol-EMI's biggest-selling records. In less than a year, label president Dave Evans

MuchMusic veejays (from left) J.D. Roberts, Erica Ehm, Christopher Ward and Michael Williams: "the nation's music station" became an instant major player in Canadian music

would be presenting Turner and her manager, Roger Davies, with a seven-times platinum award.

Before the year was out, controversy swirled around heavy-metal road warriors Iron Maiden while the band was touring the prairies. The British band's entourage had departed Winnipeg, following a December

Aquarius recording artist Corey Hart, without his evening eyewear, puts the squeeze on Capitol-EMI's Eddie Colero

concert, in two large buses. Unbeknownst to the group, one of them was carrying Capitol-EMI's Jim Maxwell, *Winnipeg Sun* pop critic Mitch Potter and two members of local radio station CITI-FM, including disc jockey Andy Frost, now best-known as the voice of Toronto Maple Leaf hockey broadcasts. What began as a joke, over many drinks, turned serious when the buses arrived the next morning in Regina. There, the stowaways were kicked off, hungover, and forced to make their own way

MuchMusic veejay Erica Ehm shares a joke with Duran Duran

home. When they did, the Winnipeg media cast them as kidnap victims, with Iron Maiden as the evil perpetrators. Potter, now arts reporter for the *Toronto Star*, still laughs when he thinks about it. "The kidnapping became kind of legendary," says Potter, "when in fact we all just wanted to party aboard a tour bus." But, he added: "I don't think Iron Maiden minded what it did for their bad-boy reputations."

Rock displayed its social conscience in 1985. The cause for concern was the Ethiopian famine, which had already prompted Bob Geldof of The Boomtown Rats to organize a fundrais-

Heavy metal road warriors Iron Maiden stopped the tour bus long enough to accept more metal from a Capitol-EMI contingent

ing single in Britain called "Do They Know It's Christmas?" An American response, the Quincy Jones–produced "We Are the World," was recorded in January. The following month, more than 50 of Canada's top recording artists gathered at Toronto's Manta Sound Studios under the name Northern Lights and recorded "Tears Are Not Enough" to benefit the cause. Among them were Capitol-EMI's Anne Murray, Tom Cochrane of Red Rider, Dalbello, Frank Mills and Zappacosta, Anthem's Geddy Lee of Rush and Aquarius's Corey Hart.

Anne Murray later spoke about the Canadian recording with *The Record*'s David Farrell. "It was a wonderful experience and a terrific day," she told him. "My only regret is they wouldn't release it in the United States. [The record company] said people had been Ethiopianed to death. In my opinion it was a good song, so why not [release it]? But at least we did our part." Meanwhile, Murray's own, world-class contribution to the recording industry was recog-

nized in May, when Capitol's U.S. president Don Zimmerman presented her with a crystal globe for global sales of 30 million records.

Corey Hart's star continued to climb throughout the year. In September, Aquarius took out a full-page ad in *The Record* noting that Hart's second album, *Boy in the Box*, had sold 500,000 copies in Canada in its first 75 days. "Aquarius," stated the ad, "thanks everyone at Capitol-EMI for this remarkable achievement." Although executives at Aquarius and Capitol Canada were loath to paint it as a competition, Hart was quite clearly giving A&M recording artist Bryan Adams a run for his money. At the Juno Awards in November, Adams took Album of the Year while Hart won Single of the Year for "Never Surrender." The neck-and-neck race

More than 50 of Canada's top recording artists, including Capitol-EMI's Anne Murray, Tom Cochrane and Dalbello, took part in the now historic Northern Lights charity song "Tears Are Not Enough" to benefit Ethiopian famine relief

continued into the following year, when *Boy in the Box* became only the second Canadian album (after Adams's *Reckless*) to go diamond, for sales of one million copies in Canada.

During 1985 and into the following year, Capitol-EMI began enjoying success with two talented international acts from both sides of the Atlantic: America's hard rockers Heart bounced back in a big way after faltering on the Epic label, while England's Pet Shop Boys shot straight to the top of the charts with their deadpan ballads and highly danceable synth pop.

"The Year of the Tiger." That's what Capitol-EMI called 1986. The billing was a confident forecast of the label's latest domestic signing:

Corey Hart ran a neck-and-neck race at the 1985 Juno Awards with fellow multiple nominee Bryan Adams

Glass Tiger. Deane Cameron remembers the first time he heard the band, then performing as Tokyo, upstairs at Toronto's famed El Mocambo club on Spadina Avenue. In particular, he recalls that the singer, Alan Frew, "blew me away." Right away, he was prepared to invest development

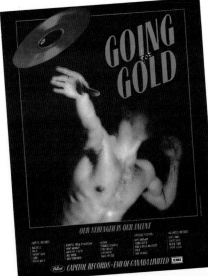

money. Meanwhile, Tim Trombley, son of Canadian radio legend Rosalie Trombley (of CKLW and Bob Seger's "Rosalie" fame), had come to work for Cameron two years earlier. Tokyo became his pet project. Together, Trombley and the band worked on demo tapes. After hearing the group again, when it opened for Culture Club at Maple Leaf Gardens, Cameron was ready for a contract. The band, renamed Glass Tiger, signed to Capitol-EMI in Canada and EMI's New York–based affiliate Manhattan Records in the summer of '85.

Glass Tiger took to the stage at Capitol-EMI's Montreal convention in June 1986, already riding high on the success of its first single. Released in February, "Don't Forget Me (When I'm Gone)" had hit the number one spot on charts at both *RPM* and *The Record*. By May, Capitol Canada

had taken out a full-page ad in the trades on behalf of the band, thanking the industry and the public for helping to make its debut album, *The Thin Red Line*, platinum in Canada (it eventually went on to sell three times that amount). Needless to say, Glass Tiger needed no introduction at the convention, which greeted the group with rapturous applause. The band enjoyed several more highlights that year: in September, its album became Capitol-EMI's first domestic CD; in October, "Don't Forget Me" reached #2 at *Billboard*; and in November, the group swept the Junos, winning Best Album, Best Single and Most Promising Group.

However, tragedy followed triumph for the company. President Dave Evans suffered a stroke at a managers' meeting in Montreal and never fully recovered. By December, the well-liked and respected executive was forced to resign, his position filled by Richard Lyttelton, who was parachuted in from South Africa by EMI head office in London. Evans had been affiliated with Capitol Canada for 18 years before his illness.

That same year, Capitol-EMI's artist roster took a walk on a wilder side when distribution deals were struck with the Nettwerk and Enigma labels. Nettwerk, a Vancouver-based company, brought cutting-edge acts like Skinny Puppy, known for its heavy industrial music, The Grapes of Wrath, Chris and Cosey and the band Moev into the fold, while Enigma, from Los Angeles, added such eclectic artists as The Smithereens,

Fela Anikulapo Kuti: the King of Afrobeat came to Canada via EMI Nigeria and his early association with Ginger Baker.

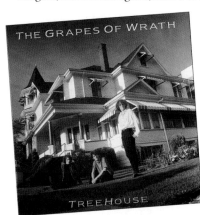

The Pogues, Mojo Nixon, The Textones and Canadian jazz legend Maynard Ferguson, who returned to the Capitol family through his Enigma-distributed *High Voltage* album on the Intima label.

Lyttelton lost no time in making headlines. "Capitol to double its A&R budget in '87," reported *The Record* in February of that year. The accompanying article quoted Lyttelton as saying that the new budget amount, estimated at $2 million, would be earmarked for A&R and marketing support. The article continued: "The company is now in the enviable position of having the number one position in the market with its Canadian roster, which includes Glass Tiger, Anne Murray, Tom Cochrane and Red Rider, Luba, The Partland Brothers, Rock & Hyde and distributed label deals which bring them Rush, Ian Thomas, The Spoons, Corey Hart, Myles Goodwyn (ex–April Wine) and The Grapes of Wrath."

Lyttelton also began rationalizing the company's operations. He transferred Capitol-EMI's now-moribund retail division, Mister Sound/Shermans, to HMV, the British subsidiary of Thorn EMI. HMV had already planned to expand into North America, using Canada as its starting point. The Mister Sound chain of stores would provide a good foundation on which to build. Then Lyttelton oversaw the development of a new distribution system, one based on a state-of-the-art, computerized carousel operation. It would take several years of careful study before it was up and running, but the carousel would eventually quadruple the company's storage capacity while making order filling dramatically more efficient.

The times were definitely changing. In July, a headline in *The Record* announced: "CD sales carrying record industry gains." The article, quoting a Canadian Recording Industry Association report, stated that the five months ending in May showed manufacturers' net sales up by more than $21 million. It added that CD sales accounted for much of the growth. Capitol-EMI, which had its CDs made by Quebec's Disque Americ until it opened its own pressing facility on American Drive, issued some notable CDs that year, including the prestigious Angel recording of Handel's *Messiah* by the Toronto Symphony Orchestra, conducted by Andrew Davis and featuring Kathleen Battle and the Toronto Mendelssohn

"Industrial" innovators Skinny Puppy brought a cutting-edge sound via Vancouver's Nettwerk Records

Choir. Most significant were the CD reissues of The Beatles catalogue, which represented the company's crown jewels. When *Sgt. Pepper's Lonely Hearts Club Band*, perhaps the brightest gem of them all, was reissued on June 1 with ads proclaiming "It was 20 years ago today," the release was greeted with appropriate fanfare.

"From sea to shining sea".

Capitol Records

In 1988, the Canadian Academy of Recording Arts and Science (CARAS) shifted the month for staging the annual Juno Awards from November to March. The change meant that for the transition period, at least, Canadian music was celebrated twice within six months. At the November '87 awards, Capitol-EMI's Luba won Best Female Vocalist for the third straight year (carrying on a tradition begun by Anne Murray), while Tom Cochrane and Red Rider took the Group of the Year award. In March, Cochrane enjoyed Composer of the Year honours and Aquarius recording artist Sass Jordan won Most Promising Female Vocalist, while Glass Tiger earned the coveted Canadian Entertainer of the Year prize, the only award voted on by the public.

There was much to celebrate when the company held its national convention that year in Ville d'Estérel, Quebec, a resort town in the Laurentians. As usual, accomplishments were reviewed and forecasts made during daytime gatherings, while evenings were more relaxed affairs involving music and socializing. Cameron and Trombley

The Partland Brothers: best known for the electric honey sound of "Soul City"

had lined up a showcase of their latest signing, an underground rock band from Toronto called National Velvet, led by singer Maria Del Mar. Trombley recalls that the band's performance didn't leave much of an impression on the convention's U.S. delegates, but the group's after-show antics certainly did. Says Trombley: "National Velvet, who were defiantly nonconformist, lived up to their reputation and trashed a couple of hotel rooms. They were the talk of the convention the next day."

Immediately following the convention, the company's parent, Capitol Industries Inc. in Los Angeles, announced that Deane Cameron would be taking over from Lyttelton as the Canadian company's eighth president, effective the beginning of November. At 34, Cameron would become the youngest leader in the Canadian music industry. *The Record*'s David Farrell made another distinction: "Cameron, a maverick talent supporter with a longstanding commitment to Canadian talent, is the first A&R director to be named to the top position at a major record company in Canada." For his part, *RPM*'s Walt Grealis felt that Cameron was a wise choice. "Deane started in the stock room and learned everything from the ground up," said Grealis. "He knows every department, from copyright and retail to marketing and accounting. The boy's got Capitol blood in his veins."

In making the announcement, Joe Smith, president of Capitol Industries-EMI, Inc., applauded Cameron's accomplishments on behalf of the company. "Deane has set new standards for the Canadian music industry," said Smith, "with his development of talent and his enthusiastic support for musicians and writers in his territory."

Legendary Canadian singer-songwriter Murray McLauchlan was one of Deane Cameron's first signings after he assumed the presidency of Capitol-EMI in 1988

One of the first things Cameron did was to instill a sense of history and company pride in his employees by having the words "Forty Years of Commitment to Canada" included on all Capitol-EMI materials. Then, as if to underscore his patriotic point, he signed legendary Canadian singer-songwriter Murray McLauchlan and announced a new distribution deal with indie label Alert Music, home of Canrock legends Kim Mitchell and Michel Pagliaro and up-and-coming acts like The Box. Cameron called Alert "a contemporary and aggressive young label" and noted that it has "a tremendous artist roster with enormous

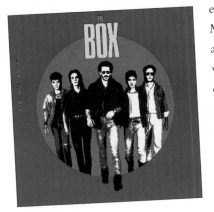

hit potential." For his part, Alert president Tom Berry said he saw Capitol-EMI as "a partner that will help us develop our artists internationally, while increasing our already successful growth rate in Canada." In other words, the two were made for each other.

Cameron made two other moves during his first full year in office that once again proved his passion for Canadian music. First, he oversaw the release of *To Kingdom Come*, a three-CD retrospective of The Band, a group that he had deeply admired, going right back to his high school days with Tom Cochrane. Then in July, he and Tim Trombley, the company's newly promoted vice-president of talent acquisition and artist development, signed Captain Canada himself, Stompin' Tom Connors. The deal called for Capitol-EMI to release the legendary musician's new *Fiddle and Song* album as well as his entire back catalogue. Connors, who had languished in the Canadian musical wilderness for too long, could not have found a better home.

As Cameron looked ahead to the 1990s, there was no shortage of challenges, including developing the company's own CD manufacturing and creating an international market for its domestic artists. At least he had inherited a financially healthy operation. The fiscal year that ended March 31, 1989, was the most profitable in Capitol-EMI's history.

National Velvet, led by sultry singer Maria Del Mar (centre), became the talk of the company's 1988 convention after the group trashed a couple of hotel rooms in Ville d'Estérel

Canada's 'Thin White Dude' Kim Mitchell moved to Alert Music and retained his connection to Capitol-EMI

GLASS TIGER

CAPITOL-EMI CANADA
1985

Group members Sam Reid, Alan Frew, Michael Hanson, Wayne Parker and Al Connelly give themselves a hand at the Junos: the 'Year of the Tiger'

"We haven't seen Capitol Canada so worked up about an album since Corey Hart's first release," stated *The Record* in its review of Glass Tiger's debut *The Thin Red Line*. "Their enthusiasm is well justified. Strong management, good visuals (including the video), sterling musicianship and the great production care of Jim Vallance makes the future of Glass Tiger look bright. What makes this record really sing is the diversity of material. There's an edge to the band reminiscent of Red Rider's *Neruda*. All passion and knockout performances. We predict Glass Tiger as one of the new Canadian bands to break this year."

British football chums Alan Frew (right) with Bruce Dickinson of Iron Maiden

The Record was right—about both Glass Tiger's eventual success and Capitol-EMI's support for the project. So confident was the record company of its new signing that it launched an extensive promotion campaign in which 1986 was proclaimed "The Year of the Tiger." "The combined musical and songwriting talents of this group were apparent from the start," Tim Trombley, the label's vice-president of talent acquisition and artist development, later wrote. "Their enthusiasm for what they did was the focal point. But most importantly, the strength of these irrepressible characters was to communicate musical vision with wit, wonder and style."

Where we gonna hang all these? Glass Tiger contemplates a wall-shortage problem, as beaming Capitol-EMI staffers look on

Glass Tiger began in the early 1980s as Tokyo, a Newmarket, Ontario–based bar band that performed a mix of original songs and Rush, AC/DC and Scorpions covers. The group—singer Alan Frew, keyboardist Sam Reid, guitarist Al Connelly, bassist Wayne Parker and drummer Michael Hanson—got its first big break opening for Culture Club at Toronto's Maple Leaf Gardens. Renamed Glass Tiger, the band then saw its fortunes rise even further when former Styx manager Derek Sutton, impressed by a demo tape, agreed to co-manage the group with Canadians Gary Pring and Joe Bamford. In 1985, Glass Tiger signed with Capitol-EMI in Canada and Manhattan Records in the United States.

The band flew to Vancouver to work with Jim Vallance, best known as Bryan Adams's co-writer and co-producer. Shortly after stepping off the plane, Frew, Reid and Vallance co-wrote "Don't Forget Me (When I'm Gone)." The song, an effervescent piece of pop, became a massive breakthrough for the band, hitting number one in Canada and number two in the United States. Vallance proved to be a most effective collaborator, co-writing much of the band's first album and producing it as well. "We really felt fortunate," Reid told *Canadian Musician*'s Perry Stern. "A lot of big name producers were offered the project, but with a debut album, if the producer puts his stamp on it you get locked in. It doesn't sound like the band, it sounds like the producer. Jim's musical sense allowed us to be Glass Tiger."

Ultimately *The Thin Red Line*, released in March, 1986, spawned five singles, including "Someday" (Top 5 in Canada and the U.S.), and sold over 1.5 million copies worldwide. The band toured for the next 18 months, opening for Tina Turner in Europe and Journey in the United States. Glass Tiger swept the 1986 Juno Awards, winning Most Promising Group, Album of the Year and Single of the Year (for "Don't Forget Me").

For its second album, 1988's *Diamond Sun*, Glass Tiger stuck with Vallance as producer but jettisoned the keyboard sheen of its debut in favour of a heavier guitar sound. The group also recruited Capitol-EMI recording artist Dalbello as a formidable backup vocalist. Like its predecessor, the album produced five singles, including the title track, "I'm Still Searching" and the stirring "My Song," which featured Ireland's The Chieftains on fiddles, flute, harp and uillean pipes. *Diamond Sun* went over triple platinum in Canada, with sales of 300,000, and earned Glass Tiger another Juno as Entertainer of the Year in 1988–89.

Even without producer Vallance and drummer Hanson, who had left the band by this point, Glass Tiger's success continued with its third album. Produced by Reid and Tom Werman, 1991's *Simple Mission* featured such hit singles as "Animal Heart" and "My Town." On the latter song, singer Frew realized the dream of a lifetime: singing a duet with Rod Stewart, one of his musical heroes. The album earned platinum status and was followed by a greatest-hits collection, *Best of the Best*, in 1993. Glass Tiger broke up after that, with Reid becoming a producer and studio owner and Frew releasing a successful solo album on EMI titled *Hold On*.

LUBA

Capitol-EMI Canada
1982

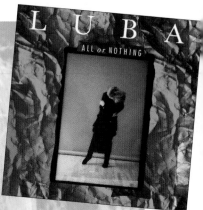

A diva before the species became ubiquitous within pop music, Luba captivated audiences in the 1980s with her big, gospel-inflected voice and polished dance sound. The diminutive Montreal singer swept the Juno Awards for three consecutive years as Best Female Vocalist while her band of the same name became a staple of the Canadian pop circuit. The accolades grew louder and Luba's star shone brighter when two of her songs were featured in the soundtrack to the film *9 1/2 Weeks*, the steamy romance starring Mickey Rourke and Kim Basinger. Even U.S. producer Narada Michael Walden, who worked with Whitney Houston, Aretha Franklin and Luba herself, proclaimed the singer "the Great White Hope of soul music."

Group members Peter Marunzak, Michael Bell, Jeff Smallwood and Luba Kowalchyk (seated): "a shimmering compendium of pop anthems"

As a teenager growing up in Montreal, Luba Kowalchyk was an unlikely candidate for pop stardom. The shy daughter of a labourer and his wife, she got her start in music singing traditional folk songs in Ukrainian Canadian communities. She even made several Ukrainian recordings before she formed a rock group with drummer Peter Marunzak and guitarist Mark Lyman while the three were still in university. After graduation, they added keyboardist Pierre Marchand and bassist Michael Bell and recorded a demo tape that came to the attention of Capitol–EMI's A&R man Deane Cameron. Impressed with the band's sound and Luba's vocals, Cameron signed them in 1982.

The group's self-titled mini-album for Capitol-EMI included "Everytime I See Your Picture," an emotional tribute to the singer's father, which reached #9 on *The Record* in 1983. *Secrets and Sins*, a full-length album produced by Daniel Lanois, came out the following year. Featuring the calypso-reggae dance hit "Let It Go," #8 on *RPM*'s Top 40 chart, and "Storm Before the Calm" (#2), the album went on to sell more than 100,000 copies. Drawing comparisons to Pat Benatar and Chrissie Hynde, Luba's vocals received the highest praise. "This is one of the timeless, great voices in rock," raved the *Montreal Gazette*, "revealing a powerhouse pair of pipes that can deliver more

Overwhelmed with Juno: "the Great White Hope of soul music"

emotion with a catch mid-phrase or a sudden intake of breath than all the mannered singers in the world."

Along with her dynamic vocals, Luba endeared herself to critics with her lack of pretension. When asked if she deliberately played down her looks to avoid feminine stereotyping, the singer was refreshingly straightforward. "I don't play them down," she told *Graffiti* magazine, "it's just me. I'm not the type of person to wear something low-cut, or running up my thighs. I love to wear big, baggy, bulky clothes. I've been called all sorts of things, even an Italian bag lady. I just feel that I can make it on my talent."

That talent shone through on Luba's 1986 album, *Between the Earth and Sky*. Featuring the stirring, gospel-flavoured "How Many (Rivers to Cross)," it received a four-star review in *The Record*. The album also drew raves from the *Toronto Star*, which called it "a shimmering compendium of pop anthems, rock ballads and new-age soul." When the *Star*'s Craig MacInnis asked her how she judged her album, Luba admitted that she was too close to the music to offer an objective analysis. "I'm the one who writes the music," she said. "I'm the one who arranges the music. I need someone outside the band to tell me the whole thing stinks."

Yet critics continued to heap on the praise. When Capitol-EMI issued a greatest-hits collection titled *Over 60 Minutes with...Luba* in 1987, *The Record* called it "one of the best pop collections on the shelf right now." The magazine pointed out that the album was topped off with Luba's live recording of the Percy Sledge favourite "When a Man Loves a Woman." The song, it noted, "has long been her concert stopper, but it took a lot of convincing for Luba to concede and let Capitol include her version for release as a single." Added the magazine: "Canada's best kept secret scores her biggest hit to date with the only new track on this 16-song Best Of."

Before the decade was out, Luba released one more album, *All or Nothing*, which hit platinum-level sales faster than any of her previous records. With her magnificent voice, the group's synth-pop sound and a string of instantly recognizable hits, Luba left a distinctive mark on the post–new wave period of Canadian pop.

Luba with Anne Murray, flanked by Marunzak and Bill Langstroth: a diva for her time

MURRAY McLAUCHLAN

CAPITOL-EMI CANADA
1988

At Toronto's Diamond club, 1988: "a writer with songs that can thrill with the shock of self-discovery and a singer who can plumb emotional depths"

When Capitol-EMI signed the 40-year-old Murray McLauchlan in the summer of 1988, the label added one of Canada's most respected and accomplished singer-songwriters to its roster. As the *Globe and Mail* noted that year: "McLauchlan is something of a Canadian institution. His songs are reprinted in school textbooks. He's won nine Juno Awards and he can be heard on the CBC both as a performer and as a host." Indeed, with his songs about farmers, winos, boulevards and timberlines, McLauchlan is every bit as Canadian as hockey or referendums. Heck, if Canadian music had its Mount Rushmore, his chiseled mug would be right there alongside Gordon Lightfoot's and Anne Murray's.

Capitol-EMI didn't sign McLauchlan for prestige alone. The label, like any responsible business, believed that signing McLauchlan was a sound investment that would pay dividends. McLauchlan recounted how the deal came about in his 1998 autobiography *Getting Out of Here Alive*. He had already recorded a collection of ten polished, country-flavoured songs, drenched in Ron Dann's weeping pedal steel. All he needed was a supportive record company. Wrote McLauchlan: "I went over to see Deane Cameron, who was head of A&R at Capitol-EMI at the time. Deane was then and is now a very active champion of Canadian music, and I got a bite right away."

What Cameron and his assistant, Tim Trombley, heard in that master tape were well-crafted songs that had a good shot at getting airplay on country radio. They were right. When *Swinging on a Star* was released, the first single, the bittersweet

At the recording of the charity song "Let the Good Guys Win," with collaborators Tom Cochrane and Paul Hyde, and MuchMusic's Denise Donlon (McLauchlan's future wife) on hand for an interview taping

ballad "My Imaginary Tree," was instantly picked up. Mind you, there wasn't a song on the record that some country programmer didn't like. The album was the "country pick" at *The Record*, which gave it a four-star review and called it a "winner" and a "real record." Even the rock-oriented *Music Express* welcomed McLauchlan's move to country. "He's no rhinestone cowboy," wrote critic Jeff Bateman, "just a writer

with songs that thrill with the shock of self-discovery (his and our own) and a singer who can plumb the emotional depths of his work in performance, just like Lyle Lovett or John Hiatt, if you're looking for a couple of Nashville reference points."

Never the sort to stay in one place for too long, McLauchlan transformed himself for his next release, 1989's *The Modern Age*. As the bio from Capitol-EMI put it: "Anyone who's grown accustomed in recent years to thinking of Murray McLauchlan as a country singer will be surprised at the discernible shift toward musical eclecticism." With a "variety of influences ranging from rock, blues and r&b to minimalist pop and even soca (!)," the bio added, "it's clear that Murray has, for the moment, outgrown the intimate, hearthside ambiance that characterized his last album."

To say the least. While *Swinging on a Star*'s strength was its personal perspective, the new album had an unmistakable social focus. The songs tackled such issues as racism, domestic violence and environmental destruction. The title track, also the album's first single, painted ominous images of oil-stained seas, clearcut hillsides and homeless people. A disturbing video for the song, featuring native dancers from the Six Nations reserve in Brantford, Ontario, went into heavy rotation on MuchMusic. An undeniable spirit of hope pervaded the album as well, best captured by "Let the Good Guys Win," on which McLauchlan was joined by Paul Hyde and Tom Cochrane. Proceeds from the song went to the United Nations for reforestation projects and feeding children.

Like Sylvia Tyson a decade earlier, McLauchlan's presence on Capitol-EMI in the '80s was a source of great pride for the label. Both artists were part of the Yorkville generation of singer-songwriters in the 1960s that first put Canada on the musical map.

PRISM

CAPITOL-EMI CANADA
1976

Left to right: Allen Harlow, John Hall, Rocket Norton, the late Dorothy Stratton and Ron Tabak, and Lindsay Mitchell. The Vancouver-born model was the subject of the group's song "Cover Girl," in 1980.

Few bands have personified a city's musical community as strongly as Vancouver's Prism. At one time or another, Prism was associated with rocker Bryan Adams and manager Bruce Allen, and included songwriter Jim Vallance, producer Bruce Fairbairn, former members of the legendary psychedelic outfit The Seeds of Time and future members of Powder Blues Band and The Payola$. Over a five-year period, the band released 6 hit albums, 16 singles and received 14 gold and platinum awards and a Juno for Group of the Year in 1980. With its bracing sound, a distinctive mix of horns, synthesizers and power chords, Prism came to epitomize West Coast Canadian rock.

Flashback to Vancouver, circa 1969. The Seeds of Time was a hippie band with a difference. As Michael Willmore noted in *The History of Vancouver Rock and Roll*: "When everyone else was smoking dope and being groovy, they were drinking beer and being obnoxious. In their time, The Seeds—Lindsay Mitchell, Al Harlow, John Hall and Rocket Norton—were hounded by the police, kicked out of the musicians' union for unbecoming behavior, banned from playing high schools and, finally, banned from the entire city of Calgary." Not bad credentials for a rock group. The band recorded two potent, Stones-ish singles, "My Home Town" and "Cryin' the Blues," before splitting up.

Jump ahead to the mid-70s. Vallance and Fairbairn, both students in the University of British Columbia's music program, form a jazz and funk band called Sunshyne. After recruiting singer Ron Tabak, former Seeds guitarist Lindsay Mitchell and changing their name to Prism, they recorded a demo of Vallance's songs, produced by Fairbairn. With Allen's managerial backing, the band landed a deal with GRT. More Seeds then joined, including guitarist Al Harlow, keyboardist John Hall and drummer Rocket Norton. Before quitting, Vallance left his mark on the band's 1977 self-title debut album, writing and performing on the single "Spaceship Superstar" and other tracks under the pseudonym Rodney Higgs.

See Forever Eyes came out the next year. But the following *Armageddon* was Prism's biggest-selling record. Produced by Fairbairn and engineered and mixed by Bob Rock (who later formed The Payola$ and Rock and Hyde), the album featured the rocking "You Walked Away

Again," written for the band by Bryan Adams before he embarked on his solo career in 1980. The title track, recorded with members of the Vancouver Symphony Orchestra, reached #8 on *RPM*'s Top 40 chart. Even bigger was the ballad "Night to Remember," which topped the Canadian charts and was later named Single of the Year by Procan, the forerunner to the Society of Composers, Authors and Music Publishers of Canada (SOCAN).

Prism kicked off the 1980s by signing with Capitol-EMI and scoring another hit: the title track from the band's *Young and Restless* album, which went Top 20. The group's next hit came from Adams and Vallance, who wrote "Don't Let Him Know" for Small Change in 1981. The album got a rave review in *The Record*, which cited "ingredients that just might work to break Prism in the United States," but by then, constant touring had begun to take its toll on the band. A conflict arose between ex–Scrubaloe Caine singer Henry Small (who had replaced a fired Tabak) and the rest of the group, many of whom quit. By the end of the tour to support Small Change, the band had fallen apart. However, they regrouped in 1983 to record one more album, *Beat Street*, before going their separate ways.

Prism's pull proved irresistible and a reunion was in the works, until Tabak was killed in a motorcycle accident in 1984 and the plan had to be shelved. They revisited the idea again three years later, when Capitol-EMI informed the group that it intended to release a Prism collection. Survivors Norton, Mitchell and Harlow recruited singer Darcy Deutsch and keyboardist Andy Lorimer, both club veterans who knew Prism's material. Together, they recorded two new songs for the greatest hits package, including the Adams-Vallance number "Good to Be Back." When Bruce Fairbairn died in May 1999, he was remembered for many things, not the least of which was his role as a founding member of Prism, Canada's quintessential West Coast rockers.

RED RIDER

CAPITOL-EMI CANADA
1978

Album sales regularly reached the gold and platinum mark, resulting in Capitol-EMI presentations like this one, attended by cheerleader Ron Robles (far right)

Tough, passionate, uncompromising. Those were the adjectives critics used in the 1980s to describe the songs and music of Red Rider. Indeed, the group's four albums on Capitol and another three recorded as Tom Cochrane and Red Rider were landmark recordings that often made reviewers' year-end lists. But they were also commercially successful. Fuelled by hit singles like "White Hot," "Lunatic Fringe" and "Boy Inside the Man," sales of those albums regularly reached the gold and platinum mark. One of the first signings by Capitol-EMI's young A&R head Deane Cameron, Red Rider did Cameron and the Canadian label proud. It also made a star of Cochrane, the band's lead singer and chief songwriter.

Cameron, in fact, played a pivotal role in bringing Red Rider and Cochrane together in the first place. Friends from junior high school, he and Cochrane had played in a country-rock, Band-influenced outfit called Harvest, with Cameron on drums. When that group broke up, Cameron went to work in the record industry while Cochrane honed his craft as a singer-songwriter. Cameron got a call at his Capitol office one day in 1978. It was Cliff Hunt, singing the praises of a Little Feat–like band he was managing at the time called Red Rider. Only problem was, Hunt told him, they need a singer. Cameron immediately suggested his old friend Cochrane. After checking the band out at Toronto's El Mocambo, Cochrane auditioned at Fryfogle's, a club in London, Ontario. He was in.

chrane: "punchy and rtinent" songs formed a nerstone for the label's nestic roster

The pre-Red Rider band Harvest, in 1973, with Cochrane (third from left) and drummer Deane Cameron (second from left)

Composed of Cochrane and Ken Greer on guitars and vocals, Peter Boynton on keyboards, Jeff Jones on bass and Rob Baker on drums, Red Rider signed with Cameron in 1978. Capitol's U.S. vice-president of A&R, Rupert Perry, flew up from Los Angeles to ratify the deal. The group's 1980 debut album, *Don't Fight It*, included three songs that became staples of FM radio: the title track, "Avenue A" and "White Hot," which reached #48 on *Billboard*. The following year's *As Far as Siam* was even more successful, producing the hit single "Lunatic Fringe," later featured on NBC-TV's "Miami Vice." Canada's *The Record*

called the album "startling," describing the songs as "punchy and pertinent," the rockers "gritty and tough." Red Rider was on its way.

Cochrane made a creative stretch with his songs on Red Rider's 1983 album, *Neruda*, which *The Record* called the group's "most cohesive, expressive and accessible yet." "I was fascinated with politics at that point," Cochrane later explained, adding that much of the inspiration came from Latin American poet Pablo Neruda. "I started reading about his life," said Cochrane. "Neruda's whole approach to writing is very mystical. [He] always seems to have one foot in the sky and one foot on the ground." For Cochrane, Neruda "tapped into something really spiritual." He added: "From then on, I always kept my eyes and ears open to things."

After the group's next album, 1984's *Breaking the Curfew*, failed to bring the much-anticipated U.S. breakthrough, Red Rider officially disbanded. A short while later, Cochrane and Greer returned to the scene, recording at Dave Edmunds's Rockfield Studios in Wales. Their next album on Capitol, *Tom Cochrane and Red Rider*, produced the radio hits "Boy Inside the Man" and "The Untouchable One" and earned them a Juno Award for Group of the Year. Between albums, Cochrane produced The Grapes of Wrath's *Treehouse*, while Greer produced The Tragically Hip's self-titled debut EP.

Victory Day, produced by Don Gehman (R.E.M., John Cougar Mellencamp), came out in 1987. The most successful single from that album was "Big League," a poignant song about a boy's hockey aspirations. It helped to win Cochrane another Juno Award as Composer of the Year. After recording *The Symphony Sessions* with the Edmonton Symphony Orchestra, Cochrane and Greer parted ways and laid Red Rider to rest. Although Cochrane continued with Capitol-EMI as an even more successful solo act, his role in Red Rider helped to make the group a cornerstone of the label's domestic roster in the 1980s.

ROCK & HYDE

CAPITOL-EMI CANADA
1986

They came from Vancouver's fertile punk and new wave scene. In the early 1980s, Bob Rock and Paul Hyde fronted The Payola$, one of Canada's most creatively potent bands. They played raw music with biting lyrics about child abuse and the futility of war. They scored Top 10 hits like "Eyes of a Stranger" and won four Juno Awards in 1983.

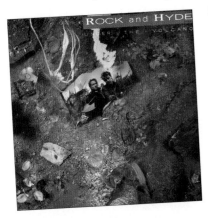

Ultimately, however, The Payola$ ran afoul of their record company, A&M, which wanted a change in the band's musical direction as well as their name. The label complained it had trouble selling U.S. broadcasters on a name that reminded them of the dreaded 1950s bribery scandal. The Payola$ and A&M parted ways and the band broke up.

Enter Capitol-EMI, who signed Payola$ principals—guitarist Rock and singer Hyde—and sent the pair into the studio with producer

Bob Rock (left) and Paul Hyde: reviews for the dynamic duo's debut album, Under the Volcano, were uniformly strong, with Maclean's declaring it "molten hot"

Bruce Fairbairn. Right away, the results were promising. The punchy chords and hard-hitting lyrics that had once given The Payola$ an edge (dulled by producer David Foster on the group's last A&M album) were back. The reviews for the duo's powerful 1987 debut were uniformly strong. "*Under the Volcano* is molten hot," raved *Maclean's* magazine. "Rock and Hyde have erupted into the mainstream." The *Toronto Sun* called it "a pop-rock record full of thick keyboard textures and lots of slashing guitar jags, while the *Globe and Mail* appreciated its "songs that tell stories on a human scale, with a point of view that is both personal and calculatedly commercial."

The album delivered two hit singles: the anthemic "Dirty Water" (not The Standells' '60s nugget) and the euphoric "I Will." Some reviewers credited Rock and Hyde's new label for the turnaround. "It's their first for Capitol Records," wrote the *Montreal Gazette*'s John Griffin, "Canuck home to Luba and Glass Tiger, and a company known for the Midas touch it gives home-grown acts." Hyde agreed. "Capitol actually likes us for the music we make," he told Griffin, "not for the music they think we can make, which is gratifying after what we've been through."

Sadly, *Under the Volcano* was Rock and Hyde's only album. The dynamic duo went their separate ways. Hyde recorded a solo album for Capitol-EMI in 1990 called *Turtle Island*, featuring the hit singles "America is Sexy" and "What Am I Supposed to Do?" Rock went on to become one of the world's top producers, best known for his work with Mötley Crüe, Metallica and Aerosmith.

The former Payola$ retained their hard-hitting lyrics

SHERRY KEAN

CAPITOL-EMI CANADA
1982

Toronto's The Sharks were one of the brightest lights of the Canadian new wave. The band, made up of singer Sherry Huffman, guitarist David Baxter, bassist Bazil Donovan and drummer Cleve Anderson, regularly packed clubs on the city's club circuit in the early 1980s. Huffman attracted the lion's share of media and record industry attention. Wrote *NOW* magazine's James Marck: "A tall, lithe woman with a voice that reflected her physique—reedy, mobile and comfortable in the upper registers—she aroused speculation not about whether she was ready for the big leagues, but when she would make the move."

The answer came in 1982. After a feeding frenzy by record labels, The Sharks' Huffman and Baxter signed with Capitol-EMI following a showcase date at Toronto's El Mocambo. The husband-and-wife team headed to New York to lay the groundwork for their debut album, while the group's Donovan and Anderson immersed themselves in Toronto's Queen Street scene, eventually joining Blue Rodeo. While in New York, Huffman and Baxter hooked up with Mike Thorne, whose success with Soft Cell's debut had earned him a reputation as one of the hottest new producers.

Mixed Emotions, a five-song EP by the newly christened Sherry Kean, came out in the fall of 1983 to glowing reviews. "A new name to watch closely," concluded *Billboard*. "A worthwhile and confident debut," stated the *Toronto Star*, adding impatiently that the EP "begs a full-length followup—soon." The *Star*'s reviewer's wish was granted in the spring of '84. Titled *People Talk*, the Thorne-produced album featured ten original songs by Kean and Baxter, including such Sharks-era favourites as the cool, clipped "Be Mine" and the gutsy rocker "I Want You Back." The latter hit the Top 10 at both *RPM* and *The Record*.

With her straight-cropped bangs of bobbed hair and stunning art deco clothing, Kean was the epitome of chic when she performed a thrilling version of "I Want You Back" on the 1984 Juno Awards show. She later won for Most Promising Female Vocalist. Although her looks created a stir, it was her voice that will be remembered as one of the most distinctive in Canadian music. "There are singers who are much better vocal acrobats," Kean admitted to the *Globe and Mail*'s Liam Lacey. "My strength is that I have the kind of tone that cuts through."

One of the most distinctive Canadian voices of the '80s

Cool, clipped favourites like "Be Mine," gutsy rockers such as "I Want You Back"

Bobbed hair and art deco clothing: the epitome of chic

STREETHEART

CAPITOL-EMI CANADA

1980

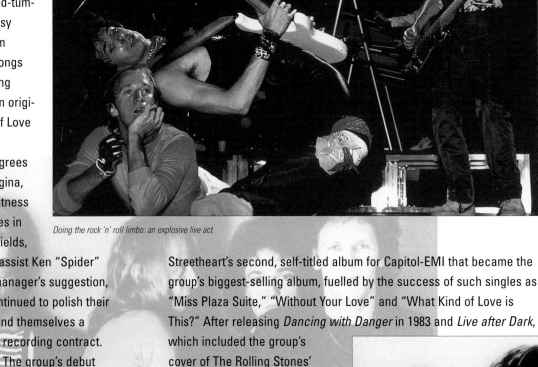

Doing the rock 'n' roll limbo: an explosive live act

Hard-rocking Streetheart was one of the most successful bands out of western Canada in the early 1980s. Although their roots were in the rough-and-tumble bar circuit, Streetheart grew to become classy arena rockers with a Juno and gold and platinum awards to their credit. Known for its covers of songs by Van Morrison, The Small Faces and The Rolling Stones, the band also scored a Top 10 hit with an original number, the bittersweet ballad "What Kind of Love is This?"

Streetheart had one of the most tangled pedigrees in Canadian music. The group was formed in Regina, when members of two popular prairie bands, Witness Inc. and Great Canadian River Race, joined forces in 1976. The initial lineup included singer Kenny Shields, guitarist Paul Dean, keyboardist Daryl Gutheil, bassist Ken "Spider" Sinnaeve and drummer Matt Frenette. At their manager's suggestion, the band's members moved to Winnipeg and continued to polish their act—enough to impress Atlantic Records and land themselves a recording contract. The group's debut album, *Meanwhile Back in Paris*, sold 100,000 copies in 1977. But then personality conflicts caused Dean and Frenette to leave for Vancouver, where they became founding members of Loverboy. After two more Atlantic albums, Streetheart signed with Capitol-EMI.

Drugstore Dancer, released in 1981, featured such crunching rockers as "Trouble" and the frenzied title track. It was

Shields letting loose at Toronto's Maple Leaf Gardens, 1980

Streetheart's second, self-titled album for Capitol-EMI that became the group's biggest-selling album, fuelled by the success of such singles as "Miss Plaza Suite," "Without Your Love" and "What Kind of Love is This?" After releasing *Dancing with Danger* in 1983 and *Live after Dark*, which included the group's cover of The Rolling Stones' "Under My Thumb," Capitol-EMI issued a greatest-hits collection. The band members then went their separate ways.

Shields formed The Kenny Shields Band, while Sinnaeve joined Tom Cochrane and Red Rider. Streetheart reunited briefly in 1996 for a tour at the same time that Dean and Frenette were doing double duty with Loverboy. Ultimately, Streetheart's strength was its concert performances during the 1980s, which often saw band members jump into the audience, in a precursor to the mosh pits of the 1990s. Says Shields: "The live act is what we're remembered for, the blood and the guts and sweat and how it was always consistent and always a good time."

Group members (back row) Daryl Gutheil, Jeff Neil, (front row) Ken "Spider" Sinnaeve, Herb Ego and Kenny Shields: a band that spawned Loverboy and, in the future, Red Rider.

HELIX

CAPITOL-EMI CANADA
1982

Group members (back row) Greg "Fritz" Hinz, Brian Vollmer, Daryl Gray, (front row) Paul Hackman and Brent Doerner: a "rip-yer-face-off style of rock"

Helix was Canada's leather-clad contribution to Capitol-EMI's international heavy-metal roster, an ear-splitting contingent that included Stryper, W.A.S.P. and Iron Maiden. The band was primarily known for what its members liked to call a "rip-yer-face-off style of rock." But they also proved themselves capable of melting hearts with the occasional tender ballad. Through the 1980s, Helix became one of Capitol-EMI's most consistent recording acts: not one of the band's six albums for the label sold less than 35,000 copies and some surpassed the 100,000 platinum mark.

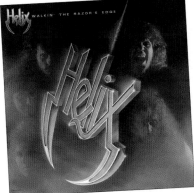

After signing in 1982, Helix set about living up to the title of its major label debut, *No Rest for the Wicked*. The band hit the road, opening for Heart, Motorhead and Molly Hatchet in the United States, while its video for "Heavy Metal Love" went into rotation on MTV. The exposure helped Helix land its first European tour, opening for Kiss on an "If this is Tuesday, it must be Rome" tour of 13 countries in six weeks. Not bad for a bunch of beer-drinkers from Kitchener, the Oktoberfest capital of Ontario.

In 1984, singer Brian Vollmer, guitarists Paul Hackman and Brent Doerner, bassist Daryl Gray and drummer Fritz Hinz released their breakthrough album, *Walkin' the Razor's Edge*. Featuring the screaming hit "Rock You" (#10, *The Record*), the album roared to platinum status in Canada during a year that saw Helix on a U.S. tour with Quiet Riot and Whitesnake and a European tour with Motorhead

and Girlschool. While the band undertook a Canadian tour with the musical outfit Triumph, it scored other hits from the album with "Gimme Good Lovin'" and "(Make Me Do) Anything You Want," a cover of the Foot in Coldwater ballad, which went to #1 at *RPM*.

Long Way to Heaven, the group's 1985 album, enjoyed a four-star review in *The Record*. Later that year, Capitol-EMI ran a seven-page advertisement on the band in *The Record*, with copy supplied by rock writer Lenny Stoute. After one more album, *Wild in the Streets*, the label issued a greatest-hits collection.

Helix remain heavy-metal diehards and have continued to record. The group's 1993 album (on Aquarius and distributed by EMI) is titled *It's a Business Doing Pleasure*.

'Don't let me fall, guys': singer Vollmer climbs aboard the Helix express

Vollmer in full roar: capable of melting hearts with a tender ballad

DAVID WILCOX

CAPITOL-EMI CANADA
1983

Wilcox, from debauchery to enlightenment: the virtuoso guitarist has evolved from raucous barroom boogies to tender, introspective ballads

L̲ike any great artist, David Wilcox has been through several incarnations in his career. There was his Crazy David phase in the 1970s when, with his waxed, Salvador Daliesque moustache, long hair and frock coat, he raffled off invisible sets of dishes to bewildered audiences. Then there was the Debauched David of the '80s, when a shorter-haired, whisky-soaked Wilcox was the life of every party, playing his cheerful barroom boogie and singing lasciviously about women. Most recently, there has been the Enlightened David of the '90s when, after a period of retirement, a head-shaven, teetotalling Wilcox returned with songs of surprising sensitivity and introspection. The only constant through it all has been his phenomenal guitar work.

A Montrealer by birth, Wilcox wound up on the Toronto coffeehouse circuit in the 1960s as a guitar-playing aficionado of bluesmen Bukka White and Robert Johnson. A major break came when Ian and Sylvia Tyson were looking for a guitarist to replace Amos Garrett in their country-rock group Great Speckled Bird. Not only did Wilcox get the job, he later got to play in the house band on Ian's weekly CTV show "Nashville North," backing guests such as Carl Perkins, Jerry Reed and Anne Murray.

After a stint in a group called The Rhythm Rockets and as a sideman with Maria Muldaur, Wilcox decided it was time to form his own group, The David Wilcox Band, in 1975. It wasn't until his second group that he began to attract a cult following. Wrote *The Canadian Composer*'s Richard Flohil: "His band, The Teddy Bears, plays exceptionally well, but Wilcox is the show—scooping the air with his Fender Telecaster, lecturing his audience and playing virtuoso slide guitar."

At first, Wilcox's show was too visual to attract major label interest. But when his independently released 1980 debut album, *Out of the Woods*, eventually sold more than 25,000 copies, Capitol-EMI took

notice and signed him. By then, the rights to the album had reverted to Wilcox. So, in 1983, *Out of the Woods* was re-released on Capitol. The album included several roadhouse favourites, including "Hot, Hot Papa" and "That Hypnotizin' Boogie," which became one of Wilcox's signature tunes both in concert and on radio and was later heard on the soundtrack of the popular Tom Cruise film *Cocktail*.

Later that year, Capitol released the first new Wilcox album, *My Eyes Keep Me in Trouble*. In its review of the record, the *Globe and Mail* wrote: "The sly wit of Wilcox's changes and crisp timing makes this second effort a treat that shows a lot more heart and warmth than most contemporary releases."

Meanwhile, *The Record* commented that his "sly, wink-behind-your-back voice works well on the title track," which quickly became another radio favourite. By the time Wilcox and his band's western Canadian tour reached Alberta, the *Edmonton Sun* was already proclaiming him "Canada's most innovative guitarist."

Bad Reputation, released in 1984, won even greater praise. "This time out," *The Record* wrote, "the combination of humour, wit, gritty vocals that sound really involved, and clean guitar playing works to make a record that succeeds on many different levels." It concluded: "The results are solid—and saleable." In fact, Wilcox became a consistently saleable Capitol artist. Each of his five albums, including *The Best of David Wilcox* (1985) and *Breakfast at the Circus* (1987), went on to platinum-level sales of 100,000 copies in Canada. After the release of *The Natural Edge* in 1989, however, the gonzo guitarist was ready for a break. EMI Music Canada paid tribute to his body of work with a three-CD collection in 1993.

When Wilcox returned in 1996 with a stripped-down, honest album titled simply *Thirteen Songs*, he was a changed man. Gone were the high-flying guitar pyrotechnics and ribald rockers like "Shake It Baby." In their place were quieter, more elegant fingerings and gentle love songs like "House By the River." "I needed time to reflect, to grow as an artist," Wilcox told the *Calgary Sun*, in explaining his six-year absence from recording and performing. "I was really into drugs and booze for a long time. It got to be too much." His agenda changed and he quit drugs and drinking. As he admitted to the *London Free Press*: "My interest is more in being in the moment. Awareness."

DAVID BOWIE

EMI America

1983

With the Cheshire-Cat-grinning Peter Frampton at Toronto's Diamond, March 1987

Adopting personas from Mannish Boy and Ziggy Stardust to Aladdin Sane and the Thin White Duke, David Bowie had already proven himself rock's quintessential chameleon. In the 1980s, Bowie found his most commercially successful persona, that of the perfectly tailored pop star. This was Bowie's rebirth, and it came after he signed with EMI America. It was also the era when Canada loomed largest in the artist's career. Bowie launched his two North American tours on Canadian soil, filmed a TV special and recorded one album here.

Onstage in Toronto, August 1987: "the biggest cabaret in history"

Bowie always had a worldly—even otherworldly—way about him. Born David Jones in London's Brixton district on January 8, 1947, he took up the guitar and saxophone in his teens and was soon immersing himself in American rhythm and blues. His first bands, The King Bees and The Mannish Boys, were named after songs by Slim Harpo and Muddy Waters, respectively. During the 1960s, Bowie's interests took him away from the pop, mod and psychedelic trends of his contemporaries and he wound up studying with mime artist Lindsay Kemp. It wasn't until 1969, when he scored his first hit single

Eleven-year-old sax player Seth Scholes, of Kingston, Ont., takes a tip from the Thin White Duke while jamming with Bowie bandmember Richard Cottle, prior to Toronto concert

"Space Oddity," that he reconnected with the pop world. His five-minute glimpse into an astronaut's alienation in outer space was chilling in its realism.

Bowie's albums through the '70s have been well chronicled. *The Man Who Sold the World*, *Hunky Dory* and *The Rise and Fall of Ziggy Stardust and the Spiders from Mars* were followed by the U.S. breakthrough *Aladdin Sane*, the nostalgic *Pin Ups* and the Orwellian *Diamond Dogs*. Then came the soulful *Young Americans* and the funky *Station to Station*. After moving to Berlin, Bowie collaborated with Brian Eno on his electronic trilogy: *Low*, *Heroes* and *Lodger*. He then headed to New York to record his paranoiac *Scary Monsters* before turning to theatre and film-soundtrack work.

In 1983, Bowie moved to the newly created EMI America label, signing one of the most lucrative contracts in history. Almost immediately, the record company's investment gamble paid off. Bowie's first album under the contract, the Nile Rodgers–produced *Let's Dance*, spawned three major hit singles: the title track, "China Girl" and "Modern Love." Album sales were further boosted by Bowie's Serious Moonlight tour, his first in five years. Bowie opened the North American leg of the tour in July in the relative quiet of Quebec City, where he performed in the 15,000-seat Coliseum hockey arena. His last Canadian date, in Vancouver (which Bowie called his favourite North American city), was recorded for a pay-TV special.

The tour, described by the *Toronto Star*'s Peter Goddard as "the biggest cabaret in history," moved on to much larger venues across Canada after Quebec City. 58,000 spectators saw Bowie at Edmonton's Commonwealth Stadium, the largest rock audience ever in western Canada.

Bowie returned to Canada the following year to record his next album, the uneven *Tonight*, at Le Studio in Morin Heights, near Montreal. And when it came time to launch his third EMI album, *Never Let Me Down*, and to announce his Glass Spiders tour, Bowie again chose Canada. He arrived in Toronto in March 1987 for a noontime press conference at the Diamond club, but when the media types arrived, they were treated to much more than expected. Bowie, backed by a band that included '70s guitar hero Peter Frampton (whose art-teacher father had once taught Bowie), performed three songs to an initially stunned and then visibly excited press gathering. Recalls Rhonda Ross, then Capitol-EMI's director of media and artist relations: "We had the international debut of Bowie and Frampton [who later appeared on the tour]. It was a real Canadian coup."

After the lush, dance-floor sophistication of *Let's Dance*, Bowie went back to the rough-and-ready sounds of 1960s music on *Never Let Me Down*. As he told *Maclean*'s: "When you get lost, you always return to the first thing that meant anything to you. For me, it was that rough, kind of excited sound of the '60s." That album would prove to be Bowie's last for EMI—and the end of his special Canadian connection. But his career resurgence while on the label was nothing short of spectacular.

CROWDED HOUSE

CAPITOL
1985

When Crowded House first came to Canada in 1986, it played at the Duke of Gloucester, a small pub on Toronto's Yonge Street. Capitol-EMI here knew that word-of-mouth on the talented pop trio would be strong, so the company was happy to start out small and let reaction grow from there. The approach paid off. Within eight months, the band had a platinum self-titled debut album and was back, playing in front of 13,000 fans at the Kingswood Music Theatre, a large outdoor pavilion north of the city. Says Rhonda Ross, then the Canadian label's director of media and artist relations: "By setting up a record that way, in an intimate setting, we got the press and retail right onside. It made everyone feel a part of it, like they were all in on the secret."

Crowded House—singer-guitarist Neil Finn, bassist Nick Seymour and drummer Paul Hester—eventually became one of the most revered groups of the late 1980s, celebrated for Finn's memorable, mellifluous pop songs. Reviews were uniformly strong, like this one from *Musician* magazine's Charles M. Young, who cited "melodies that stay in your head all day, harmonies that make you want to take singing lessons, words that make you think about love without feeling stupid, and hooks so solid you could catch fish." Despite such accolades, sales were initially slow to take off. When they finally did, they happened first in Canada, which became the group's strongest territory.

The band's origins can be traced to the New Zealand town of Te Awamutu, where Finn and his three siblings were born. Neil and his older brother, Tim, formed Split Enz, an eclectic pop band of the '70s whose appearance—"complete with glaring clownlike costumes and hairdos that made them look like parrots," according to *Rolling Stone*—often strained credibility. Still, the group earned enough of a reputation that when it disbanded in 1985 Neil found interest for his songs at Capitol in Los Angeles. After signing a deal, the younger Finn, together with Australians Hester and Seymour, moved into a small bungalow (yes, it was crowded) in Los Angeles and began writing and rehearsing.

The group's eponymous 1986 debut album, produced by Mitchell Froom, was filled with powerful, hook-laden pop. But for nearly seven months, it generated almost no North American radio play or chart action. To its credit, the record company never gave up on the album. Rhonda Ross remembers how much everyone at the label believed in the songs and continued pushing. She also credits the band with working

Drummer Paul Hester, singer-guitarist Neil Finn and bassist Nick Seymour at the University of Western Ontario, London, Ont., March 1989: sublime pop

hard to break the album in Canada. "The first time I met Neil," recalls Ross, "he got off the red-eye from L.A., where he'd flown in from Australia. He was originally scheduled to come in the day before but ran into problems. He gets off the plane, having had no sleep, and goes straight into a full day of interviews. And he did this cheerfully, without any complaint. The whole band, in fact, was a joy to work with."

Having won media converts with that intimate gig at Toronto's Duke of Gloucester pub, Crowded House returned in August 1987 to perform at the Kingswood Music Theatre. By then, "Don't Dream It's Over," a bittersweet ballad with a singalong chorus, and the more upbeat "Something So Strong" had both hit the Top 10. The group's second album, the following year's *Temple of Low Men*, was a darker, moodier record. It still featured some irresistible songs, including the yearning "Better Be Home Soon," and earned Crowded House another platinum award. Despite its growing success, the band insisted on doing another pub gig—this time at the Siboney club in Toronto's Kensington Market—as a break from its promotional tour. When the group came back in March 1989 for a month-long concert tour, it rounded out that Canadian visit with a performance on the televised Juno Awards.

The next decade was marked by personnel changes. Brother Tim joined Neil and Crowded House for 1991's *Woodface*, which did well on the modern-rock charts. After touring with the group that year, the elder Finn returned to his solo

Hester, Finn and Seymour, receiving platinum awards for Temple of Low Men *from Capitol-EMI president Deane Cameron, April, 1989: a large, devoted Canadian following*

career and Crowded House recruited American musician Mark Hart, with whom it recorded 1993's *Together Alone*. The group broke up in 1995, but left a legacy of sublime pop music.

HEART

CAPITOL
1984

Nancy and Ann Wilson, with members Mark Andes, Howard Leese and Denny Carmassi: any mousse left?

After a string of million-selling hits in the late '70s, Heart, led by singer Ann Wilson and her guitar-playing sister, Nancy, was in steady decline by the early 1980s. Its two most recent Epic albums failed to go gold and the band seriously considered packing it in. But a deal with Capitol suddenly pumped new life into Heart. The group's eponymous debut album for the label in 1985 was a stunning comeback, selling more than 5 million copies worldwide and producing four major hits. For the rest of the decade, the band remained a top seller and concert draw.

Born in California, the Wilson sisters moved to Seattle when their Marine Corps captain father retired there. Initially, Nancy worked as a folksinger while Ann fronted a local rock band called White Heart, whose name was eventually shortened to Heart. Love eventually defined the membership of the group and, ultimately, where it was based. Ann became lead guitarist Roger Fisher's girlfriend. And when Nancy wound up romantically involved with Fisher's brother Mike, the band's Vancouver-based soundman, she not only joined the group in 1974 but moved up the coast to be with him. Soon, the rest of the group relocated to Vancouver and became a regular on the club circuit in the Pacific Northwest.

Signed to Vancouver's Mushroom Records, distributed in Canada by Capitol-EMI, Heart recorded *Dreamboat Annie* in 1976. Combining high-powered rock and acoustic folk, the album reached platinum-level sales of 100,000 copies in Canada and 1 million in the United States on the strength of two hit singles: "Magic Man" and "Crazy on You." Suddenly, members of Heart were the stars of Canada's West Coast music scene and won the Juno Award as Group of the Year in 1977, while the Producer of the Year prize went to Mike Flicker for his work on *Dreamboat Annie*. A controversy erupted when Ann Wilson was quoted as saying that Heart had always been an American act and that the members' landed immigrant status was an invention of Mushroom's publicity department.

Switching to CBS and resettling in Seattle, Heart recorded several more hit

Capitol-EMI's Steve McAuley cozies up to the Wilson sisters: crazy on them

albums, including *Little Queen*, *Dog and Butterfly* and *Bebe Le Strange*. Mushroom, meanwhile, issued another platinum record with the previously recorded material on 1978's *Magazine*. Each member of the group refined Heart's unique sound, a combination of soft, Beatlesque pop and Led Zeppelin–inspired hard rock. Indeed, one critic described Ann Wilson's searing vocals as the closest a female voice could get to Robert Plant's patented Led Zeppelin wail. But 1982's *Private Audition* and the following year's *Passionworks*, both on Epic, were commercial disappointments, putting Heart at a career crossroads.

Switching producers, managers and record companies proved to be an invigorating move. The Capitol-released *Heart* in 1985 produced "What About Love?" (#7 *The Record*), "Never" (# 11 *RPM*), "These Dreams" (#6 *RPM*) and "Nothin' At All" (#2 *The Record*), sung by Nancy Wilson, the first Heart hit to feature the "other sister" on lead vocals.

With a lineup that included original founding member Howard Leese on guitar and newcomers Mark Andes on bass and Denny Carmassi on drums, Heart followed up that success with *Bad Animals*. Like its predecessor, the 1987 album was produced by Ron Nevison, whose credits included Heart's heroes Led Zeppelin. And like the Capitol debut, the new album featured three hit singles: "There's the Girl" (#2 *The Record*), "Who Will You Run To" (#8 *RPM*) and "Alone," which reached the top position on charts everywhere. That year, Heart undertook an extensive Canadian tour. "Nothing washed up about this band," understated the *Edmonton Journal* after the group's appearance there, while the *Vancouver Sun* reported that "more than 12,000 rock lovers practically blew the roof off the city's Coliseum" in appreciation of the band.

Heart continued its hitmaking into the '90s with *Brigade*, *Rock the House Live!* and *Desire Walks*. And the Wilson sisters, working as an informal acoustic group called The Lovemongers, paid further tribute to their biggest rock influence by recording a four-song EP that included Led Zeppelin's "Battle of Evermore." With a career spanning three decades, Heart remain one of rock's perennial favourites. "Heart is living proof that a band can survive any trends and fads," says Nancy. "We're proud of our longevity."

THE KNACK

CAPITOL
1979

At Toronto's the Edge, 1979: pure pop sensibilities and an onstage exuberance

On the eve of the '80s, The Knack was one of the hottest acts of the post-punk, new wave era. Dressed in white shirts, black pants and skinny ties and playing a fast, melodic brand of pop, the Los Angeles band became the subject of an intense bidding war by no fewer than 13 record companies. After the group signed with Capitol, it went on to make one of the biggest commercial debuts in rock history, with a number one single and an album that sold 5 million copies worldwide. "We were offered much more money by other companies," Knack leader Doug Fieger, "[but] we chose Capitol Records because we liked them as people. We felt that they understood the project."

The group—singer-guitarist Fieger, guitarist Berton Averre, bassist Prescott Niles and drummer Bruce Gary—formed in the summer of '78 and played its first gig at the Whiskey A Go Go in Los Angeles. By November, word of mouth had spread about the band so much, that during its two-week stand at L.A.'s the Troubador, guests such as Bruce Springsteen, Stephen Stills, Tom Petty, Eddie Money and Ray Manzarek of The Doors got up and jammed with the group. Working with producer Mike Chapman (Blondie, Pat Benatar), The Knack recorded its 1979 debut album in 11 days for the no-frills price of $17,000.

Get the Knack, featuring the lascivious single "My Sharona," went gold in 13 days and platinum in 6 weeks, making it the fastest debut to platinum in history. "My Sharona" shot straight to number one in July 1979 and stayed there for six weeks. A second single from the album, "Good Girls Don't," went Top 10. The band undertook a European tour, playing England, France and Germany, and then arrived in Canada for the first time. In Toronto, the group's appearance at the Edge was attended by Capitol-EMI's A&R director Deane Cameron, who was impressed by the band's exuberance and pure pop sensibilities.

By December 1979, The Knack had travelled to New Zealand, Australia and Japan and completed its first sold-out North American tour. That month, the group recorded its second album, *...But the Little Girls Understand*, this time in just seven days. After winning two Grammy Award nominations and watching "My Sharona" win honours as *Billboard*'s song of the year, The Knack's *Little Girls* was released in February 1980. The album went gold in Japan and the United States; in Canada, where the band enjoyed a strong following, it sold platinum-level sales of 100,000 copies.

Ultimately, the stress of being labeled pop's "next big thing" took its toll, and the band took a year off due to exhaustion and dissent within the group. The Knack re-emerged in the summer of '81 and began recording its third album with producer Jack Douglas (Aerosmith, John Lennon). This time, however, the album took five months to complete. *Round Trip*, released in the fall, sold poorly and the band broke up shortly afterwards.

During their meteoric run, The Knack suffered a backlash in the early '80s from critics who charged that the group had appropriated The Beatles' image (the back cover of *Get the Knack* mimicked the Fab Four's studio shots on *A Hard Day's Night*). Although the group had intended the imitation to be an homage to The Beatles, some people labelled the band corporate sellouts and frauds. A "Knuke the Knack" movement arose in the same Los Angeles club scene that had spawned the band. Recalls Fieger: "At that point it seemed that nothing we could say would stop the avalanche of misperceptions, so we said nothing, naively believing that the truth would out." For many years, it didn't.

The band reunited briefly in the 1990s, with Billy Ward on drums, and recorded one more album, *Serious Fun*. The group's members went their separate ways again, with Fieger taking on a small role in the hit TV series "Roseanne" and recording a solo album produced by Don Was. The group's legacy lives on. "My Sharona" received the ultimate pop compliment: a satirical treatment by Weird Al Yankovic, titled "My Bologna." The song also reached a new audience after being featured in the 1994 movie *Reality Bites*.

PET SHOP BOYS

PARLOPHONE
1985

"i've got the brains, you've got the looks let's make lots of money"

Tennant and Lowe: deadpan lyrics and danceable synth-pop

Smart, stylish and unashamedly commercial, England's Pet Shop Boys neatly personified the 1980s. With their deadpan lyrics and danceable synth-pop, Neil Tennant and Chris Lowe managed to become one of the most popular acts of the "Me Decade." From 1986–88, the duo scored five consecutive Top 10 singles and did, in fact, make lots of money. But Pet Shop Boys was also a critical success, earning kudos for the clever ambiguity that lay behind what was essentially a good disco beat. Wrote John Leland in the *New York Times*: "Gay or straight, ironic or sentimental, battered or bored, hip or square, they were all at once."

Tennant was a journalist and Lowe an architecture student when the pair met in 1981. After discovering they could write songs together,

Receiving Platinum for Actually *in November 1988 from EMI Canada president, Deane Cameron*

the two decided to form Pet Shop Boys. Their first break came when Tennant, then working for pop-music magazine *Smash Hits*, landed an assignment to cover The Police in New York. Although not enamoured of Sting's blond trio, Tennant took advantage of being in the Big Apple and arranged to meet Eurodisco producer Bobby "O" [Orlando], whose work he admired. Together, they record-

ed a Tennant-Lowe composition called "West End Girls," which became a hit in Belgium when it was released on Epic.

Signed to EMI's Parlophone in early '85, Pet Shop Boys recorded "Opportunities (Let's Make Lots of Money)," but, in Tennant's own words, "it flopped." The duo then wisely decided to remix "West End Girls" and the new, more polished version shot to number one in Britain before topping the charts in both Canada and the United States. *Please*, the group's 1986 debut album, contained a remixed version of "Opportunities," which enjoyed a second life as well. Realizing the rewards of recasting previously released songs, Tennant

and Lowe issued *Disco*, an entire album of their dance remixes.

By 1987, the Pets were Britain's most successful pop duo since Wham! *Actually*, the group's next album immediately outsold *Please*. In Canada, it reached platinum-level sales by year's end on the strength of the hit single "It's a Sin," Tennant's ode to his strict Catholic upbringing. By the following spring, the album had produced two more hits: "What Have I Done to Deserve This?" a duet with Tennant's favourite female singer, Dusty Springfield (#2 *The Record*), and "Always On My Mind," a buoyant remake of the Elvis Presley ballad, which hit number one at both *RPM* and *The Record*.

Until the early '90s, neither Tennant nor Lowe expressed any interest in touring as a live act. But that didn't stop them from striving for mainstream acceptance. As Simon Frith, writing in the *Village Voice*, pointed out: "For them, stardom meant smart pix and silly interviews in the teen magazines [and] that their public appearances be limited to well-orchestrated TV spots." Capitalizing on video, the Pets made eye-catching clips that enjoyed heavy rotation at MTV and MuchMusic. Rhonda Ross, then Capitol-EMI's director of media and artist relations, remembers MuchMusic devoting a full hour to the duo in the mid-80s. "An hour on Much was novel in those days," says Ross, "but the Boys played so well to the camera, with Neil being the talkative one and Chris acting as his silent sidekick. Much just loved them."

Skilled studio technicians, Pet Shop Boys continued making albums, including *Introspective* (1988), *Behavior* (1990) and *Very* (1993), that were both commercially and critically successful. And Tennant and Lowe continued their track record of scoring hits with disco remakes of songs by other artists. After segueing U2's "Where the Streets Have No Name" with Frankie Valli's "Can't Take My Eyes Off of You," Pet Shop Boys redid The Village People's "Go West," complete with a striking video of costumed, marching men. It became an uplifting anthem for AIDS victims, proving once again the power of clever, well-crafted pop.

TINA TURNER

CAPITOL
1983

When Tina Turner's *Private Dancer* came out in the summer of '84, there was no sign of the phenomenal breakthrough that lay in store. True, the veteran rhythm-and-blues singer had already begun her comeback, opening tours for Rod Stewart and The Rolling Stones and scoring a modest hit with her steamy cover of Al Green's "Let's Stay Together." But all of that paled in comparison to the commercial success that awaited her. Within a year, *Private Dancer* spawned four hit singles, earned three Grammy Awards and

Turner: the comeback queen of rock 'n' roll

sold eight million copies worldwide. At 46, Turner was suddenly one of the hottest acts in show business. As she kicked off her world tour in Canada, with a performance in St. John's, Newfoundland, Turner told *Maclean's*: "They ask me when I'm going to slow down, and I tell them I'm just getting started."

In fact, Turner had started out many years before as Annie Mae Bullock, the daughter of a Baptist sharecropper-father and a half-Cherokee mother. Growing up in tiny Nutbush, Tennessee, she picked cotton and sang in the local church choir until she moved with her mother and older sister to St. Louis. There, she saw her first big-city band, Ike Turner and his Kings of Rhythm. After grabbing the microphone one night and belting out a B.B. King blues number, the 16-year-old girl dazzled the bandleader and was promptly conscripted. Soon after, she changed her name to Tina and eventually married Turner.

During the late 1960s, the Ike and Tina Turner Revue, backed by three scantily clad female backup singers known as the Ikettes, became a major soul act. Its popularity with white audiences was boosted by appearances on tours by The Rolling Stones. In 1975, Tina turned her frenetic, sexually charged stage moves into a role as the Acid Queen in Ken Russell's movie version of The Who's *Tommy*. The following year she left Ike, whom she later described in her autobiography as a chronic wife beater. With just 36 cents and a handbag to her name, Tina set about rebuilding her life. It began with a solo career launched in Las Vegas.

Turner moved from supper clubs to rock stages with the help of Roger Davies, the Australian manager who took over her career in 1982. A deal with Capitol Records soon followed. After her Al Green cover became a hit in Britain, Capitol gave her $150,000 and two weeks to come up with an album. Davies quickly solicited songs from a variety of sources, including songwriters Mark Knopfler, Rupert Hine and Terry Britten, and arranged for the recording of *Private Dancer*. With songs like the title track (#10 *RPM*), "Better Be Good to Me" (#3 *The Record*) and "What's Love Got to Do With It," a number one hit in Canada and the rest of the world, it established her primarily as a singer, as opposed to a dancer or stage performer. Add a starring role with Mel Gibson in *Mad Max Beyond Thunderdome*, which produced another number one hit in Canada with "We Don't Need Another Hero," and Turner's career transformation was well underway.

A number of duets with male rockers—including Mick Jagger, who shamelessly ripped off her skirt at Live Aid—sealed her stardom. After a sold-out Canadian tour in the summer of '85, Turner returned to Canada in November to perform on the Junos with Bryan Adams. With Turner playing sexy older woman to Adams's not-so-innocent boy next door, the pair delivered a scorching duet of "It's Only Love," which they'd recorded for his *Reckless* album. Adams, who returned the favour by writing "Back Where You Started" for Turner's next album, *Break Every Rule*, recalled seeing the singer in his hometown of Vancouver years before. As Adams admitted to *Musician* magazine: "I'd be the guy standing on the table, howling at the moon. I just couldn't believe that a woman would get up in front of maybe two or three hundred people and just give everything she had. It was pretty inspirational." No wonder he was happy to join Turner for 20 dates on her European tour.

Throughout the '80s, which saw three more Turner albums, including *Foreign Affair*, a live recording and greatest-hits collection, the veteran performer's profile was further boosted through videos. John Martin, then MuchMusic's programming director, felt that her image perfectly suited the times. "Her success corresponds with a new way of looking at sexy, self-assured women," Martin told *Maclean's*. "She's doing it on her own and she's a heroine because of that."

Turner came back to EMI when she signed with Virgin. Paul Shaver, Virgin's Director, National Promotion & Artist/Media Relations, posed with her in 1999.

Canadian Affiliate Labels

ANTHEM

Anthem Records was born out of the success of one of Canada's most enduring rock groups—Rush. Unable to land the band a recording deal, manager Ray Danniels formed Moon Records, which eventually became distributed worldwide by Mercury/Polydor. By 1977, with the territory of Canada back in his hands, Danniels created Anthem as the new Rush outlet. Within a year, the label was distributed by Capitol, where it remained until 1990. Throughout the '80s, Anthem and Danniels's SRO Management were Canada's leading sources of domestic rock, new wave, heavy metal and comedy albums.

Together, Anthem and Capitol enjoyed a string of triumphs, beginning with the weird and wonderful Max Webster. Led by singer-guitarist Kim Mitchell, Max Webster became one of Canada's favourite touring rock groups. With albums such as *Mutiny Up My Sleeve* and *A Million Vacations*, featuring the single "Let Go the Line" (#1 on *RPM*'s Top 40), the band built on a fanatical following. Other acts landed hits, including singer Ian Thomas ("Chains," #5), heavy-metal rockers Coney Hatch ("Hey Operator," #8) and new wavers Boys Brigade ("Melody," #3) and B.B. Gabor ("Nyet Nyet Soviet," #14 at Toronto's CHUM). Meanwhile, the label scored a comedy coup with Bob & Doug McKenzie, played by Rick Moranis and Dave Thomas, of SCTV fame. The hoser duo's debut album, *Great White North*, featuring "Take Off," went four times platinum with sales of 400,000 copies and established Bob and Doug as true (if ironic) Canadian icons.

Rush's Geddy Lee, Alex Lifeson and Neil Peart: Anthem giants

But Anthem's biggest success story with Capitol remained Rush. The progressive-rock power trio of Geddy Lee, Alex Lifeson and Neil Peart ruled Canadian music through the 1980s, with nine multiple platinum albums, dozens of Juno nominations and several Juno Awards for Group of the Year and, in 1990, Group of the Decade. A truly international phenomenon, Rush had, by that year, sold 30 million records worldwide and played thousands of concerts in a dozen countries to over six million fans. "Virtuoso musicians," *Rolling Stone* called them, noting that "the three regularly place high in musicians' magazines readers' polls." The band that spawned Anthem has earned its place in music history, according to *Rolling Stone*, as "an inventive thinking-man's hard-rock group."

AQUARIUS

A Montreal-based label formed in 1970 by principal owners Terry Flood and Donald Tarlton, Aquarius Records earned a reputation for developing Quebec-based Anglo rock and pop artists. London Records initially distributed the company's first recordings, by the rock group April Wine. But Aquarius's biggest success came in the 1980s, after signing a deal with Capitol-EMI. Along with April Wine's international breakthrough, Capitol-EMI contributed to the phenomenal rise of singer Corey Hart, whose 1985 album, *Boy in the Box*, became one of the best-selling Canadian albums of the decade.

It was Deane Cameron, Capitol-EMI's then newly appointed director of artists and repertoire, who brought Aquarius into the fold in 1978. Just as he had done that year with Anthem Records and Max Webster, Cameron was able to attract Aquarius by offering them a U.S. deal for April Wine. Beginning with *First Glance* and following with the *Greatest Hits*, *Harder Faster* and *Nature of the Beast* albums, April Wine's international star rose steadily higher. No sooner had the band recorded its last album, 1984's *Animal Grace*, than Aquarius and Capitol-EMI scored a U.S. hit (#7, *Billboard*) with Corey Hart's *Sunglasses at Night*. Another star was born.

April Wine's Myles Goodwyn (seated) and (rear) Gary Moffet, Steve Lang and Jerry Mercer: Aquarius kingpins

Aquarius began developing other acts, such as Walter Rossi, Tease and Sass Jordan, who won a Juno Award for most promising female vocalist in 1988. Under new company president Keith Brown, Aquarius and EMI Canada have continued presenting new talent in the

'90s, including Jerry Jerry & the Rhythm Orchestra, Lindy and Bif Naked. But Hart's *Boy in the Box* remains the label's crowning achievement: a million-selling album that made Hart only the second Canadian artist to enjoy diamond status in his own country.

Novelties

Drugs in My Pocket

A pseudo-punk band from England, The Monks were actually refugees from the progressive-rock era of the early and mid-70s. John Ford and Richard Hudson had been members of The Strawbs, a group best known for the Ford-Hudson composition "Part of the Union," which became a novelty hit in 1973. After forming The Monks in the late '70s, Ford and Hudson further displayed their penchant for tongue-in-cheek humour with the band's EMI debut *Bad Habits*. The album featured the thinly veiled Sex Pistols putdown "Johnny B. Rotten" and the blatantly sexist "Nice Legs, Shame About the Face," which became a surprise hit in Britain.

In Canada, however, where the album was released on Capitol-EMI, The Monks enjoyed success with an entirely different track. There—and only there—"Drugs in My Pocket" became the album's hit single, reaching #16 on *RPM*'s Top 40. Curiously, the song, which appeared to fit the Cheech & Chong variety of tunes celebrating herbal or pharmaceutical indulgence, actually took an anti-drug stance, albeit cloaked in satirical humour. Ford and Hudson were laughing all the way to the bank. The success of "Drugs" led to another Monks album, *Suspended Animation*, which came out in exclusively in Canada on Polydor. That recording went 5x platinum and prompted a sellout tour of large stadium venues. Only in Canada.

Take Off

A satirical response to the CBC's request to make the already successful SCTV comedy program more Canadian, the "Great White North" segment was a hoser's dream come true. Featuring Rick Moranis and Dave Thomas as the betoqued and beer-chugging McKenzie Brothers, the two-minute spot quickly snowballed into a CanCon phenomenon known as hosermania. Like a pair of moose run amok on the Trans-Canada, Bob (Moranis) and Doug (Thomas) McKenzie charged off down the road to fame, dazzled by the glare of recording deals and Hollywood offers.

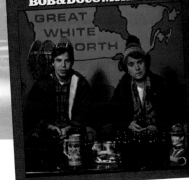

Signed to Toronto-based Anthem Records in 1981, Bob and Doug recorded only one album of songs and comedy sketches. But what an album, eh? Released in the fall and distributed by Capitol-EMI, *Great White North* included "Take Off," a single featuring Geddy Lee of Rush on lead vocals. With Lee screeching "it's a beauty way to go," the song did literally take off, topping the Canadian charts and reaching #16 on *Billboard*. In Canada, Capitol-EMI's staff had to work hard to keep up with the demand: in less than a month, the album sold more than 300,000 copies. Some staff members still fondly remember the Hoser Day parade, held in Toronto that November. Beginning in suburban Scarborough and ending at the A&A (as in "Eh and Eh") record store downtown, it attracted an astonishing 5,000 hoseheads, many swilling beers and dressed in toques and parkas themselves.

By the time the McKenzie movie *Strange Brew* opened in theatres in 1983, the craze had already run its course. The actors behind Bob and Doug had to admit they were somewhat relieved. As Thomas told one interviewer: "It's really tough because on the one hand they did buy my album and they are fans and I owe them something. But on the other hand, do I really want to be chugging a beer at 9 a.m. with these guys?"

Wankers' Guide to Canada

Buoyed by the success of *Great White North*, Anthem and Capitol-EMI teamed up on another comedy album. Drawing again on the fertile, twisted minds associated with SCTV, *Wankers' Guide to Canada* featured Rick Moranis, Dave Thomas, Catherine O'Hara, Martin Short and Eugene Levy. The 1986 album also boasted musical performances by The Nylons, Ian Thomas and The Hummer Sisters in

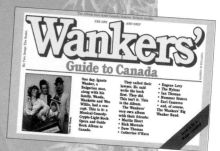

what Anthem called a "musical-comedy-crypto-light-rock-opera and guide book album to Canada." Like a cross between Monty Python and Spinal Tap, the album mixed humour and music while taking a satirical look at such Canadian issues as immigration, bilingualism and the CBC.

Levy plays babbling Syd Dithers, a senile Jewish-Canadian immigration lawyer who advises the Wanker family from Bulgaria on their entry to Canada. From East Indian–Canadian immigration officers in Newfoundland to sickeningly smooth FM deejays in Vancouver, the Wankers encounter Canadians of all kinds from coast to coast. Along the way, the family, who are in the process of recording an album, perform a variety of songs about their experiences. Highlights include Dave Thomas's funky "Robert Service at Your Service," The Nylons' doo-wop ransom note "We Have Your Daughter" and Ian Thomas's head-banging "Is Your Metal Heavy?" Although it failed to duplicate the success of *Great White North*, *Wankers' Guide to Canada* was nonetheless a welcome addition to the genre of Canadian comedy recordings.

CHAPTER FIVE

Innovation and Celebration:

1990 - 1999

CHAPTER FIVE

INNOVATION AND CELEBRATION:
1990 - 1999

EMI
MUSICCANADA

TM

From the pioneering 1950s to the adventurous '80s, Capitol-EMI had faced each decade with a well-tuned ear for music and a fine eye for the bottom line. This mix of art and commerce was by no means contradictory. While it had always been applauded for its commitment to developing new Canadian talent, the company was increasingly earning respect for its financial health, having rounded out the '80s with the most profitable year in its history. At the dawn of the '90s, with a youthful, energetic president at the helm, Capitol-EMI was about to embark on what would turn out to be its most fruitful decade to date.

Quick to seize on a growing musical trend, the label made news in March 1990 when it created a new staff position: Black Urban Dance product manager. In a front-page article, *The Record* reported: "Capitol-EMI of Canada has become the first company to formally acknowledge the success of black music nationwide by installing a manager full-time (20-year Capitol veteran Ron Robles) to handle product exploitation." The article quoted Ron Scott, then Capitol-EMI's marketing director, on the significance of the new position. Said Scott: "This

MC Hammer with Capitol-EMI's Ron Robles and Deane Cameron, 1990: please Hammer, don't hurt 'em

should send a strong message that Capitol is very serious about [urban music] in the '90s."

Ice Ice Baby: Capitol-EMI staffers chill out with white rapper Vanilla Ice (fourth on left)

The timing couldn't have been better. Capitol-EMI was poised to become an industry leader, with some of rap's first pop-crossover artists as well as Canada's pioneer rappers. First out of the gate was MC Hammer, whose album *Please Hammer Don't Hurt 'Em* catapulted the Oakland, California–born rapper into pop's stratosphere. That recording eventually sold 10 million copies worldwide and remained at #1 on *Billboard*'s pop album charts for an unprecedented 21 weeks. But he was quickly followed by another Capitol act (via the U.S.-based SBK Records label, which EMI had purchased the year before). Vanilla Ice edged out Hammer in November for the number one position with his album *To the Extreme*. The white rapper's "Ice Ice Baby" also became the first rap tune to top the pop single charts.

Rap was also a driving force on one of the year's top-selling soundtracks, *Teenage Mutant Ninja Turtles*, released on SBK. Along with MC Hammer, the soundtrack featured Technotronic and Spunkadelic, a Canadian hip-hop act comprising Ray and Ali from Brampton, Ontario. Soon, Capitol-EMI was showcasing two other domestic rap acts: Simply Majestic, featuring B Kool, and MCJ and Cool G.

The *Pretty Woman* soundtrack was also a winner. That success, combined with hit albums by MC Hammer, Heart, pop metal band Poison and '60s offspring Wilson Phillips, led to another front-page piece in *The Record*. Headlined with the Ninja Turtle catchphrase "Cowabunga," the article reported that "Capitol is on a roll, the likes of which only WEA has achieved in recent years. The company holds down fully 50 per cent of the Top 10 on the Top Retail Album chart and scores an

impressive 60 per cent in the Top Five." On a roll, indeed. By year's end, Capitol-EMI was proclaiming 1990 its biggest year ever.

That success was reflected the following March at the Canadian Music Industry Awards, where Capitol-EMI was named Major Record Company of the Year and label president Deane Cameron was chosen Music Industry Executive of the Year. Meanwhile, the company's promotion team, led by Peter Diemer, took the top award in its category.

Leslie Spit Tree-o's Frank Randazzo, Pat Langer, Laura Hubert, Joel Anderson and Jack Nicholsen

At the Junos, held in Vancouver that month, awards went to the label's Leslie Spit Tree-o for Most Promising Group and to Andy Curran for Most Promising Male Vocalist. Capitol-EMI's rap breakthrough was recognized with awards to MC Hammer, and to Simply Majestic, featuring B Kool. Hammer, who also performed on the show, won for Best Selling International Album, while Simply Majestic took best r&b/soul-recording honours.

Rap was not the only type of music with which Capitol-EMI excelled in the early '90s. A two-page colour advertisement in *The Record*, titled "Welcome to Capitol Country—a new commitment to an old tradition," signalled the marketing priority that the label was giving albums by Garth Brooks, Glen Campbell and Anne Murray. Brooks, in particular, was a commercial phenomenon. The Oklahoma native's 1991 album, *Ropin' the Wind*, made music history by becoming the first album to enter both

Poison lead singer Brett Michaels: an intoxicating noise

The three grinning girls of Wilson Phillips, (from left to right) Chynna Phillips, Carnie and Wendy Wilson, with equally cheerful SBK and Capitol guys

Billboard's country and pop charts at number one. And Brooks, who eventually went on to sell more than 100 million albums worldwide, blazed a trail for a whole wave of new country artists in the '90s, including Clint Black, Billy Ray Cyrus, Reba McEntire and Canada's own Shania Twain.

Pure pop at the label came in the form of Sweden's Roxette. Made up of vocalist Marie Fredriksson and guitarist and songwriter Per Gessle, Roxette was one of the major international acts of the early '90s. From the start, the duo enjoyed a particularly strong following in Canada, which eventually became its most successful territory outside of Sweden. The *Look Sharp!* and *Joyride* albums both topped the Canadian charts and "It Must Have Been Love," from the *Pretty Woman* soundtrack, became a hit single. "We've always had a special connection with Roxette," recalls Rob Brooks, then Capitol-EMI's international marketing manager and now the company's vice-president of marketing and operations. "Marie, in particular, never forgot how we were the first country outside of Sweden to release their debut album."

Richard Marx (middle) with (left to right) Capitol-EMI's Val D'Amico, Richard Gamache, Ron Scott and Steve McAuley: four times platinum for Repeat Offender

Capitol-EMI was further boosted by the success of such international acts as singer Richard Marx, veteran blues-rocker Bonnie Raitt, South Africa's groundbreaking multiracial band Johnny Clegg and Savuka, and heavy-metal artists Iron Maiden. Distribution deals with Chrysalis (Sinead O'Connor), Enigma (The Cramps) and I.R.S. (Concrete Blonde, The Infidels) only added more depth and eclecticism to the roster.

On the domestic side, two Toms led the label in the early '90s. Tom Cochrane, former lead singer with Red Rider, released his solo debut,

Mad Mad World, in September 1991. Featuring the anthemic hit single "Life is a Highway," the album went on to achieve diamond status in Canada with sales of more than one million copies, making Cochrane only the fifth Canadian artist in history to reach that lofty status. Meanwhile, country legend Stompin' Tom Connors kicked off the decade with a 70-date national tour and Capitol-EMI began reissuing the singer's extensive back catalogue. Suddenly, the man behind such Canadian classics as

Roxette's Marie Fredriksson, looking sharp: from Sweden with love

"Bud the Spud" and "Sudbury Saturday Night" was back in the spotlight.

At the 21st annual Junos, held the following March in Toronto, Cochrane swept the awards, winning in the male vocalist, songwriter, album and single categories. Cochrane's "Life is a Highway" even topped Bryan Adams's "(Everything I Do) I Do It For You," prompting the media to paint a supposed rivalry between the two singers. Cochrane refused to take the bait. Meanwhile, Capitol-EMI artists earned several other awards. Garth Brooks won for Foreign Entertainer of the Year and Vanilla Ice's *To the Extreme* was the best selling album by a foreign artist. Domestically, Renee Rosnes won the best jazz album prize and I.R.S. recording artists The Infidels, led by singer Molly Johnson, was the year's most promising group. For the second consecutive time, Deane Cameron was named Executive of the Year at the Canadian Music Industry Awards.

Blues guitarist Bonnie Raitt: rock's comeback queen

Before the next Junos, several significant changes took place at Capitol-EMI. First, after four decades of a maturing A&R policy, the label began spreading its wings and found an innovative way of bringing in new repertoire. By signing a manufacturing and distribution deal with two Toronto-based labels, Intrepid and fre, Capitol-EMI was able to diversify its domestic roster. Intrepid, founded by British expatriate and former Bruce Cockburn road manager Stuart Raven-Hill, released albums by such promising Canadian acts as National Velvet, The Rheostatics and Meryn Cadell. Meanwhile, fre, run by former Aquarius co-owner Terry Flood and ex-Spoons' drummer and former Enigma Canada manager Derrick Ross, brought The Skydiggers and Jim Witter into the Capitol-EMI stable. Similar deals later in the decade would allow the company to expand into the aboriginal, urban and Celtic-based music fields.

Then, in September 1992, right after Capitol U.S. celebrated its 50th anniversary, EMI Music Publishing announced that Michael McCarty would become its president in Canada. McCarty, a Canadian, took over from American-born Hank Medress, who had opened the publishing company's Toronto

Molly Johnson and Norman Orenstein of I.R.S. recording artists The Infidels: promising

Wayne Stokes, Josh Finlayson, Andy Maize, Ronnie von Johnny and Peter Cash of Enigma's The Skydiggers: into the Capitol-EMI stable

Newfoundland native and EMI recording artist Kim Stockwood presses the flesh with Prime Minister Jean Chrétien

office two years earlier (Medress was best known as one of the voices of The Tokens, whose doo-wop version of the African folk song "The Lion Sleeps Tonight" was a number one hit in 1961). Within a few months, McCarty signed Vancouver band Moist, St. John's singer-songwriter Kim Stockwood and former Glass Tiger singer Alan Frew to publishing deals. As McCarty told *The Record*: "Our job is to find and develop songwriters." But, he added, "our mandate is to become an important source of music for the world."

Capitol-EMI's artist roster grew substantially in January 1993 with the addition of Virgin Records, which had been purchased by EMI the previous June. Before that, Virgin had the distinction of being the world's

largest independent label, with a long and illustrious history. Formed by Richard Branson, Simon Draper and Ken Berry, Virgin was launched in the summer of 1973 with four adventurous albums: Mike Oldfield's *Tubular Bells*, Gong's *The Flying Teapot*, *Manor Live*, a jam session featuring Robert Palmer, and *The Faust Tapes*, by a German group called Faust. *Tubular Bells* became the breakthrough release, hitting number one in the U.K. and going gold in the U.S., where it won a Grammy for Best Instrumental Composition. Through the '70s and '80s, Virgin broke such top acts as The Sex Pistols, Phil Collins, Culture Club, Simple Minds and an assortment of reggae and African acts, including Peter Tosh and Chief Ebeneezer Obey.

Initially, there were fears that Virgin Canada would be swallowed up by Capitol-EMI's head office on American Drive. But the management team decided to keep Virgin at its own downtown location—and then gave Doug Chappell, Virgin president, the responsibility of handling I.R.S. and Chrysalis as well. Maintaining the spirit of

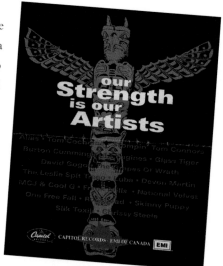

an aggressive independent label, Virgin added such top-selling international acts as The Rolling Stones, Janet Jackson, Lenny Kravitz, Smashing Pumpkins and UB40 to the EMI roster, while continuing to work with domestic artists like Rita MacNeil and The Northern Pikes. The label's first certification after the purchase by EMI was the platinum-plus-selling debut album by Right Said Fred. From that point onward, Virgin helped to greatly diversify its parent company's artistic roster.

On March 1, 1993, Capitol-EMI announced that it was changing its name to EMI Music of Canada, to reflect the legacy of

Tom Cochrane, at his landslide Juno victory, 1992

the EMI logo throughout the world, and to better define the broad line of internationally owned labels that it marketed. In a two-page advertisement in *The Record*, published during Canadian Music Week, the company displayed its new logo with the heading "Tradition in an Age of Change—the New Era Begins!" It also instructed readers to "Know Us by the Company We Keep," before listing more than 25 associated labels, including Alert, Apple, Aquarius, Blue Note, Charisma, Curb, Ensign, Eureka, fre, I.R.S., Intrepid, Liberty, Lupins, Manhattan and Nettwerk.

In the case of Curb Records, EMI had joined forces with the most sucessful independent record company in the United States.

Virgin recording artist Lenny Kravitz, at a Molson Canadian Rock "Blind Date," 1996

Formed by Mike Curb, a former musician and politician whose band Mike Curb Congregation had a 1971 Top 10 hit with "Burning Bridges," the label boasted best-selling packages by The Righteous Brothers, Dean Martin, The Stray Cats and Gladys Knight & the Pips. But mostly, Curb was known for country music. Among Curb's best-selling country acts— many of whom toured Canada during the '90s—were LeAnn Rimes, Tim McGraw and Sawyer Brown. The label, which often dominated the *Billboard* country music charts, was also the home of Canadian country star Jim Witter.

Almost immediately there was a flurry of new signings, as A&R vice-president Tim Trombley moved to diversify and expand the company's domestic roster. First up was The Tea Party, an adventurous three-piece rock band from Trombley's hometown of Windsor, Ontario. Then, following her induction into the Canadian Music Hall of Fame, Anne Murray signed directly with EMI Music Canada, in a major deal that included her entire discography. Already, the label had begun building a strong association with Atlantic Canadian music, through the signing and acquisition of two fine Cape Breton acts: The Rankin Family and Rita MacNeil.

LeAnn Rimes with Capitol-EMI's Eddie Colero: country prodigy

Celtic and aboriginal music—true cornerstones of Canadian culture— were to become the foundation on which Deane Cameron and his staff would build EMI Music Canada's own, unique identity.

By November, the company had signed a distribution deal with First Nations/Wawatay, a label formed by Cree singer-songwriter Lawrence Martin (who at the time was the mayor of Sioux Lookout, Ontario) and Vic Wilson, a music consultant and former co-manager of Rush. A launch at Toronto's Bamboo club featured

The Tea Party's Stuart Chatwood, Jeff Burrows and Jeff Martin at Toronto's Ultrasound bar: an electrifying live presence

performances by the country-flavoured Martin and blues-rocker Murray Porter, a native of the Six Nations Reserve. "There was a definite sense of excitement," reported *The Record* of the event, "as a full slate of EMI employees, a number of natives, a handful of politicians, half-a-dozen television crews, miscellaneous industry-ites, the usual print media suspects and a *Kung Fu*-clad and dancing David Carradine packed the club."

EMI Music Canada's vision was rewarded at the next Junos in March, as The Rankin Family swept the awards with four wins, including single, group, country group and the coveted Canadian Entertainer of the Year, while Lawrence Martin took the award in the newly created Best Music of Aboriginal Canada Recording category, for his debut album *Wapistan*. Once again, Deane Cameron was named Music Executive of the Year at the Canadian Music Industry Awards, and EMI Music Canada, which led the industry with 21 per cent market share of retail albums, was cited once more as Major Record Company of the Year.

Anne Murray receives her Canadian Music Hall of Fame Award, 1993: a national treasure

Meanwhile, the label bolstered its domestic roster in 1994 with the alternative-rock signings of Vancouver's Moist and Econoline Crush. On the urban side, where the company had already signed Devon, a talented Toronto rap and funk artist, it added The Dream Warriors, one of the most innovative and acclaimed rap acts ever to emerge from Canada. The label also signed rockers I Mother Earth and musical cross pollinators King Cobb Steelie. It then landed a prestigious artist with the signing of radiant Inuit singer Susan Aglukark, from Arviat, Northwest Territories. Said Tim Trombley, vice-president of talent acquisition and

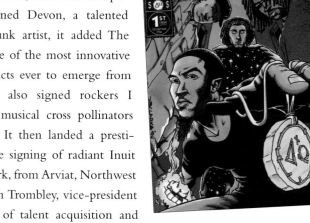

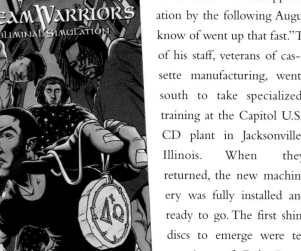

artist development: "Canada's a vast country with distinct cultural and regional differences. We try to reflect that with the roster at EMI. We also try to keep the roster diversified so we don't end up competing with ourselves in the marketplace."

The year 1995 proved to be one of the biggest yet for EMI Canada. In February came the news that a recording of The Beatles, *Live at the BBC*, had sold an astonishing 450,000 copies in Canada since its release in December. With the future release of the *Anthology* series, the company would experience a bit of déjà vu, as a second wave of Beatlemania rolled across Canada—more than 30 years after the original had struck. At the Junos, held in Hamilton, Ontario, that March, Aglukark and Moist were both winners, while 1960s legends Robbie Robertson and Buffy Sainte-Marie, both released by EMI in Canada, were honoured with a Producer of the Year award and a Hall of Fame induction respectively. By June, the company had reported its eighth consecutive year of highest sales and profits for the fiscal year ending March 31.

But one of EMI Music Canada's proudest achievements came in August, when the company opened its own CD plant. Hugh Wiets, vice-president of manufacturing, recalls with pride how the facility was up and running in

record time. "We had approval in December and we were in operation by the following August," says Wiets. "No other CD plant I know of went up that fast." To prepare for the new operation, some of his staff, veterans of cassette manufacturing, went south to take specialized training at the Capitol U.S. CD plant in Jacksonville, Illinois. When they returned, the new machinery was fully installed and ready to go. The first shiny discs to emerge were test pressings of Bob Seger's *Greatest Hits.* But the first CDs actually produced and shipped out of the Canadian plant on American Drive were copies of U.S. country singer John Berry's *Standing on the Edge.*

In many ways, Wiets felt that *he* was the one standing on the edge. While still growing accustomed to the new manufacturing process, Wiets and his staff had to face one of the heaviest fall production periods in recent memory. Large orders for The Beatles' *Anthology*, in particular, had forced the company to bring in extra staff to handle the packaging. "We were cutting our teeth on CD manufacturing while coping with an extremely busy schedule," recalls Wiets. "It was a really steep learning curve, but

Moist's Jeff Pearce, Mark Makoway, David Usher, Kevin Young and Paul Wilcox, receiving 1995 Juno for Best New Group: bold new sounds from the coast

somehow we managed to get through it." In fact, within three short years the plant had achieved an impressive annual output of 11.3 million units. Concludes Wiets: "We're a very tight group, in tune with our needs for marketing and distribution. We can turn things around really quickly. Ultimately, having our own manufacturing makes us a more complete record company."

Although working with vastly different technology, Wiets was mirroring the pioneering efforts of Ken Kerr with vinyl production, at the company's London, Ontario, plant in the '50s.

In April 1996, Vancouver-based Nettwerk Records returned to EMI

Canada's fold after a two-year absence. The deal involved EMI manufacturing and distributing Nettwerk releases, including those by rapidly rising Canadian star Sarah McLachlan. It followed a venture announced three months earlier that saw Nettwerk distributed in the U.S. through the EMI-owned CEMA, and certain EMI Canada artists receiving a marketing push south of the border through Nettwerk's representatives there. "It's a pleasure to be working with Nettwerk again," stated Deane Cameron at the time. "We look forward to continuing the growth of this prestigious label in both the Canadian and U.S. markets."

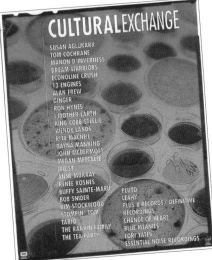

That month, when EMI's board of directors flew into Toronto from the U.K. and the U.S. for the company's first annual general meeting held outside of England, Cameron treated his guests to some first-rate Canadiana. His staff arranged a private concert, featuring the label's prized singers Rita MacNeil and John McDermott at the prestigious Wintergarden Theatre. And each visitor received a gift pack that included bottles of award-winning Canadian wines, a book on Canadian heritage, the *Oh What a Feeling* box set (comprising 30 years of Canadian hits) and a

commemorative CD of the Wintergarden concert that was mixed, produced and manufactured overnight. The music and hospitality that EMI extended at this event made an impression on all who attended.

Just as Capitol had ushered the British Invasion into Canada

Legendary EMI France recording artist Charles Aznavour receives Prime Minister Jean Chrétien and his wife, Aline, in his dressing room

in the mid-60s, EMI led the way with English pop acts in the mid-90s. Besides The Beatles, The Rolling Stones (via Virgin) and Kate Bush (who remained loyal to EMI in Canada even after signing with

Columbia in the U.S.), the Canadian company boasted such cutting-edge bands as Blur and Radiohead, who the media touted as a modern-day Pink Floyd. Then, in December 1996, The Spice Girls' self-titled debut album landed from Virgin, launching a Spice-craze phenomenon.

Ladies' night at the 1995 Junos: (left to right) Alannah Myles, Sass Jordan, Anne Murray, her daughter, Dawn, Buffy Sainte-Marie and Susan Aglukark

Featuring the smash hit single "Wannabe," the album debuted at #1 at *The Record* and was almost instantly named the top retail album of the year. Suddenly, girls across Canada and the world were dressing as their

favourite Spice member, either Ginger, Scary, Sporty, Baby or Posh.

Ginger and company also spiced up EMI Canada's profit picture after disappointing results in the 1996–97 fiscal year. Garth Brooks (the best-selling solo artist in music history) and Canada's

Sarah McLachlan came to EMI via Nettwerk Records: an ethereal presence

own Sarah McLachlan, whose *Surfacing* album had debuted at #1 at *The Record* also brought in substantial revenues. In the magazine's year-end review of industry leaders, Deane Cameron noted that the whole pre-recorded music market had showed an encouraging 10 per cent increase over 1996. He added that he and his company, with a domestic roster of 26 acts, were further encouraged by the "continuing strength of Canadian music on the charts."

In a joint venture with Universal and Warner Music Canada, EMI had also reaped a Canadian commercial bonanza in compiling youth-oriented pop collections. Featuring the leading hits of the day, compilations like *NOW!* and *Big Shiny Tunes*, heavily promoted on MuchMusic, became some of the top-selling releases among the 15–24 age group. By the end of '97, all three record companies were able to report that sales for the compilations, each with three volumes, had surpassed five million copies.

Not content to rest on its pop laurels, EMI Canada also expanded its roster in the jazz and classical fields. The company now had several artists signed to the prestigious, New York–based Blue Note jazz label, which it distributed, including legendary Cuban pianist Chucho Valdes, singer-songwriter Shirley Eikhard (returning to the EMI fold after 25 years) and pianist Renee Rosnes, who in March had won her second Juno Award in the Best Mainstream Jazz Album category for *Ancestors*. To top it off, Maynard Ferguson—Capitol's first Canadian jazz artist—received long-overdue recognition when he was inducted into the Canadian Music Hall of Fame.

On the classical side, EMI Canada signed a licensing deal with the Toronto-based Marquis Classics, a label that released such breakthrough albums as *Bach Meets Cape Breton* by Puirt a Baroque, the self-titled debut by Quartetto Gelato and *Slow Fox* by cabaret singer Patricia O'Callaghan, who combined a penchant for Kurt Weill with a love of Leonard Cohen songs. Meanwhile, EMI Classics scored a hit with the reissue of *Healy Willan at the Church of St. Mary Magdalene Toronto*, an internationally acclaimed recording of sacred organ and choir music made between 1965–67.

Other top classical releases in the '90s, with sales of more than 50,000, included: *Canto Gregoriano*, Sarah Brightman, Nigel Kennedy's *Four Seasons*, Vanessa Mae's *the Violin Player*, Maria Callas's *La Divina* and such compilations as *Best Classical Album in the World*, *Best Opera Album in the World*, *Most Relaxing Classical Album in the World* and *Movies Go to the Opera*. In 1998, Canada's highly acclaimed St. Lawrence String Quartet became the first classical act to be signed directly to the label.

At the beginning of '98, the company was greeted with the news that EMI Music Publishing was ranked as the world's largest major music publisher, ahead of Warner Chappell, with 1997 earnings of $550 million U.S. Then, at the Junos in March, EMI Music Canada, together with Virgin Music Canada and associated labels, was again a major winner. Nettwerk's Sarah McLachlan enjoyed a clean sweep, winning five awards, including female vocalist, songwriter, producer and album (*Surfacing*) and single ("Building a Mystery"). Virgin's latest platinum-plus domestic signing, the nine siblings known as Leahy, won for Best New Group and Instrumental Artists of the Year, while The Spice Girls' *Spice* won for the year's best-selling album.

Coinciding with the Junos was the launch of *Silent Radar*, the EMI debut album by Winnipeg's The Watchmen, who left Universal after racking up two platinum awards and one gold for its first three albums. "Overall, EMI seemed like a better fit for the band," manager Jake Gold told *The Record*. "Working with EMI's A&R department was a great experience for both the band and myself."

Virgin Canada made significant breakthroughs in urban music in the late '90s. The label signed promising

rapper Choclair, the first Canadian hip-hop artist signed to a major record company in either Canada or the United States. Virgin's Urban Department, led by Russ Hergert, spearheaded an aggressive national campaign that helped to make Canada the top territory for such urban acts as Daft Punk and Fat Boy Slim. And in three short years, the department—which included a "street team" of 14 working in various Canadian cities—pushed annual sales of Virgin's urban recordings from 30,000 to 600,000 copies, to the point where the label had captured 25 per cent of the urban market.

According to Tim Trombley, urban music represents one of the last frontiers for the Canadian music industry in the '90s. "Maybe it will take a Canadian act breaking through in America first to open the doors here," admits Trombley, "but once that happens the hip-hop kids will accept Canadian urban music on its own terms." He added: "If that happens within the next couple of years, and I believe it will, then I can walk away from this job quite happily."

Perhaps the last true frontier for the global music industry in the final days of the twentieth century—and its greatest challenge—was the growth of the Internet and the development of downloadable music capabilities. EMI Recorded Music, the third largest music company in the world, was quick to play a leading role in this field with its announcement in June 1999 that it had signed a deal with Liquid Audio. A leading provider of Internet software and services for delivering music on-line, Liquid Audio was selected to encode

EMI's entire catalogue. Said Ken Berry, president of EMI Recorded Music: "EMI is leveraging the global reach of the Internet to make our artists' music available to millions of fans online and generate additional income from our extensive library."

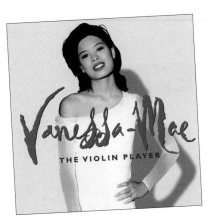

The announcement coincided with the news that EMI had also struck deals with both musicmaker.com, the leading Internet CD-compilation company, and Digital On-Demand, a company that specializes in digital distribution of recordings into retail stores. "The Internet is the ultimate means of direct marketing to the consumer," said Jay Samits, EMI's senior vice-president of New Media. The deal with musicmaker.com, he added, is simply "one of a number of opportunities for EMI to generate additional income from our extensive back catalogue. This agreement will also benefit consumers who will be able to enjoy music in a new way by creating the albums they have always dreamed of owning."

As EMI Music Canada approached its 50th year, there was much to celebrate. Canada's first adult contemporary video channel, MuchMoreMusic, was launched in September 1998, giving much-needed exposure to such EMI artists as Susan Aglukark, Tom Cochrane, Anne Murray, The Rankins and Robbie Robertson. Then in January, Blue Note Records celebrated its 60th anniversary, an occasion marked by a large party in New York and several commemorative releases.

But all of that paled in comparison to what followed in 1999. Celebrating its own golden anniversary in June, EMI Music Canada threw a lavish, old-fashioned picnic for 750 guests in a large park west of Toronto. Under glorious sunny skies, the company's staff—from all the branches—and their families from Vancouver, Edmonton, Calgary, Winnipeg, Kitchener, Toronto, Ottawa, Montreal, Quebec City and Halifax—were treated to a gourmet barbecue, hayrides, outdoor games and live musical performances. Deane Cameron, cognizant of the event's historical significance, invited past executives Ed Leetham, Arnold Gosewich, Paul White and Pierre Dubord. Among the special guests were EMI Europe president Rupert Perry, who flew in from London, and company founders Ken Kerr and Harvey Clarke.

Deane Cameron presents Capitol Canada founders Harvey Clarke (left) and Ken Kerr with honorary awards: true pioneers

EMI Canada president Deane Cameron addresses the 50th anniversary picnic: "a brave entrepreneurial spirit"

through 8-track and cassette tapes, to CDs and CD-ROMs—we've sold nearly 350 million units of music in this country. Over the same period, we've employed literally thousands of Canadians in every area of the business, from A&R and marketing to manufacturing and distribution.

"Meanwhile, we've kept pace with new technologies—and sometimes become industry leaders in them. When our parent, EMI Records, celebrated its 100th anniversary in 1997, the company acknowledged its origins back in the earliest days of recorded sound. At first, it took decades to change configurations, to go from cylinder to disc and then through various forms of disc and tape. As the century draws to an end, the pace of events has only taken a few short years for the whole digital opportunity, with on-line, downloadable music, to be suddenly upon us. We are traversing an exciting and challenging time. And EMI Music Canada will meet the challenge head-on."

"Throughout our history runs a brave, entrepreneurial spirit," Cameron told the crowd, following a stirring rendition of the national anthem by John McDermott. "It's there, in the first releases our company ever issued from a converted wire and nail factory in London, Ontario. It's there, during the pre-CanCon era of the '60s, when Ed Leetham and Paul White first put together a viable, domestic roster. And it's there in the flag-waving days of the '70s, when Arnold Gosewich and Pierre Dubord took part in the Maple Music Junket and Sounds Canadian campaigns. As a record company, we may not have always been the biggest, but we've consistently strived to be the best. And we've done that by developing our own, distinctly Canadian music.

"Since 1949, our company—between direct signings and associated labels—has featured the music of upwards of 350 Canadian artists. With recordings covering numerous formats—from 78s, 45s and 33s,

EMI Music Canada's management team honors Capitol Canada founders Harvey Clarke (fourth on left) and Ken Kerr (fourth on right)

Then, before introducing musical performances by Anne Murray and her daughter, Dawn, singers Damhnait Doyle, Dayna Manning and Kim Stockwood, and Virgin's latest signing, Quebec's La Bottine Souriante, Cameron brought his speech to an emotional climax. "I now want to invite to the stage Ken Kerr and Harvey Clarke,"

Virgin Canada's La Bottine Souriante inject some Québecois spirit into the proceedings

Anne Murray sang Snowbird

John McDermott sang our National Anthem

Impromptu trio Dayna Manning, Kim Stockwood and Damhnait Doyle, after performing a stirring rendition of The Beatles' "Yesterday" at the picnic

EMI Music's management team gathers to celebrate the anniversary

he said. "These are the founding fathers of this wonderful, truly Canadian, record company. And each of them deserves a hero's welcome for the legacy they have left us." Cameron and his management team—including vice-president of human resources Sharon MacDonald, who had organized the successful picnic celebrations—presented Kerr and Clarke each with a commemorative plaque and a diamond ring in the design of the old Capitol logo.

It was a fitting end to a jubilant day. EMI Music Canada would spend the rest of the year marking its anniversary with other significant events, including the release of several retrospective CD packages and the com-

pletion of this book. But nothing quite matched the emotion in Ken Kerr's voice when, in a short, impromptu acceptance speech, he told the picnic gathering of his genuine surprise at the legacy of which Cameron spoke. "We had no idea we were giving birth to all of this," Kerr said, stretching his arms out, as if to encompass 50 years of music making. "I'm just proud to have been a part of it all."

It was a remarkable accomplishment. From that converted wire and nail factory in London, Ontario, EMI Music Canada has grown into one of the world's great record companies. Its passion and commitment has taken Canadian music across the country and around the globe.

The Campbell Brothers piped in the day

Still crazy after all those years: Paul White, Maurice Zurba and Pierre Dubord share old war stories

SUSAN AGLUKARK

EMI CANADA
1993

At the 1995 Junos: a treasured artist and a shining role model to the Inuit people of the North

An aboriginal heroine of the '90s, Susan Aglukark has become a role model to the Inuit people of the North. Since signing with EMI Music Canada, Aglukark has also become one of the country's top recording artists, with Juno and MuchMusic video awards to her credit. While she realizes the significance of her stature, she is also wary of being turned into a cultural icon. "This is the thing in my career that I'm most afraid of," Aglukark once admitted to *Canadian Musician* magazine, "that people won't let me make my mistakes, that they'll put me on a pedestal. And they won't give me the space to grow."

One of seven children born to an Inuit Pentecostal minister and his half-Inuit wife in Churchill, Manitoba, Aglukark grew up in various Inuit communities in the Keewatin region. Around the age of 12, her family settled in Arviat, Northwest Territories, a small town with a population of 1,300 on the northwestern shore of Hudson Bay. Aglukark, who had begun expressing interest in singing at church, soon learned to play guitar, bass and keyboards. Although both of her parents had recorded gospel songs at one time, a career in music seemed a remote possibility.

Schooling in the North posed its own sets of challenges. Aglukark began high school in Iqaluit, Baffin Island, but dropped out for three months to attend Bible School over in Cambridge Bay. She then completed her high school studies in Yellowknife, where she earned her diploma. It wasn't until after graduation that Aglukark performed publicly for the first time outside of church, taking to the stage at a festival in Arviat. For the next several years, however, she put her musical aspirations on hold as she moved to Ottawa to work as a translator for the federal Department of Indian and Northern Affairs, and then as an executive assistant for an Inuit lobby group.

Aglukark's first musical break came when CBC producer Randall Prescott heard a tape she submitted for a compilation of northern artists the radio network was assembling. Prescott was so struck by her sweet, gentle vocals that he quickly arranged a recording session. Aglukark then released her own tape of gospel recordings, *Dreams of You*, which CBC Radio began playing throughout northern Canada. Aglukark then produced a video for the song "Searching," which won a MuchMusic Award for outstanding cinematography in 1991. Her second album, *Arctic Rose*, was released the following year and sold 14,000 copies through mail order. Sung in both English and her native Inuktitut, its songs reflected both traditional Inuit values and the social realities of life in the North.

Impressed by her commercial success and artistic stance, EMI Canada signed Aglukark and released a self-titled collection of Christmas carols sung in Inuktitut in December 1993. The following April, EMI re-released *Arctic Rose*, which went on to sell an additional 30,000 copies. The first single and video, "Song of the Land," and the second single, "Still Running," were specially re-recorded for the label. The latter dealt with the aftermath of sexual abuse, something Aglukark herself had been subjected to by a family friend at the age of nine (she later testified against him in court). *Arctic Rose* earned Aglukark her first music industry recognition, including the Canadian Country Music Association's Rising Star Award and two Junos, for Best New Solo Artist and Best Music of Aboriginal Canada Recording.

In 1995, EMI Canada released Aglukark's next album, *This Child*. Produced and partly co-written with Chad Irschick, best known for his work with labelmates The Rankin Family, the album struck a balance between traditional Inuk chants and contemporary country-pop melodies. Once again, Aglukark bridged two worlds with songs like "Shamaya," about the traditions of the Inuit hunt, and "Kathy I," about the

tragedy of a friend's suicide. But it was the joyful single "O Siem" that took Aglukark to the top of the adult contemporary charts, hitting the #1 position at both *RPM* and *The Record*. After its initial launch at a reception in Yellowknife, *This Child* went on to achieve triple-platinum sales of 300,000 copies in Canada.

Aglukark needn't have worried about not being allowed to grow creatively. In 1999, EMI Canada released her album *Unsung Heroes*, which featured a contemporary, rhythm-oriented pop sound. With her singular talent and inner strength, a trait common to Inuit people, Canada's Arctic rose has emerged as one of the country's most treasured artists.

TOM COCHRANE

EMI CANADA
1987

Few solo careers have soared as dramatically as that of Tom Cochrane. But for Cochrane, the son of a Canadian bush pilot and former frontman for the band Red Rider, things didn't really get off the ground until he returned from a 1990 trip to East Africa, where he witnessed starvation and turmoil. "I saw a lot of very, very heavy things," Cochrane admitted. "And yet I discovered something I wasn't prepared for, and that was the resilience of the people, their ability to find joy in the simple things, to live for the moment. That was a big inspiration for me because we find all sorts of things to complain about in our society and don't realize how lucky we are. Life is short, no matter where you live it."

The experience led to "Life is a Highway," the lead-off single from Cochrane's solo debut album *Mad Mad World*. The anthemic song, which perfectly captured a feeling of joyful abandon, topped the charts at *RPM* and *The Record* in the fall of '91 and later hit the Top 10 at *Billboard* the following summer. More significantly, it kick-started Cochrane's whole solo career and led to two world tours, four Juno Awards and several more singles from *Mad Mad World*, which eventually sold more than one million copies in Canada and two million around the world. Although he had recorded seven albums with Red Rider, it took just one solo album to make Cochrane an international superstar.

With fellow EMI recording artist Kate Bush, in 1993: 'Life is a Highway' sent his career racing into the fast lane

Born in Lynn Lake, Manitoba in 1953, Cochrane and his family eventually settled in the Toronto suburb of Etobicoke, where Tom soon gravitated to music, buying his first guitar at the age of 11. In the early '70s, while dividing his education between music and journalism, he performed in coffeehouses, under the influence of Bob Dylan and such Yorkville folkies as Bruce Cockburn and Murray McLauchlan. By 1973 he landed a record deal and released his first single, "You're Driving Me Crazy," under his surname Cochrane on the Toronto label Daffodil Records. Even with a debut album, *Hang On To Your Resistance*, under his belt, Cochrane was still struggling to make ends meet.

Heading out to Los Angeles, he found work writing theme music for

At work in the studio: a consummate singer-songwriter, capable of penning deeply personal material

Xaviera (the Happy Hooker) Hollander's movie *My Pleasure Is My Business*. Then, back in Toronto, Cochrane drove taxi for several years before passing an audition to join Red Rider in 1978. Signed to Capitol-EMI in Canada, the band went on to become one of Canada's top rock groups during the 1980s, with Cochrane as lead singer and chief songwriter. With the departure of guitarist Ken Greer, with whom Cochrane recorded Red Rider's final album, *The Symphony Sessions*, Red Rider was no more.

With the massive success of *Mad Mad World*, Cochrane found his life suddenly turned upside down. "It was like living in a hurricane for two or three years," the singer-songwriter told *The Record*, later admitting that his newfound celebrity—not to mention touring practically nonstop for 30 months—placed a strain on his marriage. Fortunately, Cochrane emerged as a wiser individual, and he and his wife were able to reconcile. "I basically sat down and tried to get my life back in balance," he said. "Part of it involved writing an honest record, probably my most personal record in many ways." That record became *Ragged Ass Road*.

Released in 1995, the rootsier *Ragged Ass Road* did indeed feature some of Cochrane's most personal songs, including the hit singles "I Wish You Well," about a failed relationship, and "Wildest Dreams," about long-term love. The title track, meanwhile, was about a rough stretch of road in Yellowknife, Northwest Territories, that Cochrane felt was part of his heritage. "Oddballs, adventurers, pioneers, artists, misfits—some of them going back generations—live there," he said at the time.

True to his word, Cochrane proved himself an adventurer in the summer of '97, when, in a move that would have made his father proud, he got his pilot's licence and bought himself an airplane. Two years later, while touring in support of his latest album, *xray sierra*, his Cessna crashed at a small airport north of Montreal. No one was injured and Cochrane was able to resume touring. "I was a little shook up," he later admitted about the crash, "but God was smiling on us." Like the message of his breakthrough hit single, *Life is a Highway*, Cochrane knows all about living for the moment.

STOMPIN' TOM CONNORS

EMI CANADA
1989

Getting patriotic with the legendary Stomper, at Toronto's Matador club, for the release of his 1995 autobiography, Before the Fame: the true north strong and Tom

The legend was back. In the spring of 1990, Stompin' Tom Connors took to the stage in a high school auditorium in Owen Sound, Ontario, and performed his first concert in 13 years. It was a memorable night. In front of a backdrop of a giant Maple Leaf, the gaunt-faced, wiry country singer, dressed from Stetson to boots in black, thrilled his audience of 700 by launching straight into "Around the Bay and Back Again," his tribute to Georgian Bay and the people of the surrounding towns of Tobermory, Collingwood and Owen Sound itself. Instantly, the crowd was on its feet, singing and stomping along. A similar scene was acted out on stages throughout his 70-date national tour, as Connors claimed to have a song for almost every town he visited.

An ardent nationalist, with a gift for writing simple, honest (and often funny) songs about Canada and its people, Connors had stopped performing and recording in 1976 in protest to the music industry's lack of support for Canadian talent. His disappearance from the music scene was treated as a national tragedy by his fans. And celebrities, from broadcaster Peter Gzowski to comedian Dan Aykroyd, publicly pleaded with him to return. His comeback began in 1988, but it was a gradual process. First he performed several times on Gzowski's *Morningside* show on CBC Radio. Then he appeared on a k.d. lang TV special the following year. It wasn't until his national tour and the deal with Capitol-EMI, which included reissuing his entire back catalogue, that Connors appeared ready to resume his role as patriotic troubadour. "The guy is a national treasure," said Capitol-EMI president Deane Cameron at the time. "Like the Group of Seven, he captures the very essence of Canada."

The national treasure started out as a lonely orphan who became a restless drifter. Born in 1936, Saint John, New Brunswick, to an unwed teenage mother, Connors began hitchhiking with his mother at the age of three and was begging on the streets at four. Soon, he was taken in by the Children's Aid Society and placed in an orphanage, where he was often physically abused. Although adopted by a family in Skinner's Pond, Prince Edward Island, at nine, he ran away four years later and, living a hitchhiker's transient life, worked as a tobacco picker, gravedigger and short-order cook. Ultimately, music was his salvation. On a rainy night in Timmins, Ontario, in 1964, Connors found himself a nickel short for a beer at the Maple Leaf Hotel. The manager told him he could make up the difference singing a few songs with his guitar, which he'd picked up and learned to play along the way.

That performance led to a 14-month run at the Timmins hotel—and to Connors's rising fame. It was there that he earned his nickname "Stompin'", for his foot-pounding performances on stages that were often reduced to splinters. He began recording singles about tobacco workers ("Tillsonburg") and potato-hauling truck drivers ("Bud the Spud"). One of his best-known songs, "Sudbury Saturday Night," dealt with the lives of miners ("*Well, the girls are out to bingo/And the boys are getting stinko/And we'll think no more of Inco/On a Sudbury Saturday Night*"). Soon, Connors was performing at Toronto's Horseshoe Tavern and, eventually, in the prestigious Massey Hall. By 1971, Connors could afford to form his own label, Boot Records, and to release albums by other Canadian artists.

Connors's unbridled patriotism has always taken precedence, sometimes at the cost of his career. In 1975, he boycotted the Canadian National Exhibition when he learned he was to be paid $2,500 for a two-hour concert while American country singer Charley Pride received $35,000 for performing six songs. When he stopped performing the following year, he returned all seven of his Juno Awards because, he said, the music industry was honouring too many "border jumpers," Canadian artists who lived and worked in the United States.

During the lead-up to the 1995 Quebec referendum, Connors's album *Long Gone to the Yukon* and his autobiography *Stompin' Tom: Before the Fame* were released with much flag-waving fanfare at Toronto's Matador club. EMI Music Canada staff and artists, including Susan Aglukark, John McDermott and Kim Stockwood, turned out in full force. On referendum day, EMI bought full-page Stompin' Tom ads in the *Sun* chain of newspapers and the *Vancouver Province* to encourage people to request Canadian music on their favourite radio station.

The hats have it: comparing brims with admirer Kim Mitchell, before indulging in a little Crown & Anchor

Ever the rebel, Connors—whose *Hockey Song* became a staple in arenas across North America in the '90s—remained fiercely committed to his cause. As he told *Maclean's*: "They says you get older and mellower, but, by Jesus, I'm just the same way I've always been."

ECONOLINE CRUSH

EMI CANADA
1993

Morfitt, Robert Wagner, Ziggy, Ken Fleming and Hurst (squatting): a penchant for pop hooks and rock guitars

Vancouver's Econoline Crush has endured a few too many comparisons to industrial group Nine Inch Nails. While there are similarities, including a hard-edged sound and raw, Trent Reznor–like vocals, Econoline Crush has distinguished itself with a penchant for pop hooks and rock guitars. During a European tour in 1996, the band actually found itself being pegged as a crossover act. "Industrial music has a lot of its origins in Germany, where they're industrial purists," Econoline Crush singer Trevor Hurst told the *Calgary Sun*. "We have lead guitars and songs, so they call it crossover because they feel it's pop-rock meets industrial."

Formed in 1992, Econoline Crush came together when Hurst responded to an ad seeking a vocalist who could sing over a bed of electronic music. Within a few months, Econoline Crush was making a noise around Vancouver with a lineup that included Hurst, guitarist Robbie Morfitt, bassist Daniel Yaremko and drummer Gregg Leask. After a cross-Canada tour in '93, the band recorded an independently released six-song EP titled *Purge*, and managed to earn themselves a Juno nomination.

After landing a record deal with EMI Music Canada in 1994, Econoline Crush recorded its first full-length album, *Affliction*, which came out the following year to positive reviews. But the band then suffered numerous changes that saw the entire lineup, save Hurst and Morfitt, depart. Hurst admitted that he almost packed it in at that point, before deciding to establish a new commitment to the band. The new, improved Econoline Crush got serious and recorded *The Devil You Know*, released in 1997. Produced by Sylvia Massy (Red Hot Chili Peppers, Tool), the album boasted the same tough sound as its predecessors but with more of a pop-flavoured melodic edge.

Fuelled by the infectious hit singles "Home" and "All That You Are," the album went on to hit platinum-level sales of 100,000 copies.

By late '98, Econoline Crush had hooked up with Vancouver-based powerhouse manager Bruce Allen and toured North American stadiums with glam-metal rockers Kiss. For Hurst, it was a thrilling and educational experience. "Kiss has always been about bringing on bands that they think are gonna break, like Stone Temple Pilots," he said. "For Kiss, it keeps them in touch with what's going on. For us, it's arena rock 101. Learn some chops."

Frontman Hurst (left) raises a glass at the 1998 Junos with actor (and Barenaked Ladies director) Jason Priestley

THE WATCHMEN

EMI CANADA
1997

Like other Winnipeg bands, including The Guess Who and Crash Test Dummies, The Watchmen developed in glorious isolation from Canada's major music centres. "We jammed every single day," singer Daniel Greaves told reporter Mike Ross. "It would be minus 40, we'd go to our rehearsal space and jam for hours with a case of beer and discover our craft together." Added guitarist Joey Serlin: "We were just Winnipeg kids doing what felt right at the time. It definitely affects things if you're from a community that's far away from anywhere else, especially the whole Toronto thing."

The Watchmen's rehearsal space was the furnace room of Winnipeg's McLaren Hotel. So when it came time to find a name for the band's 1992 debut album, *McLaren Furnace Room* seemed highly suitable. Signed to The Tragically Hip's management company, the group—including bassist Ken Tizzard and drummer Sammy Kohn—recorded two more albums, the platinum-selling *In the Trees* and the gold-status *Brand New Day*, before joining EMI Music Canada for its fourth full-length recording, 1998's *Silent Radar*. That album, produced by Adam Kasper (R.E.M., Soundgarden) and featuring the hit single "Stereo," broke new ground for the band with its darker tones and themes about the alienating effects of technology.

But, as Tizzard told *The Record*, "even though much of the song 'Stereo' is about a fear of technology, the band has no doubt about

Sammy Kohn, Ken Tizzard, Daniel Greaves and Joey Serlin: breaking new ground with dark tones and themes about the alienating effects of technology

ters, for their unique camaraderie onstage. "People establish their identity on their own here," said Serlin, about Winnipeg. "All we did was play, every single day for years. Being outside during the winter simply wasn't an option."

embracing it." Indeed, *Silent Radar* was the first to feature CD-Active, which enabled listeners to unlock "private" Web pages on the band's Web site through a CD-ROM drive and the Internet. CD-Active allowed users to play back the album from within a Web browser while synchronizing the song "Stereo" with behind-the-scenes video footage, private photos, song lyrics not found on the CD, exclusive interviews and a fan contribution area. Added Tizzard: "We believe in using new technologies to help our fans get a fuller experience from our new album and connect with us more easily."

Ultimately, the band's strongest connection with its fans has come from its concerts. And The Watchmen, an intense live act with a soulful rock sound, credit Winnipeg roots, including the city's infamous win-

Jamming with Canrock giant Randy Bachman: "Winnipeg kids doing what felt right at the time"

JOHN McDERMOTT

EMI CANADA
1992

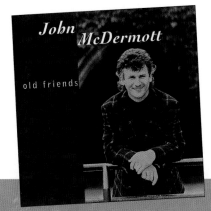

He has one of the world's most mellifluous voices, yet, surprisingly, John McDermott never expected a singing career. Early in 1992, he was still working in the circulation department of the *Toronto Sun* newspaper. By night, he sang the national anthem at Toronto's Maple Leafs and Blue Jays home games and often performed traditional Celtic songs for friends at parties and weddings.

Born in Glasgow, Scotland in 1955, McDermott was one of 12 children born to an amateur singer and his wife, who emigrated to Canada in 1965. The McDermott household in north Toronto was always filled with music. Saturday nights were spent with friends and neighbours all trading old songs. Often, McDermott's father, Peter, led the way. And afterwards, John and his brothers and sisters were asked to sing one for their dad before bedtime, in exchange for a piece of candy.

While singing at functions for the *Toronto Sun*, McDermott caught the ear of publishing mogul Conrad Black, who asked him to sing at a 1989 dinner where the guests included Brian Mulroney and Ronald Reagan. Later, when McDermott decided to record his first album, as a 50th wedding anniversary present for his parents, he approached Black with his plans. With a cheque to finance the CD, McDermott signed to EMI Music Canada and recorded *Danny Boy*, named for the Irish ballad that had become his trademark. Featuring mostly war-themed standards, such as "And the Band Played Waltzing Matilda" and

McDermott goes heavy metal with EMI Canada staffers in the warehouse, 1994: platinum and gold awards for one of the world's most mellifluous voices

"Christmas in the Trenches," the album reached platinum status in Canada in 1993 and went triple platinum in New Zealand after McDermott made a promotional tour there. "We knocked Bryan Adams

out of first place for about a week," the singer proudly told *The Record*. "I had him, Meat Loaf and (Michael) Jackson in the back seat. I looked kind of funny."

Buoyed by that success, EMI in 1994 released *Old Friends*, a collection of old and modern classics, including "The Skye Boat Song" and "The Dutchman." It, too, enjoyed platinum-level sales in Canada, where McDermott became a staple of CBC Radio, and earned him a Juno nomination for Best Male Vocalist. That same year, McDermott recorded a holiday album, *Christmas Memories*, in response to requests from his audiences. Then came *Love is a Voyage* in '95, a collection of traditional and contemporary songs, including numbers by John Prine, Ron Hynes and Murray McLauchlan. McDermott dedicated the album to the memory of his father, who died that year. And he included a recording of his dad singing in a smoky Glasgow pub in 1957. His father, McDermott wrote in the liner notes, was "my greatest musical influence and my best friend."

Each year brings a new spate of recordings and related projects. In '96, EMI released *The Danny Boy Collection*, mixing songs from both *Danny Boy* and *Old Friends*. Following Rita MacNeil's lead, McDermott produced an infomercial for U.S. television as a marketing strategy south of the border. The compilation went on to near gold-level sales of 500,000 copies there. Then, in '97, McDermott recorded *When I Grow Too Old to Dream* and launched a 60-date Canadian tour, and the following year produced a collection of war songs titled *If Ye Shall Break the Silence*, honouring veterans. The recording was renamed *Remembrance* for its release in the United States later that year. McDermott toured extensively throughout Canada and the United States, singing songs from the album, donating a portion of the proceeds to local veterans' charities and a proposed Second World War memorial in Washington.

As the decade wound to a close, McDermott was riding high as a member of The Irish Tenors, a trio that included Anthony Kearns and Ronan Tynan singing Celtic favourites, backed by a 60-piece orchestra. That project included a 12-city North American tour and a CD recorded live in Dublin that attained gold-level sales in the United States. The broadcast of the concert was the most successful PBS program in 1999. In the midst of all that, McDermott's modesty remained intact. "I wouldn't say I'm surprised by my success," he told the *Edmonton Sun*. "I mean, these songs I'm doing are so wonderful, I think they sell themselves."

MOIST

EMI CANADA
1994

"Moist," reads the band's first bio, "is five musicians, a road manager, a sound guy, a roadie with a bad haircut, 1,000 pounds of gear, five or six magazines, a well-worn copy of *Hammer of the Gods*, over 400 comic books, a goldfish and a hell of a lot of T-shirts stuffed in a van travelling at danger-ously high speeds down narrow roads in the middle of the night."

The description could fit any number of young groups. The difference with Moist—singer David Usher, keyboardist Kevin Young, guitarist Mark Makowy, bassist Jeff Pearce and drummer Paul Wilcox—is that, shortly after hitting the road, they found the fast track to stardom. Formed in November 1992, Moist came together when Usher, Young, Makoway and Pearce, all originally from Kingston, Ontario, met at a party in Vancouver. Almost immediately, they began writing songs and played live for the first time in January 1993. The following month, they recorded a self-titled independent cas-sette and began criss-crossing the country in a dilapidated Ford Econoline van. Within a year, the band recorded its debut CD, *Silver*, and hit number one on the Canadian indie retail charts, thanks, in part, to the popularity of its video for the song "Push." Signed worldwide to EMI Music Canada in April 1994, the band was suddenly Canadian pop's Next Big Thing.

Moist (they chose the name, Young said, because "it's evocative, provocative and impossible to forget") immediately set itself apart from other bands with a readily identifiable sound built around Usher's keen-ing vocals and Makowy's bright guitar playing. Distinctive videos didn't hurt either. "Push" was a masterpiece of simplicity and stunning visu-als, while "Silver" was shot like a Shakespearean drama. The video for "Believe Me," boldly tackled the subject of teenage suicide. By December 1994, Moist was jetting back and forth across Canada, the United States and Europe and watching as *Silver* hit double platinum at home for sales of 200,000 copies (it eventually sold twice that amount).

The band then developed a strong base in Thailand, of all places. Rob Brooks, the label's vice-president of marketing and operations, dis-covered that Usher, whose mother was from there, could actually speak Thai. Seizing the opportunity, Brooks quickly set up phone inter-views with the Thai press and sent the band over. When Moist arrived,

Moist: "evocative, provocative and impossible to forget"

there were TV crews and screaming girls waiting for them at the airport. After that, it only made sense for Moist to re-record some of its songs with Usher singing the lyrics in Thai, much the way The Beatles had converted their material into German in the early '60s.

Creature, the band's next album, easily matched *Silver*'s success. Released in 1996, the album featured the hit singles "Resurrection," "Leave It Alone," "Tangerine" and "Gasoline." After extensive worldwide touring with such diverse artists as Neil Young, Green Day and Hole, Moist topped off their head-lining arena tour for *Creature* with an outdoor show in Montreal before 85,000 people. When the band took a break from touring and recording, Usher released a solo album with EMI titled *Little Songs*. His dark good looks and attractive mixed heritage made the singer one of Canadian pop's biggest heartthrobs. More than 800 screaming fans jammed into a Montreal record store in 1998 when he appeared there for a live interview and autograph session.

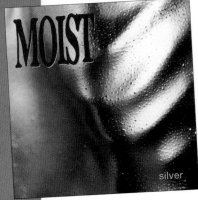

In the summer of '99, Moist released its third full-length album, *Mercedes Five and Dime*. Produced by David Leonard (Barenaked Ladies, Prince), the album was a departure for the band, with its use of acoustic guitars, percussion instruments, synthesizers and loops. It was also written differently. "In the past," explained Pearce, "people would bring in riffs and we'd just jam on them for a while. This time, we were all bringing in songs that were closer to being com-pleted. Having songs that fully realized allowed us to experi-ment more with the arrange-ment and sounds in the studios." That eclecticism became evi-dent on songs such as "Fish," "Mandolin," "Pleasing Falsetto"

Makowy, Usher, Wilcox, Young and Pearce, at the 1995 Junos: suddenly Canadian pop's Next Big Thing

and the infectious first single "Breathe." "Moist is very much a group of writers," concluded Usher, "and we're always looking for a new outlook, a new way to present the material as a collective."

THE RANKINS

EMI CANADA
1992

The forerunners of Canadian Celtic music in the '90s, The Rankins' roots run deep. Seventh-generation Scottish Canadians, the group is part of a large family of 12 children, who grew up in the tiny town of Mabou, on the west coast of Cape Breton Island.

Five of the siblings—Jimmy,

Cookie (fourth from left), John Morris, Raylene, Jimmy and Heather Rankin: taking Celtic music from the tiny town of Mabou to the international stage

John Morris, Cookie, Raylene and Heather—began performing together at an early age, often in the tartan kilts of their clan. Soon, clear but interchangeable roles emerged within the group. Jimmy stood out as the natural leader, handling much of the songwriting as well as singing and playing guitar. John Morris was the quiet brother who played fiddle and piano while taking on the group's arranging. And sisters Cookie, Heather and Raylene provided intricate harmonies and electrifying step-dancing, along with their own share of the songwriting. Many of the group's first songs, featured on two independent albums, were either traditional fiddle tunes or original ballads that drew on their Cape Breton upbringing.

When combined sales of *The Rankin Family* and *Fare Thee Well Love* reached 60,000 and the group earned three Juno nominations in the spring of 1992, Capitol-EMI stepped in and signed them. The label reissued both recordings and released the group's next album, *North Country*, in 1993. The Rankins' Celtic sound then swept the Juno Awards in early '94, as the quintet won all four categories they were nominated in: Country Group or Duo of the Year, Group of the Year, Single of the Year ("Fare Thee Well Love") and the coveted Canadian Entertainer of the

Jamming on "Patio Lanterns" with guitarist Kim Mitchell for the Kumbaya Festival at Toronto's Ontario Place

Year. When asked to explain the group's formula for success, Jimmy's answer was short and simple. "We keep our traditional side quite pure," he said.

Within a year, despite sales of more than one million for those recordings, and constant touring of North America and Europe, Jimmy and the group were restless. Unhappy with their image as quaint purveyors of traditional Celtic song, the Rankins sought the help of Nashville producer John Jennings, best known for his work in transforming Mary Chapin Carpenter from folksinger to country-pop star, for their fourth release, 1995's *Endless Seasons*. While still steeped in Celtic sounds, the album boasted a livelier, looser feel than their previous releases. It included Jimmy's boisterous country tune "You Feel the Same Way Too." With Jimmy singing "*We may drink too much, we may lose our fancy touch*," it sounded like just the tonic the group needed.

The following year, EMI Music Canada released *Collection*, a 13-track compilation that featured such early Rankin classics as "Orangedale Whistle" and such recent material as "Grey Dusk of Eve (Portobello)," a traditional Scottish Gaelic boat song sung as a duet between Cookie and Liam O'Maonlai of the popular Irish band Hothouse Flowers. By this time the label, inspired by the Rankins' success, had signed numerous East Coast acts, including Ron Hynes, Bruce Guthro, Kim Stockwood and Damhnait Doyle, and struck a distribution deal with Duckworth/Atlantica.

The Rankins' shift toward a country-pop sound continued in '97 with the album *Do You Hear...*, which won them another Juno Award for Country Group or Duo of the year. Their next recording, *Uprooted*, was produced by Grammy Award–winner George Massenberg and stretched the Rankins' definition of Celtic sounds.

Canada's finest Celtic outfit was evolving as a result of its exposure to other types of music, from its constant travelling, touring and playing with other people. By September 1999 the Rankins announced that they were going to pursue independent careers and interests. Jimmy began work on a solo record, Cookie continued songwriting and recording projects, Heather appeared in the 1998 movie *The Hanging Garden* and John Morris was planning to freelance as a multi-instrumentalist and composer before his tragic death in January 2000. The Rankins will remain artistic forces for many years to come.

ROBBIE ROBERTSON

CAPITOL

1993

Having led The Band into rock 'n' roll history on Capitol Records in the 1960s, Toronto-born Robbie Robertson returned to the label in the '90s with a pair of powerful solo albums. Rather than draw from the American South for his material, Robertson looked to his heritage as a Mohawk whose mother was raised on the Six Nations Reserve near Brantford, Ontario. It was on that reserve, where he spent summers as a teenager, that he was first taught how to play guitar. "It was [also] my first contact with spiritual people who had this connection with Mother Earth," said Robertson. "They could sniff the air and say it would rain in four hours. It was astonishing to me."

For Robertson, it took a long time to get back to those roots. After The Band gave its farewell concert, captured in the 1978 Martin Scorsese movie *The Last Waltz*, Robertson ventured into the world of film. Collaborating with Scorsese, he worked on the soundtracks for such movies as *Carny* and *Raging Bull*. It was while living in Santa Monica, with his wife and three teenage children, that Robertson first began exploring his connection to native culture.

Robertson used his native voice with the 1987 release of his eponymous solo debut. Released on Geffen Records, the album offered such

native-inspired tracks as "Showdown at Big Sky," "Hell's Half Acre" and "Broken Arrow." The latter, featuring the sound of native drums, spoke of a spiritual quest in the best tradition of The Band. The following year, Robertson reunited with The Band at the Juno Awards, where the group was inducted into the Canadian Music Hall of Fame. His next album, 1991's *Storyville*, seemed less explicitly focused on native themes, and its songs were primarily set in New Orleans, where the album was also recorded. Yet Robertson featured members of The Wild Magnolias and The Golden Eagles, two of the most prominent tribes of New Orleans Indian musicians.

Commissioned to produce a soundtrack for *The Native Americans*, a six-hour documentary television series, Robertson immersed himself in aboriginal music two years later. The resulting album, *Music for the Native Americans*, involved writing and collaborating with such First Nations artists as Kashtin, sisters Rita and Priscilla Coolidge, The Silver

Accepting his Toronto Music Award in 1991: a local legend returns home

Cloud Singers, Douglas Spotted Eagle, Ulali and a group Robertson called The Red Road Ensemble. With its Canadian release on EMI Music Canada in 1994—the same year The Band was inducted into the Rock and Roll Hall of Fame—the album enjoyed sales of more than 75,000 copies with little or no video or radio airplay.

Where that album was relatively conservative in its sounds, Robertson's next album was positively experimental. Blending native chants, raw guitar riffs and a set of diverse electronic textures created by such DJ-mixers as Howie B and Marius de Vries, 1998's *Contact from the Underworld of Redboy* stretched the boundaries of native music. "Native traditions meet ambient techno," proclaimed *The Record* in a feature on the album. On the one hand, it featured the gorgeous, otherworldly sounds of singers Primeaux and Mike, peyote healers from the controversial Native American Church. "Making a Noise," on the other, included Robertson's spoken verse over moody dance rhythms.

One of the highlights of the album, which won the Juno Award for Best Music of Aboriginal Canada Recording in 1999, was "Stomp Dance." Robertson described the track and its personal significance in the publicity material accompanying the album. "It's a unity song that The Six Nations Women Singers performed for me at the conclusion of my return visit to the reserve," explained Robertson, "combined with a song I wrote about what it felt like going back to where it all started for me."

With First Nations performers: stretching the boundaries of native music

THE TEA PARTY

EMI CANADA

1993

"The only way something like rock music can go forward," Jeff Martin once ventured, "is by interpreting other cultures." Over the course of four albums, Martin and his Tea Party partners Jeff Burrows and Stuart Chatwood have done exactly that—push the limits of rock 'n' roll in the '90s while exploring global sounds from North Africa, the Middle East, South Asia and all points in between. "We perceive ourselves as citizens of the world," Burrows added. "With the advent of the global village, it was only a matter of time before someone would try to bridge gaps that exist between personal taste and personal expression in a musical sense. That's one of our goals."

The concept was forged one night in 1990, after a marathon jam at the Cherry Beach Rehearsal Rooms on Toronto's waterfront. Martin, Burrows and Chatwood had all played together in a variety of bands while growing up in Windsor, Ontario. Singer-guitarist Martin, son of a local blues musician, was fed a steady diet of blues, like B. B. King and Elmore James. His education soon extended into the English folk of Bert Jansch, Roy Harper and John Renbourn and the wide-ranging field of world music. By the time Martin teamed up with bassist Chatwood and drummer Burrows, they all shared a common musical vision: to mix acoustic and Middle Eastern influences with straight-ahead rock and blues for a heavy, groove-oriented vibe.

Courted by several record labels, The Tea Party ultimately chose EMI Music Canada in early '93 because, according to Chatwood, "they gave us artistic control when others wouldn't." The label's confidence in the group was rewarded when its debut album, *Splendor Solis*, quickly went gold on the strength of its first single, "The River." The album eventually sold more than 160,000 copies, as the band worked like road warriors to promote it, playing 374 shows in 134 cities in 10 countries between 1993–94. The group took a unique approach in establishing itself around the world: creating a buzz in select markets by playing club dates, then returning to perform at larger, often sold-out venues. In this way, The Tea Party eventually gained release in more than 20 countries. The only negative was the constant critical refrain that Martin resembled The Doors'

The Tea Party: exploring global sounds from North Africa, the Middle East, South Asia and all points in between

Jim Morrison vocally and physically and that his band sounded like Led Zeppelin. No wonder "retro" became, for The Tea Party, a dirty word. Those comparisons didn't completely die with *The Edges of Twilight*, the group's 1995 album, but by then, critics could hardly deny that The Tea Party had found a large audience for its sound. Fuelled by several hit singles, including "Fire in the Head" and "Sister Awake," the album, co-produced by Martin and Ed Stasium (The Ramones, Living Colour) quickly passed the platinum mark of 100,000 in sales. Listeners seemed entranced as much by Martin's intense vocals and mystical lyrics as by the group's growing musical palette. *Edges* employed 31 different stringed and percussive instruments, including sitar, sarod, santoor, djembe, dumbek and hurdy-gurdy. "We felt going beyond the standard guitar, bass and drums was key," says Chatwood. "The instruments brought with them a new way of seeing and expressing how we felt."

In 1996, EMI released a six-song, multimedia-enhanced CD that also featured full-length videos, acoustic performances and interviews. To promote the release, the group undertook a club tour, setting up computers in the rooms to allow fans to view the CD's multimedia track.

With the industrial crunch of the following year's *Transmission*, all the comparisons were gone as The Tea Party won over new fans and critics alike. Featuring the hit singles "Temptation," "Release" and "Babylon," it became the band's biggest-selling album to date, entering the album charts at #4 and hitting the double-platinum mark. The band continued to tour extensively, joining that year's Edgefest lineup and headlining the same festival in '98, which included playing to 41,000 people in Barrie, Ontario.

Maintaining its momentum as one of Canada's most popular rock acts, The Tea Party released its fourth major-label album, *TRIPtych*, in 1999. A potent mix of accessible tracks that seemed guaranteed to widen the band's audience while satisfying the group's long-standing fans, the album included the hit single "Heaven Coming Down." But anyone who thought the band had abandoned its love of global grooves only needed to check out tracks like "Samsara" and "The Halcyon Days." Utilizing such exotic instruments as the esraj and the oud, those songs helped to keep The Tea Party in the forefront of rock's global village.

GARTH BROOKS

CAPITOL
1988

When Garth Brooks came to Canada in the fall of 1991, the singer had already made music history for having the first album to enter both *Billboard*'s country and pop charts at number one. That album, *Ropin' the Wind*, had knocked heavy hitters Guns N' Roses and Metallica out of the top spot on the *Billboard* album chart. Combined with his other two albums, it brought the singer's worldwide sales to close to 10 million. Brooks was a country-music phenomenon, and Capitol Canada intended to treat him accordingly. Prior to Brooks's concert at Toronto's Maple Leaf Gardens, the label lined up an afternoon press conference at the hockey shrine that included a declaration by the mayor welcoming him to the city and a meet-and-greet with media and fans.

But all did not go as planned. Brooks had been unavoidably delayed leaving his hotel. Then, while the mayor and the press were in the Gardens' Hot Stove

Country music superstar gets the Royal Canadian treatment

Lounge waiting, a tour bus—not the easiest thing to steer through city streets—arrived and parked behind the arena. As *The Record* reported, "Brooks had driven it over himself with no more thought than if it

was a rented car. Those that know Brooks would just shrug and tell you, 'That's just the way he is.'" And the way he was when he arrived at the lounge made up for his lateness. According to Roger Bartel, of Capitol Canada's promotion and marketing team, "[Brooks] spent about an hour and a half in that room meeting every single person, signing every single autograph and kissing every single baby." Added Bartel: "I've never worked with an artist who spent so much time making sure that everybody that came to see him got what they needed. He had his picture taken with everybody."

The common touch came naturally to Garth. Born in 1962 to Ray Brooks, a working-class draftsman and his wife, Colleen Carroll, a former Capitol Records artist, he grew up in a supportive family and developed a love of both music and sports. Although he attended Oklahoma State University on a track scholarship, as soon as he graduated he set off for Nashville in 1985 with guitar in hand. After less than a day in Music City, however, Brooks returned home discouraged and disillusioned. His mother convinced him to go back and try again. When he did, Brooks caught the attention of Capitol Nashville, who signed him in 1988. Later, the singer credited his mother for her sage advice. "I feel like I'm pickin' up a baton for Mom," Brooks told Nashville writer Robert K. Oermann, "because she was on Capitol Records, and I feel like I'm part of the reason she gave it up."

Brooks's race up the charts began with his 1989 self-titled debut album, which peaked at #2 on the country album charts and produced four Top 10 country singles: "Much Too Young (To Feel This Damn Old)," "If Tomorrow Never Comes," "Not Counting On You" and "The Dance." By the time Brooks came to Toronto

Filling EMI Canada's warehouse with awards, fans and at least three Santas

two years later, Capitol Canada was presenting him with a double-platinum award for his second album, *No Fences*, and a platinum for his latest, *Ropin' the Wind*. In accepting the awards, the singer cited his fans, retail, radio and the record company for his success. "It's just one happy family," Brooks said, "and without any key element of this family, this whole thing wouldn't work."

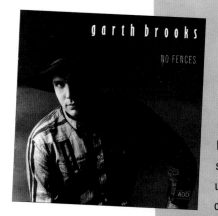

A sensitive songwriter and an explosive performer, Brooks possessed all the ingredients to become a major music star. His socially conscious lyrics, particularly, set him apart from the countless other "hat acts" that were coming out of Nashville at the time. Brooks bravely portrayed the reality of domestic violence in "The Thunder Rolls" (from *No Fences*) and defended homosexuals in "We Shall Be Free" (from his fifth album, *The Chase*). "I pride myself in doing songs about real life," he said. "Sometimes real life is sad, sometimes it's pretty funny. I like to keep people guessing." By the end of '92, Brooks had become the first artist in 25 years to have three albums simultaneously on the *Billboard* Top 15. The last act to do that had been The Beatles.

The following year, while touring in support of his album *In Pieces*,

Jetting across Canada with CTV's Wei Chen

Celebrating backstage with EMI staffers, September 1996: breaking box office records across Canada

Brooks broke numerous box office records. In western Canada, his shows at the Vancouver Pacific Coliseum and Calgary's Olympic Saddledome became the fastest-selling, same-day, multi-city sellouts for Ticketmaster Canada. In Saskatoon, the high demand even blew a fuse in the city's phone system. Brooks's chart domination continued through the rest of the '90s, with such hit singles as "Standing Outside the Fire" and "One Night a Day." In 1998, he returned to Canada and flew across the country aboard a private jet to promote his latest album, *Sevens*—all in a single day. Brooks visited Toronto, Winnipeg and Calgary, all topped off in Vancouver with a live CMT special.

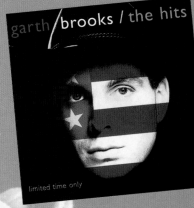

The man who took country music into the mainstream saved his most intriguing release until the following year. *In the Life of Chris Gaines* appeared to be the soundtrack for a future film titled *The Lamb*, about a wildly eccentric pop superstar from the '80s and '90s named Chris Gaines—with songs by that character. But Gaines turned out to be Brooks, who wrote and performed all 12 songs in a variety of styles including folk, country, funk and what Brooks described as "Prince meets Aerosmith." "If I ever get to do movies," Brooks once said, "I'd like to play somebody who is just totally nuts." With *Chris Gaines*, he got his wish.

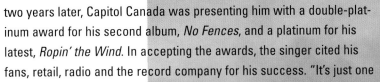

JOHNNY CLEGG & SAVUKA

CAPITOL
1987

Three years before Paul Simon brought South African music into pop's mainstream with *Graceland*, Johnny Clegg was already charting similar waters with Juluka, a racially mixed group from Johannesburg. With its blend of Zulu chants and English style folk-rock, Juluka won a faithful western audience. But it died when Clegg's Zulu partner Sipho Mchunu left in 1985. Two years later, Clegg resurfaced with a new band, Savuka, and new recording deal with Capitol-EMI. Shifting to a more electric, rock-oriented format, while still retaining its Zulu roots, Clegg and Savuka became one of the most potent forces in world music in the late '80s and early '90s. Along with recording four first-rate albums for the label, the group performed a now-legendary concert at the Montreal Jazz Festival that had 50,000 delirious fans dancing in the streets.

A unique product of his cross-cultural roots, Clegg was born in England but raised in his mother's native land of Zimbabwe before emigrating to South Africa at the age of six. His mother was a cabaret singer, while his stepfather was a journalist with a passion for kwela music and a hatred of apartheid. Clegg, who learned to speak the Bantu language Ndebele before he could speak English, began to play guitar at 14 after moving to South Africa. His teacher was a Zulu cleaner who played street music near Clegg's home. For two years, he learned the fundamentals of Zulu music and traditional dancing at hostels and shebeens. But his involvement with black people was frowned upon by law, and Clegg was arrested for entering black areas without the necessary permits.

Still, Clegg pursued his love of Zulu culture and developed a reputation in the competitive street music scene. Word of his talent reached Mchunu, a migrant Zulu worker and musician, who challenged Clegg to a guitar competition, sparking off a friendship and musical partnership. Initially, the two performed as an acoustic act known as Johnny and Sipho, combining Zulu mbaqanga music with traditional Zulu inhlangwini dance steps. But, under apartheid's harsh gaze, they were subjected to racial abuse, threats of violence and police harassment. Meanwhile, Clegg, who had a bachelor's degree in social anthropology, pursued an academic career, lecturing at the University of Natal.

With Juluka, formed in 1979, Clegg and Mchunu fused English lyrics and western melodies with Zulu musical structures. A six-piece group, comprising three white and three black members, Juluka released seven albums in South Africa, several of which went gold and platinum there. In '82 and '83, Juluka toured the United States, Great Britain,

Germany, Scandinavia and Canada, where the group was signed to Warner Bros. and its single "Scatterlings of Africa" became a minor hit. With Savuka, which means "We have awakened," Clegg built on that success.

Savuka's debut album on EMI, *Third World Child*, achieved phenomenal worldwide success, selling more than two million copies. It featured two singles, a reworking of "Scatterlings" and "Asimbonanga (Mandela)," a moving tribute to the imprisoned South African leader Nelson Mandela that became a major hit despite being banned by South African radio. Savuka's follow-up album, *Shadow Man*, continued to reach wider audiences, as the group toured as the opening act for Steve Winwood in the United States and George Michael in Canada. Clegg also joined Bruce Springsteen, Sting, Peter Gabriel and Tracy Chapman for one of the Amnesty International concerts on the Ivory Coast.

While recording his third album with Savuka, Clegg found his schedule interrupted by his marriage to Jenny, in a traditional Zulu tribal wedding, and the assassination of his long-time friend and fellow critic of apartheid, David Webster. Several of the songs Clegg subsequently wrote and recorded, including the album's title track, "Cruel, Crazy Beautiful World," "One (Hu)man One Vote" and "Woman Be My Country," were linked to Webster's death. In 1992, Savuka's percussionist Dudu Zulu, with whom Clegg performed the acrobatic Zulu dances, was murdered during factional warfare between Zulu tribes. The following year, Clegg and Savuka recorded *Heat, Dust & Dreams*, which included "The Crossing," a tribute to the fallen band member.

In Canada, Clegg and Savuka will always be best remembered for the 1988 appearance at the Montreal Jazz Festival. The massive crowd, which filled the city's downtown streets for the group's hour-long set, came in all shapes, colours and sizes. As John Griffin wrote in the *Montreal Gazette*: "There were old people and young people, black, white, red, Oriental and all the colors in between. There were straights and gays, punks and preps; people who spoke French, people who spoke English and all the mother tongues on earth." For Clegg, who had always stood for racial unity, the concert was a dream come true.

MC HAMMER

CAPITOL
1988

"U Can't Touch This": hip hop's first superstar does his thing at Toronto's Skydome, 1990

With a number one pop album, a Saturday-morning cartoon show and a toy doll made in his likeness, rapper MC Hammer reigned supreme in the early '90s. While others, including L.L. Cool J, Run-D.M.C. and Jazzy Jeff & The Fresh Prince, had experienced mainstream acceptance, Hammer had clearly crossed over to become hip-hop's first superstar. He did this by striving to be viewed as an all-round entertainer, with a big band, a flamboyant wardrobe and elaborate, choreographed dance moves. "When people think of Hammer," he told writer David Nathan, "I want them to think of music. I want to change the narrow thinking that rap and rappers are one-dimensional."

Born Stanley Kirk Burrell in 1963, one of seven children in a poor family from Oakland, California, Hammer acquired that ambition while growing up in a drug- and crime-ridden neighbourhood. "We were definitely poor," he told *Maclean's* magazine in 1990. "Welfare. Government-aided apartment building. Three bedrooms and seven children living together at one time." After working as a bat boy for the Oakland Athletics baseball team, and after a short stint in the U.S. navy, Hammer (the Oakland A's Reggie Jackson gave him the nickname because of his resemblance to baseball star "Hammerin'" Hank Aaron) formed a religious-rap duo. With $40,000 invested by two Athletics players, he formed his own record company, Bust It Records. "Ring 'Em," the first single from his album *Feel My Power*, sold 50,000 copies—enough to attract the attention of Capitol Records.

Signing the rapper to a multi-album deal, Capitol released *Let's Get it Started*, which included re-recorded tracks from *Power* and several new cuts. That album, which eventually sold two million copies and won Hammer two American Music Awards, set the stage for his 1990 follow-up, *Please Hammer Don't Hurt 'Em*. Recorded on the back of his tour bus for less than $10,000, the album spawned three hit singles, "Have You Seen Her," "Pray" and the anthemic "U Can't Touch This," and held the #1 position on the *Billboard* pop album charts for 21 weeks. It sold 15 million copies worldwide, including nearly one million in Canada. By the time Hammer toured that summer, performing to 14,000 at Toronto's Skydome, he and his large entourage were travelling by private Boeing 727 jet.

The album sales and tour, which included stops in Europe, Japan, Australia and the Caribbean, helped Hammer become a household name. So, too, did the fall '91 launch of *Hammerman*, an

ABC-TV cartoon show that depicted an aspiring rap and dance star who transformed into a superhero, and the Hammer doll, which Mattel Inc. introduced to Barbie's "celebrity friend" line. The cartoon series and dolls opened up new marketing avenues for Capitol, including the ability to place Hammer's recordings next to the dolls in Toys "R" Us and Kmart outlets. And they helped to pave the way for Capitol's launch of the rapper's next album, *Too Legit to Quit*.

Capitol pulled out all the stops for the launch, committing $500,000 for a TV ad campaign that included cross-promotional tie-ins to the $20-million campaign behind the release of the movie *The Addams Family*. Hammer's presence in the Paramount Pictures release was substantial; he appeared in the pre-sell TV teasers and had four songs from his album, including the theme song, "Addams Groove," featured in the film. For the launch, Capitol Canada flew down president Deane Cameron, national promotions vice-president Peter Diemer, urban dance product manager Ron Robles, Ontario branch promotions representative Liz McElheran and artist relations manager Steve McAuley, who all attended a private party and took part in marketing meetings for the album's release.

Too Legit to Quit, which saw Hammer drop the "MC" from his name, expanded on the artist's musical vision. Gone was the sampling that had characterized his earlier work. In its place were original songs that spanned jazz hip-hop ("Good to Go"), dance ("Gaining Momentum," "This is the Way We Roll") and spiritual numbers ("Do Not Pass Me By"). Although the album sold a more-than-respectable three million copies worldwide, it was seen as a disappointment in the wake of its predecessor. Meanwhile, Hammer's success had provoked a backlash from other rappers, who publicly dissed his mainstream style and ostentatious attire that included billowy harem-style pants. In short, Hammer had peaked. But in his heyday he had managed to do what no other rapper had managed: take hip-hop to the masses.

JANET JACKSON

VIRGIN
1991

Getting "Intimate & Interactive" at MuchMusic: a pop-funk diva to be reckoned with

Growing up in the shadow of the self-proclaimed King of Pop could not have been easy. Nor, likely, was it a piece of cake being the baby in pop's most famous family. But somehow Janet Jackson found a way to assert her talent and forge an identity all her own. Although brother Michael was a bigger commercial phenomenon and sister LaToya could boast a more sensational profile, Janet, with her savvy dance-pop recordings and admirable message of social and sexual freedom, was easily the most respected of the nine Jackson siblings.

Jackson joined her older brothers and sisters on the stage at the tender age of seven, pushed by her overbearing father, Joseph. Still, she went on to land parts on the popular sitcoms *Diff'rent Strokes* and *Good Times*, after TV producers saw her perform with the entire family on a 1976 summer-replacement show on CBS. Signed to A&M in 1982, Jackson then released two mediocre albums: her self-titled debut and *Dream Street*. She took a bold step in marrying singer James DeBarge, of the rival DeBarge sibling act—much to her father's chagrin. Although the marriage was annulled less than a year later, "the seeds of Jackson's independence from the family dynasty" *Rolling Stone* said, "had been firmly planted."

Her breakthrough came in 1986 with *Control*. Produced by Jimmy Jam and Terry Lewis of The Time, the album bristled with infectious energy and a distinct, Prince-like funk sound that spawned several songs that topped both the pop and r&b charts, including "Nasty," "Let's Wait Awhile" and "What Have You Done For Me Lately." Jackson's ascendancy was boosted immeasurably by her distinctive videos, featuring heavily choreographed dance moves that rivalled those of brother Michael. The follow-up album, 1989's *Rhythm Nation 1814*, expressed more social themes. Yet it still managed to produce a number of genre-crossing hits and led to Janet's first major tour.

Proof that Janet had come of age—and become a pop-funk diva to be reckoned with—was her lucrative 1991 signing to Virgin Records. When her Virgin debut, *janet.*, was released two years later, it was apparent that Jackson's interests had shifted from the social to the sexual. As music journalist David Ritz accurately described it, *janet.* traced "a seamless pattern established by Marvin Gaye, who followed the socially conscious *What's Going On* with the erotic *Let's Get It On*."

The album also became Jackson's most successful project to date, with the seductive hits "That's the Way Love Goes," "If" and "Again." Canada quickly became the singer's strongest market in the world, with sales hitting the triple-platinum mark of 300,000 copies.

Ultimately, with *janet.*, Jackson had an album that produced more top-five singles than any other singer—including her brother Michael. Refreshingly competitive, Janet made it no secret that she'd love to break her brother's record of the best-selling album of all time, which he held for 1983's blockbuster *Thriller*. Although Janet failed to pull off that upset, there were no hard feelings. In fact, in 1995 she teamed up with Michael to sing the duet "Scream" for his double-CD retrospective *HIStory: Past, Present and Future*.

Jackson's examination of sexuality deepened with 1997's *The Velvet Rope*. Featuring songs about bondage, body piercing and bisexuality, the album was so explicit that the media labelled the entire collection S&M, a judgment that angered Jackson. "It's so much deeper than that," the singer told the *Toronto Sun*'s Jane Stevenson in September 1998. When pressed about the song "Rope Burn," however, Jackson did concede that she likes to experiment. "Okay, I'm not into bondage," she admitted to Stevenson. "That isn't sexy to me. But there are certain things that I just think are so incredible, and one of them is being blindfolded. Having your hands bound, anticipating your lover's every move, that to me is sexy. I'm getting goose bumps just thinking about it."

Jackson's astonishing candor was repeated a few days later when she appeared on MuchMusic in an "Intimate & Interactive" special. Interviewed by veejay Juliette Powell, before a largely teenage studio audience, Jackson confessed that she considers herself a sexual being. And she added that exploring one's desires—stressing the need to practice safe sex—is a healthy part of growing up. With *The Velvet Rope*, the 34-year-old Jackson had clearly grown up to become a mature and highly accomplished artist.

RADIOHEAD

PARLOPHONE

1991

Yorke, in full tortured scarecrow mode

Few albums have garnered the widespread critical acclaim of Radiohead's *OK Computer*. Released in 1997, the dark, sprawling collection of songs about technology and alienation made every Top 10 list that year. The respected British music magazine *Q* even went so far as to name it "the best album ever recorded." And, largely on the strength of the surreal, cinematic recording, Radiohead—once dubbed "the new U2" but more often a "Pink Floyd for the '90s" and "the future of rock 'n' roll"—was named band of the year by both *Spin* and *Rolling Stone*, which hailed the album as "an art-rock tour de force." Not bad for a group that four years earlier was written off as a one-hit wonder for its angst-ridden, self-loathing single "Creep."

Formed in 1988 by five Oxford University students, the group initially called itself On a Friday until its members—singer Thom Yorke, guitarists Ed O'Brien and Jonny Greenwood, bassist Colin Greenwood and drummer Phil Selway—settled on Radiohead for a name. Not long after releasing an independent EP titled *Drill*, the group signed with EMI's Parlophone label. Its debut album, *Pablo Honey*, gained some attention, largely on the strength of "Creep," which became a slacker anthem to rival Beck's "Loser." On the back of the single's success, Radiohead toured the U.S., opening for the likes of Belly and Tears for Fears. As the single grew to become a Top 10 hit, the group found itself, in 1994, on an extensive world tour.

All smiles, no paranoid androids among them

Sensitive to the criticisms that it was only capable of a lone hit, Radiohead enlisted the services of producer John Leckie to record their follow-up album, *The Bends*. Released in 1995, the album was a more ambitious affair that drew on Yorke's choirboy vocals and introspective, tortured lyrics. Nothing on it resembled "Creep." According to guitarist Ed O'Brien, that was deliberate. "There was a lot of serendipity involved [in a hit single]," he told the *Toronto Sun*. "It kind of captured the mood of the times or whatever. But the last thing we want is to be formulaic." Critics lauded the album for the group's deeper, more mature sound, and Radiohead began moving into the forefront of the Brit-pop movement, alongside Oasis and EMI labelmates Blur and Supergrass. But in North America, at least, the band still had to settle for a cult

following, opening for R.E.M. on its *Monster* tour and winning such celebrity fans as Madonna, Courtney Love and Marilyn Manson. In 1996, while opening for Canada's Alanis Morissette (who covered *The Bends*' "Fake Plastic Trees" early in her own tour), Yorke and company began writing and working out material that would eventually appear on *OK Computer*. When it came time to record, the band retreated to the English countryside and rented actress Jane Seymour's house outside Bath. There, in that rather bucolic setting, Radiohead's dark vision of a post-industrial wasteland devoid of spirituality began to take shape. Some of the inspiration for the album came directly from cyberspace, as the band's members surfed various Radiohead-related Web sites and discussion groups and found lyrics for the album that hadn't even been recorded yet. According to guitarist Jonny Greenwood, fans had taken bootleg recordings of the band and written down what they thought Yorke was singing. Laughed Greenwood: "If Thom was ever stuck for lyrics, he'd occasionally go to these sites and steal all this kind of garbled, mistranslated singing he was doing."

OK Computer was released in June 1997, featuring the first single "Paranoid Android." That month, the band played at Toronto's Opera House, where tickets sold out in an astonishing 46 seconds. The group returned in August for a full Canadian tour, performing other subsequent hits from the album, including "Karma Police" and "Subterranean Homesick Alien." During an interview with the *Ottawa Sun*, drummer Phil Selway admitted that EMI's reaction to the album was initially lukewarm. "Their first reaction was more or less 'commercial suicide,'" he said. But he credited the label's support, which included an unorthodox advertising campaign featuring full-page ads with Yorke's cryptic lyrics printed on a blank background, with helping to break the album commercially.

The album eventually sold more than four million copies worldwide, and went double platinum in Canada, where the band had long enjoyed a strong following, with sales of 200,000. Although *OK Computer* lost out in the '98 Grammy Awards' Best Album category to Bob Dylan's *Time Out of Mind*, it still managed to win Radiohead an award for Best Alternative Performance. In the spring of '99, Radiohead continued breaking new ground when it issued *Meeting People is Easy*, a behind-the-scenes tour video that marked EMI's first venture into simultaneous VHS and DVD release.

BONNIE RAITT

CAPITOL

1989

Bonnie Raitt hit rock bottom around 1986. Dropped by Warner Bros., and suffering from a serious alcohol and drug habit developed after years on the road, the red-headed singer-guitarist reached a turning point after injuring her hand in a skiing accident and using the time off to reassess her life. "I remember thinking to myself," Raitt told Los Angeles writer Kristine McKenna, "'I'm 37 years old and I don't have a relationship with someone I love. I don't have a record company that believes in my work, and radio isn't interested in my music.' It was pretty depressing."

Raitt kicked the bottle, gave up drugs and landed a new deal with Capitol Records. After two decades of critically acclaimed albums, Raitt's Capitol debut, the aptly titled *Nick of Time*, finally proved to be her commercial breakthrough. The album topped the charts, sold four million copies worldwide and won a Grammy Award for Album of the Year—one of four won by a visibly overwhelmed Raitt at the 1990 gala. As she told McKenna: "What got me through it was the fact that I really love my job. I feel so lucky to get to do this and the thrill has never worn off. I guess I got it in my blood from my dad."

The daughter of Broadway musical star John Raitt was born in Los Angeles in 1949 and started playing guitar at age 12. Although she moved to Boston in 1967 to attend Radcliffe College, she dropped out after two years to pursue her deep love of blues music. Within a short time, she developed a following in the area's clubs and coffeehouses and was regularly performing with the likes of Howlin' Wolf, Mississippi Fred McDowell and other blues legends. After signing with Warner Bros. in 1970, Raitt enjoyed a long string of rave reviews and minor hits with a career built around her fluid voice, soulful guitar playing (including a formidable bottleneck technique) and clever choice of material.

Raitt's career was also marked by a political consciousness resulting from her Quaker upbringing. She was a founder of M.U.S.E. (Musicians United for Safe Energy), which held a large anti-nuke benefit concert at New York's Madison Square Garden in 1979, featuring such artists as Jackson Browne, James Taylor and The Doobie Brothers, and led to a popular three-album set. Raitt also later co-founded the Rhythm and Blues Foundation, dedicated to raising money for musical pioneers—many of them her blues heroes—left impoverished by bad record deals and no health insurance.

Onstage in Toronto, 1991: giving audiences something to talk about

After being abruptly dropped by Warner Bros. in 1983, Raitt nearly went broke herself as she struggled to keep her band on the road. Her luck changed when several executives who had worked with her at Warners resurfaced at Capitol and promptly signed her. With a new lease on life, not to mention her new-found sobriety, Raitt went from strength to strength. The Don Was–produced *Nick of Time* featured a potent cover of John Hiatt's "Thing Called Love," the reggae-flavoured "Have a Heart" and two Raitt originals: the title track, about the passage of time symbolized by the female biological clock, and "The Road's My Middle Name." Her Was-produced follow-up album, 1991's *Luck of the Draw*, repeated the pattern of its predecessor, selling more than four million copies and winning Raitt three more Grammys.

One of the best things about *Luck of the Draw* was the single "Something To Talk About." Written by Canada's Shirley Eikhard—herself a former Capitol artist whose songs had been covered by the likes of Anne Murray, Emmylou Harris and The Pointer Sisters—the buoyant single hit #2 on the *Billboard* chart, became the title track for a movie starring Julia Roberts as well as the theme song for a TV show. (Along with Raitt's success with it, "Something To Talk About" also did wonders for Eikhard's career. With her considerable earnings from the song, Eikhard was able to finance the album of her dreams. Titled *Going Home*, a collection of 12 original jazz songs, the album brought the Sackville, New Brunswick, native back into the Capitol-EMI family when it was released in 1998 on the prestigious Blue Note label.)

Raitt's winning ways continued with two other strong releases for Capitol-EMI. In 1994, she and Was co-produced the platinum-selling *Longing in Their Hearts*, a collection of originals and covers, including a stunning version of Richard Thompson's "Dimming of the Day." Then in 1998, working with Mitchell Froom and Tchad Blake, Raitt produced *Fundamental*, which featured her version of bluesman Willie Dixon's "Round and Round" and Raitt's own "One Belief Away," written with Irish songwriters Dillon O'Brian and Paul Brady.

Raitt's unwavering love of music had conquered her demons; her signing to Capitol-EMI led to her triumph.

SMASHING PUMPKINS

VIRGIN

1991

Iha, Wretzky, Corgan and Chamberlain: mixing dreamy pop with harder edged sounds to become leaders of the post-Nirvana, alt-rock era

The rise of Chicago's Smashing Pumpkins mirrored the mainstream success that alternative rock enjoyed generally throughout much of the 1990s.

Singer-guitarist Billy Corgan got his musical start in Florida after moving there at the age of 19 with his goth-metal band The Marked. The group failed to catch on and Corgan moved back home to Chicago, where he began working in a used-record shop. There, he met graphic arts student James Iha and the two began collaborating on guitars with the backing of a drum machine. When bassist D'arcy Wretzky joined them in 1989, they christened themselves Smashing Pumpkins and began developing a guitar-driven sound that was more melodic and polished than that of its grunge counterparts. The turning point came when a club owner booked them to open for Jane's Addiction. On the eve of that crucial show, they hired Jimmy Chamberlain as the group's full-time drummer.

After recording several successful independent singles, the Pumpkins found themselves in a major-label bidding war. Cognizant of the risk of losing indie credibility, Corgan and company signed with Virgin Records, which offered them an alternative outlet through its Caroline subsidiary label. The strategy worked: the group's debut album, *Gish*, became a hit at college radio after its release in the spring of '91. With its mix of hard rock and dreamy pop, the album went on to gold-level U.S. sales of 500,000 copies. But it wasn't until the Pumpkins switched over to Virgin for their second album, 1993's *Siamese Dream*, that the band experienced a mainstream breakthrough. Led by the singles "Cherub Rock," "Today" and "Disarm," *Siamese Dream* became one of the top-selling albums of the mid-90s. The Pumpkins became headliners on the Lollapalooza tour in 1994, during which the band also released its

Braving the elements on MuchMusic's outdoor stage, 1998

B-sides and rarities collection, *Pisces Iscariot*.

With 1995's ambitious double album, *Mellon Collie and the Infinite Sadness*, Canada became the Pumpkins' most significant market. It was the first territory in the world where *Mellon Collie* was certified double platinum, selling 200,000 units in just two months. It came as no surprise when the band announced it would be staging a mini-tour in early '96 and Toronto was chosen as the launching point, with two shows at the Phoenix Theatre. *Mellon Collie* had a little bit of everything, from folk and psychedelia to metal and orchestral pop. The sprawling collection eventually achieved diamond status (for sales of one million copies) in Canada alone. The Pumpkins returned to Canada for a stadium tour later that year, by which time the group had lost its touring keyboardist Jonathan Melvoin, who died of an overdose while taking heroin with Chamberlain. The band subsequently fired Chamberlain and recruited a replacement for the remainder of the tour.

The Pumpkins returned to Canada in 1998. After releasing *Adore*, a kinder, gentler album that year, the group appeared at MuchMusic headquarters in Toronto for the station's first outdoor "Intimate & Interactive" special. Just a few hours before the Pumpkins were to perform, Toronto was hit with an extreme weather warning. A second, indoor stage, complete with all the necessary equipment, had to be hastily assembled as backup. By showtime, lightning, rain and 80 kilometre winds had indeed forced the Pumpkins inside. But, with a crowd of 6,000 gathered in the station's parking lot and surrounding streets, the band moved back outside as soon as weather permitted—to resounding cheers.

The group's Canadian connection continued the very next evening when the Pumpkins performed a special charity event at Toronto's Massey Hall. After the show, the band donated all of the proceeds from its sold-out concert to Street Outreach Services, a local organization set up to help troubled youth, especially those involved in prostitution.

Late in 1999, Smashing Pumpkins received an injection of CanCon, as Montreal-born Melissa Auf der Maur, formerly of the band Hole, replaced Wretzky as the group's bassist.

THE ROLLING STONES

VIRGIN

1991

Virgin Records founder Richard Branson remembers well the mixed emotions he felt in 1991 on signing the world's greatest rock 'n' roll band. On the one hand, he was euphoric. "Signing The Rolling Stones was the culmination of everything I had ever wanted to do at Virgin Music," he later wrote in his autobiography, *Losing My Virginity*. "We had been fighting to sign them for twenty years and now at last we had [them]." On the other, having just paid a princely sum for the veteran rockers' contract, Branson was more than a little worried when his 10-year-old daughter asked who they were. "Are they some kind of pop group?" she inquired. "For a moment," he recalled, "I wondered whether I had made a ghastly mistake."

As it turned out, the signing proved to be a stroke of brilliance. Although Branson sold Virgin to EMI before The Rolling Stones released their debut album on the label in 1994, the Virgin deal seemed to breathe new life into the band. *Voodoo Lounge* was widely hailed as the Stones' best recording since the 1970s. It was, Mick Jagger told *Maclean's*, his group's attempt to make "a more human record" by moving away from "the slick sound of the Eighties." To achieve this, producer Don Was recorded the tracks more directly, with fewer overdubs. Filled with exuberant, *Some Girls*–style rockers like "Sparks Will Fly" and "You Got Me Rocking" and such vintage-Stones balladry as "Out of Tears," *Voodoo Lounge* sold an impressive five million copies worldwide—including triple platinum–level sales of 300,000 copies in Canada alone.

Canada, in fact, loomed large in the life of the Stones throughout the '90s. Canadian concert promoter Michael Cohl, who had been behind the group's comeback tours in 1989 and '90, brought Jagger, Keith Richards, Charlie Watts and Ron Wood to Toronto for six weeks in the summer of '94. Working out of Crescent School, a private boys school in North Toronto, the Stones held daily rehearsals for their ambitious *Voodoo Lounge* tour. *The Toronto Star* set up a "Stones watch" to track the numerous sightings of band members in parks, stores and restaurants around town.

By the time the group gave a surprise concert at RPM, a downtown nightclub, on July 19—their first Toronto club date since the infamous El Mocambo gig attended by Margaret Trudeau in 1977—the city was abuzz with Stones hysteria. Bill Banham had just been hired the day before as Virgin Music Canada's director of national promotion. As luck would have it, he got to be one of the 1,100 fortunate souls who witnessed the now-historic RPM gig. "The energy inside the club was absolutely amazing—a total sweatbox," recalls Banham, now the label's vice-president and general manager. "And the band put on a fabulous show, ripping through both early and more recent stuff. I'll never forget that night as long as I live."

After releasing 1995's *Stripped*, a live acoustic souvenir of the tour featuring such classics as "Angie," "Wild Horses" and "Street Fighting Man," the Stones returned in '97 with another studio album of new material, *Bridges to Babylon*.

Watts, Wood, Jagger and Richards: the world's greatest—and oldest—rock 'n' roll band shows no signs of letting up

And when it came time to stage the accompanying world tour, the band once again chose Toronto as its home base. This time, the group used the Masonic Temple as its rehearsal space. When the *Toronto Sun*'s Jane Stevenson asked what the city meant to him, Richards—recalling his 1977 heroin bust there, the subsequent court case and benefit concert for the blind—answered: "It's a good town. The people are always great to us. They're used to us being in and out, and after all, my own relationship with the town is kind of special, anyway. People were always real cool with me, no matter what was going on inside the courthouse. So for me, hey, I've got a warm spot."

And, proving their fondness for the city, the Stones once again treated hard-core fans in Toronto to another surprise club show. On September 4, the band delivered a thrilling 70-minute set at the Horseshoe Tavern, performing everything from an opening cover of Chuck Berry's "Little Queenie" to the brand-new "Out of Control," from *Bridges to Babylon*. The Stones toured Canada in both '97 and '98 and played one last, triumphant date in early '99 at Toronto's new Air Canada Centre. At the dimming of the millennium, the world's greatest—and oldest—rock 'n' roll band still showed no signs of letting up.

THE SPICE GIRLS

VIRGIN

1995

Chisholm (Sporty), Bunton (Baby), Addams (Posh), Brown (Scary) and Halliwell (Ginger): defying the odds and their critics

Girl power. They proved they had it by becoming the first all-female band in England to enter the charts with a debut single in the top position. One-hit wonders. They showed that they weren't by repeating the feat with their second single. Staying power. They proved they had that, too, even after one of the group's members went solo. In fact, every step of the way along their highly celebrated careers, The Spice Girls defied the odds and their critics. With their infectious brand of dance-pop and their playful image as flirtatious feminists, they became the pop music phenomenon of the '90s. What male band could boast, as they did, that they'd sold 30 million albums—and pinched Prince Charles's bottom in the process?

Massive success often breeds critical backlash. In the case of The Spice Girls, there was also skepticism about their talent because of the manufactured nature of the group. In March 1993, an advertisement ran in a British entertainment trade magazine seeking five "lively girls." It began: "R.U. 18–23 with the ability to sing/dance? R.U. streetwise, outgoing, ambitious and dedicated?" The successful candidates—Geri Halliwell, Melanie Brown, Victoria Addams, Melanie Chisholm and Emma Bunton—initially became Touch. Their managers, who had

Onstage at MuchMusic: flirtatious feminists with an infectious brand of dance-pop

placed the ad, put them up in a house outside London and provided them with generic songs and matching costumes. In October, after changing their name to The Spice Girls, the five young women walked out, paying off the managers' expenses with a loan. They spent more than a year writing, recording and dancing before signing with Annie Lennox's manager, Simon Fuller, in March 1995. Seven months later, The Spice Girls landed a lucrative deal with Virgin Records.

From the outset, image was a key element in the group's success. Each member took on a distinctive name and personality: Halliwell became Ginger Spice, the sexy one; Brown, with her pierced tongue, was Scary Spice; Addams became Posh Spice, because of her wealthy background; the athletic Chisholm was obviously Sporty Spice; and Bunton, who often wore her blond hair in bunches, was christened Baby Spice. Oddly enough, neither Fuller nor the girls themselves came up with the names. They were invented by a British teen magazine

called *Top of the Pops*. Almost immediately, The Spice Girls began garnering regular coverage in the British music and tabloid press.

"Wannabe," the group's first single, was released in the summer of '96 and spent seven weeks at number one in England (in fact, the foursome went on to score ten consecutive number one singles in the U.K.). By the end of the year, it was number one in 21 other countries, including Canada. The debut album, *Spice*, which came out in Canada in early '97, featured another number one single, "Say You'll Be There," and such tracks as "2 Become 1," "Mama" and "Naked" (ultimately, the group landed ten consecutive singles in the Top 5 in Canada).

By the fall, The Spice Girls had made one North American promotional trip, including a stop at Canada's MuchMusic, but had still not toured. Concerts would have to wait until after the film *Spice World*, and the debut album, *Spice*, hit the market in November and January '98, respectively. The album, featuring such Latin-flavoured tunes as the first single, "Spice Up Your Life," and the ballad "Viva Forever," quickly shot up the charts. And the movie, which billed itself as a Spicy version of The Beatles' *A Hard Day's Night* and Rob Reiner's mocumentary *This is Spinal Tap*, did boffo box office.

When Ginger announced in June, on the eve of the group's first North American tour, that she was trading in her push-up bras and platform sneakers for a solo career, little girls everywhere wept buckets. To no avail. When The Spice Girls kicked off their 40-city tour on June 14, the formerly fab five were a foursome. Still, the Montreal show, which opened with the *Star Trek*–borrowed announcement "Spice, the final frontier—they will boldly go where no woman has gone before," was a screaming success. So, too, were sold-out shows in Toronto and Vancouver.

When Virgin Canada's vice-president Bill Banham and his staff lined up an "Intimate & Interactive" appearance at MuchMusic for the four Spices, an estimated crowd of 5,000 lined the streets surrounding the TV station to try to catch a glimpse of their heroes. A smaller, but nonetheless devoted, crowd gathered at the station in the spring of '99 when ex-Spice Geri Halliwell came through to promote her solo debut album on EMI, *Schizophonic*. Even in the aftermath of the split, it seemed, girl power was alive and well.

Canadian Affiliate Labels

ALERT

Alert Records came together in 1984, when Toronto's Tom Berry and Montreal's Marc Durant joined forces to form a new Canadian independent label. Berry had been with Anthem Records, while Durant had managed the band Men Without Hats. For its first five years, PolyGram distributed Alert. But from 1990–97, after Berry became the sole owner of the label, Alert moved over to EMI Music Canada.

Beginning with The Box, Alert and EMI released the Montreal-based band's fourth album, *The Pleasure and the Pain*, featuring the single "Carry On." The partnership also handled *I Am a Wild Party*, the 1990 live album by Kim Mitchell, who *The Record* called "Canada's own Thin White Dude" in its four-star review of the recording. Mitchell's solo career soared from then on, touring incessantly and releasing his sixth album, *Aural Fixations*, in 1992.

The real jewel in Alert's crown in the '90s was Holly Cole. Starting with her debut album, *Girl Talk*, the sultry, jazz-tinged singer and her sidemen, pianist Aaron Davis and bassist David Piltch, began captivating audiences in both Canada and around the world. That album, along with 1991's *Blame It On My Youth* and 1993's *Don't Smoke in Bed* all enjoyed platinum-level sales of 100,000 copies in Canada. *Temptation*, Cole's 1995 collection of Tom Waits songs, failed to match that,

Alert vocalist Holly Cole: a smoky, jazz-tinged presence

with still respectable gold sales of 50,000. But by then, Cole had established herself at home and abroad with her distinctive voice and interpretive skills.

NETTWERK

Vancouver's Nettwerk Records is one of the great success stories of Canadian music. Formed in 1984, Nettwerk sprang up around a local techno-pop band called Moev. Its original owners included the group's manager Terry McBride, its guitarist Mark Jowett, and Brad Saltzberg, the owner of a music store that specialized in imported records. In the summer of '84, Nettwerk launched its first releases. Two years later, Ric Arboit replaced the outgoing Saltzberg as the third owner, and the company joined the Capitol-EMI family of affiliated labels. By that time, Nettwerk had signed a young Halifax singer named Sarah McLachlan. The '90s have proven to be Nettwerk's, McLachlan's and (with the exception of a two-year gap, when Nettwerk was handled by Sony) EMI's decade.

McLachlan, the jewel in Nettwerk's crown, juggling Junos at the 1998 awards: an international superstar

Following releases by Moev, the industrial combo Skinny Puppy and acoustic rockers The Grapes of Wrath, Nettwerk branched out into the ambient dub of Tackhead, the ethereal global strains of Single Gun Theory and the impossible-to-describe sound of MC900 Ft. Jesus. The label pioneered new media within the music industry, becoming one of the first record

companies to develop interactive CD-ROMs and artist Web sites in Canada. With McBride as CEO, Arboit and Jowett as co-presidents, Nettwerk continued going from strength to strength. But it wasn't until McLachlan rose to international fame that the label had a bona fide superstar.

McLachlan's star climbed steadily with her albums and singles, starting with 1988's *Touch*, featuring "Vox," and followed by 1991's *Solace* ("Into the Fire" and "Drawn to the Rhythm") and 1993's *Fumbling Towards Ecstasy* ("Possession" and "Hold On"). With 1997's multiple Grammy and Juno award winning *Surfacing*, its single "Building a Mystery" and the Lilith Fair all-women's rock festival she conceived and headlined beginning that summer, McLachlan's star was suddenly catapulted into the pop stratosphere. Nettwerk's vision and commitment, nurturing of new talent, and grassroots approach to devel-

oping its artists has proven to be fruitful not just for Sarah McLachlan, but also for other established artists such as Delerium, Gob and Tara MacLean.

BLUE NOTE

Bruce Lundvall (at the time president of Blue Note Records/now president of Capitol Classics and Jazz) celebrates the Blue Note signing via EMI Music Canada of Shirley Eikhard and legendary Cuban jazz pianist Chucho Valdes, along with Deane Cameron, November 1997

One of the world's most revered jazz labels, Blue Note was founded by German émigré Alfred Lion to "serve the uncompromising expressions of hot jazz or swing," as Lion put it in the company's 1939 statement of purpose. Through Blue Note's golden age, from the mid-50s to the late '60s, the company achieved that goal with many classic recordings by such artists as Art Blakey, Dexter Gordon, John Coltrane, Herbie Hancock and McCoy Tyner. Although it stumbled somewhat in the '70s, the label bounced back with its 1985 acquisition by EMI and the instal-

Blue Note recording artist Renee Rosnes (second from left) with Archambaults' Shelley Steinsacks and his wife Doreen and EMI Canada's vice-president of sales, Al Andruchow (far right): elegant jazz

lation of Bruce Lundvall as president. Through the '90s, Blue Note has resumed its role as an influential jazz label, with the signings of some of the world's top players, including several Canadian artists.

Under Lundvall's leadership, Blue Note became known as a source of inventive, jazz crossover acts such as Us3, which re-mixed Hancock's '60s tune "Cantaloupe Island" to become "Cantaloop (Flip Fantasia)," an international acid jazz/hip-hop hit in 1993. It also became the home of vocalists Dianne Reeves and Cassandra Wilson, alto saxist

Greg Osby, multi-reed star Joe Lovano, guitarists John Scofield and Charlie Hunter, neo-funk-fusionists Medeski, Martin & Wood and Cuban piano virtuoso Gonzalo Rubalcaba. In fact, Latin jazz and Cuban music, in particular, has become one of Lundvall's specialties. Along with Rubalcaba, he has signed such Cuban artists as pianist Chucho Valdes and the band Irakere and, through Metro Blue, groups like Los Van Van and NG La Banda.

Oddly enough, it was Lundvall's love of Cuban music that led him to Canada, with the signing of Toronto-based reedist Jane Bunnett, who had won a 1998 Juno nomination for her first EMI Music Canada/Blue Note recording, *Chamalongo*. Since then, a number of artists who Lundvall has signed also happen to be Canadian, including pianist Renee Rosnes, singer Shirley Eikhard and

singer-songwriter Marc Jordan. As he told *Downbeat* magazine: "If you can sign someone with a voice of their own and you feel that they're going to leave an important legacy, I think that's the most that any of us can expect to do."

Novelties

The Hockey Song

Originally issued in 1971 on Stompin' Tom Connors' Toronto-based Boot label, "The Hockey Song" has become the battle cry at hockey arenas across North America in the '90s. It all started when the tune, with its description of players storming the crease "like bumblebees," caught on like "a burning flame" during the Ottawa Senators' first 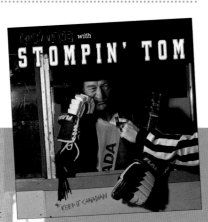 season at the Civic Centre in 1996. That same year, Vancouver punk band the Hanson Brothers recorded a slamming interpretation of the song on its hockey-themed *Sudden Death* album. From there, the song's popularity grew to anthemic proportions. When Stompin' Tom sang it himself, at the closing ceremonies of Toronto's Maple Leaf Gardens, there was scarcely a dry eye in the house.

Hockey music has become a fine Canadian tradition, dating back to Maple Leaf goalie Johnny Bower's "Honky the Christmas Goose" on Capitol in 1965. Two years later, Leaf tough guy Eddie Shack was immortalized in "Clear the Track, Here Comes Shack," by Douglas Rankin and the Secrets. Other classic hockey songs include "Fifty Mission Cap" by The Tragically Hip, "Gretzky Rocks" by The Pursuit of Happiness, "The Ballad of Wendel Clark, Parts I and II" by The Rheostatics and "Big League" by EMI recording artist Tom Cochrane.

But Stompin' Tom's own version has become the rink-rat tune of choice among most hockey fans. Featured on several of his CD compilations on EMI, including *Souvenirs: 25 of the Best Stompin' Tom*, *Once Upon a Stompin' Tom* and *KIC★ Along with Stompin' Tom* (★Keep It Canadian), it remains one of the ardent nationalist's most revered and covered songs. In 1999 alone, it was recorded by country singer Terri Clark for Sportsnet's N.H.L. broadcasts and by alternative rockers Rusty as the theme song on the CTV series *Power Play*. With its simple but heartfelt depiction of Canada's national game, Stompin' Tom scored a winner.

Appendix I

AT THE HELM

During its 50-year history in Canada, EMI has been headed by just ten
presidents or executive officers. Here are their names and their tenures:

Lockwood Miller
>(President, 1949)

Ken Kerr
>(General Manager, 1949–1953)

Harold Smith
>(General Manager, then President, 1954–1962)

Geoffrey Racine
>(President, 1962–1966)

Edward Leetham
>(Executive Vice-President 1966, President 1968)

Ron Plumb
>(Executive Vice-President and General Manager, 1968–1970)

Arnold Gosewich
>(President, 1970–1977)

Dave Evans
>(President, 1977–1986)

Richard Lyttelton
>(President, 1986–1988)

Deane Cameron
>(President, 1988-present)

Appendix II

THE 6000 SERIES OF 33 1/3 RPM (LP) VINYL DISCS

(based on research compiled by Piers Hemmingsen; Copyright 2000)

Between 1960 and 1987, Capitol Records Of Canada issued the unique "6000" series of LP records for the Canadian market. The series encompasses the very best of Canadian popular music of the era, as well as an incredibly broad range of the very best European and American EMI artists tailored for the unique tastes of the Canadian record buying public, including The Beatles early and later Canadian-only releases. The 6000 series was boosted initially by Paul White and the decline of the 6000 series in the 1980s coincided with the arrival of the "global format" compact disc. The 6000 series has become famous among music collectors worldwide.

This brief "discography" attempts to list all of the known releases of Capitol Records of Canada 6000 Series. The first Capitol of Canada LP was T 6000 "Freddy Gardner: The Unforgettable."

"The 6000 Series" logo could be found on the front of the sleeve under the Capitol Records logo.

THE 6000 SERIES OF 33 1/3 RPM (LP) VINYL DISCS

Catalogue Number, Release, (EMI Vault Record Release Date), Artist, Album Title

THE "6000" SERIES

T-6000	(1960), Freddy Gardner, *The Unforgettable*
T-6001	Ruby Murray, *Endearing Young Charms*
T-6002	George Formby, *When I'm Cleaning Windows*
T-6003	The Glasgow Orpheus Choir, *The Glasgow Orpheus Choir — Conducted By Sir Hugh Roberton*
T-6004	US Air Force Drum & Bugle Corps, *Searchlight Tattoo*

T-6005	Matt Monro, *Love Is The Same Anywhere*
T-6006	Peter Dawson, *A Life Of Song*
T-6007	The Glasgow Orpheus Choir, *Volume II*
T-6008	Eddie Calvert, *Vive La Piaf!*

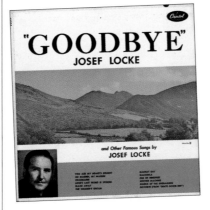

T-6009	Josef Locke, *Goodbye And Other Famous Songs*
T-6010	The George Mitchell Minstrels, *Your Minstrel Sing Along Show*
T-6011	The Billy Cotton Band Show, *Wakey Wakey...*
W-6012	Lois Marshall, *Lois Marshall Sings Folk Songs*
T-6013	(June 8, 1962), Noel Coward And Gertrude Lawrence (aka Noel And Gertie), *Scenes And Songs From Private Lives...*
T-6014	Brendan O'Dowda With Norrie Paramor And His Orchestra, *By Special Request*
T-6015	Django Reinhardt & Stephane Grappelli, *Django And Stephane Originals*
T-6016	Joan Hammond, *Oh My Beloved Daddy*
T-6017	Peter Dawson, *The Boys Of The Old Brigade/A Song For Everyone*
T-6018	Ruby Murray, *Irish And Proud Of It*

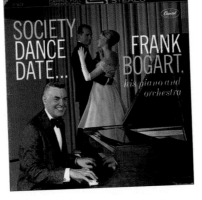

(S)T-6019	Frank Bogart, His Piano & Orchestra, *Society Dance Date*
(S)T-6020	Helen Shapiro, *Sings The Big Hits Of The 60s*
T-6021	Charlie Drake, *Fun Songs For The Whole Family*
T-6022	Legarde Twins, *Twincerely Yours*
T-6023	Jan 63 (January 1963), Elaine And Derek, *How Great Thou Art—Hymns For The Family*
(S)T-6024	Jan 63 (January 1963), Mrs. Mills with Geoff Love, *Plays The Roaring Twenties*
(S)T-6025	Feb 63 (February 1963), Frank Ifield, *Frank Ifield Sings*
T-6026	Matt Monro, *Matt Monro Sings Hoagy Carmichael*
T-6027	Mike Sarne, *Come Outside*
T-6028	Jan 63 (January 1963), Rich Little with Les Lye, *My Fellow Canadians*
(S)T-6029	Mar 63 (June 3, 1963), Cliff Richard & The Shadows, *On Your Mark...Get Set...Let's Go!*
T-6030	Mar 63 (April 1, 1963), Helen Shapiro, *12 Hits And A Miss Helen Shapiro*
(S)T-6031	May 63 (May 6, 1963), Andy Stewart, *Andy Sings Songs Of Scotland*
T-6032	(July 22, 1963), Jimmy Shand, *Scottish Country Dances*
T-6033	(July 22, 1963), Jimmy Shand, *Jimmy Shand's Party*
(S)T-6034	(April, 1963), Cliff Richard & The Shadows, *Summer Holiday*
(S)T-6035	(July 22, 1963), Band Of The Irish Guards, *The Big Parade*
W-6036	July 63 (July 22, 1963), Richard Tauber, *My Heart And I*
T-6037	(July 22, 1963), Various Artists (Comedy) (Spike Milligan, Peter Sellers, Jonathan Miller, Peter Cooke), *Bridge On The River Wye*
T-6038	(September 3, 1963), Brendan O'Dowda With Philip Green And His Orchestra, *The World Of Percy French*
T-6039	(July 29, 1963), John Bird, Eleanor Bron, etc., *The Establishment*

(S)T-6040 (September 3, 1963), Various Artists, *Jazz In The Making (1923-1930)*

(S)T-6041 Sep 63, (September 3, 1963), Vera Lynn with Tony Osborne, *Sings The Hits Of The Blitz*

(S)T-6042 (September 3, 1963), Victor Silvester, *Victor Silvester In France*

T-6043 Sep 63, (September 3, 1963), Cliff Richard & The Shadows, *Living Doll*

(S)T-6044 Oct 63, (September 30, 1963), Frank Bogart, *Steppin' In Society*

(S)T-6045 (September 30, 1963), Ross Smith, *Laugh Of The Party*

(S)T-6046 Oct 63, (September 30, 1963), Rolf Harris, *Tie Me Kangaroo Down Sport*

T-6047 (September 30, 1963), BBC (various comedy: David Frost, Millicent Martin, Lance Percival, Roy Kinnear, etc., *That Was The Week That Was*

(S)T-6048 (October 15, 1963), Dr. William McCauley, *Show Stoppers From O'Keefe Centre*

T-6049 Nov 63, (November 25, 1963), Rich Little, *Scrooge And The Stars*

T-6050 (December 30, 1963), Harry Douglas & The Deep River Boys, *Presenting*

T-6051 Nov 63, (December 2, 1963), The Beatles, *Beatlemania*!

T-6052 Feb 64, (February 3, 1964), The Shadows, *Dance On With The Shadows*

T-6053 Feb 64, (February 3, 1964), Helen Shapiro, *Helen Shapiro In Nashville*

T-6054 Feb 64, (February 3, 1964), The Beatles, *Twist And Shout*

(S)T-6055 Feb 64. (February 3, 1964), Mrs. Mills with Geoff Love, *Everybody's Welcome At Mrs. Mills Party*

T-6056 (February 3, 1964), Andy Stewart, *North Of The Border*

(S)W-6057 Nov 63, (December 16, 1963), Margaret Ann Ireland, *Plays Villa-Lobos & Granados*

(S)W-6058 (December 16, 1963), Margaret Ann Ireland, *Plays Schubert & Rachmaninoff*

(S)T-6059 Mar 64, (March 2, 1964), Vera Lynn, *The Wonderful Vera*

(S)T-6060 (March 2, 1964), Victor Silvester, *Victor Silvester's Sing And Dance Party*

T-6061 Mar 64, (March 2, 1964), Billy J. Kramer & The Dakotas, *Listen To*

T-6062 (April 13, 1964), The Dave Clark Five, *Session With The Dave Clark Five*

T-6063 May 64, (April 27, 1964), The Beatles, *Long Tall Sally*

(S)T-6064 Apr 64, (April 13, 1964), Ron Goodwin, *Elizabethan Serenade*

(S)W-6065 May 64, (May 19, 1964), Margaret Ann Ireland, *Plays Music Of Polish Masters (Chopin)*

(S)W-6066 May 64, (May 19, 1964), Paul Brodie, *The Saxophone In Concert*

(S)T-6067 May 64, (May 19, 1964), Cliff Richard, *It's All In The Game*

T-6068 May 64, (May 11, 1964), The Dave Clark Five, *Bits And Pieces*

T-6069 Jun 64, (May 25, 1964), The Swinging Blue Jeans, *Hippy Hippy Shake*

T-6070 May 64, (May 4, 1964), Gerry & The Pacemakers, *I'm The One!*

(S)T-6071 Jun 64, (June 1, 1964), The York University Choir, *From Bach To Rock*

T-6072 Aug 64, (August 10, 1964), Andy Stewart, *Scottish Soldier*

T-6073 Jul 64, (July 20, 1964), The Hollies, *Stay With The Hollies*

(S)T-6074 (August 10, 1964), Larry Dubin's Big Muddys, *At The Ports Of Call*

T-6075 Aug 64, (August 10, 1964), The Esquires, *Introducing The Esquires*

T-6076 (July 20, 1964), The Luton Girls Choir, *Best Loved Songs*

JAO-6077 (July 20, 1964), Ann Stephens, etc., *Alice In Wonderland And Through The Looking Glass*

T-6078 (October 5, 1964), Various Caribbean Artists, *Caribbean Treasure Chest*

T-6079 Sept 64, (September 8, 1964), The Shadows, *Shindig With The Shadows*

T-6080 Jun 64, (June 15, 1964), Various Artists, *Smashin' Smashers From England*

T-6081 (August 8, 1964), Cliff Richard & The Shadows, *Wonderful Life*

(S)T-6082 Sep 64, (September 14, 1964), Mrs. Mills & Russ Conway, *Let's Have A Party*

T-6083 Sep 64, (September 14, 1964), The Dave Clark Five, *On Stage With The Dave Clark Five*

(S)T-6084 Nov 64, (November 2, 1964), Matt Monro, *Great Songs From The Movies*

T-6085 Oct 64, (October 5, 1964), Freddie And The Dreamers, *I Love You Baby*

(S)T-6086   Nov 64, (November 2, 1964), Ron Goodwin, *The Smooth Sounds Of Ron Goodwin*

T-6087   (January 4, 1965), Lucio Agostini, *Action With Agostini*

(S)T-6088   (October 5, 1964), Parsons And Poole, *Play Brahms*

T-6089   (October 5, 1964), Various Artists, *Your Favourite TV And Radio Themes*

T-6090   (September 14, 1964), Ebony Rhythm, *Ebony Rhythem [sic]*

T-6091   Oct 64, (October 5, 1964), Billy J. Kramer & The Dakotas, *Top Twelve Hits*[1]

T-6092   Sep 64, (September 21, 1964), The Animals, *Including Their Single, House of the Rising Sun*

T-6093   Oct 64, (November 2, 1964), Manfred Mann, *The Five Faces Of Manfred Mann*

T-6094   (November 2, 1964), Mrs. Mills, *It's Party Time*

(S)T-6095   (January 4, 1964), Tony Osborne, *Nights To Remember*

T-6096   (February 1, 1965), Ken Jones, *Music Of Galt McDermott*

T-6097   (January 4, 1965), David Curry, *My Ireland Volume II*

T-6098   Jan 65, (January 4, 1965), Robert Wilson, *Tribute To Robert Wilson*

T-6099   (February 1, 1965), Various Artists, *Holiday In Italy*

T-6100   (February 1, 1965), Vera Lynn, *Among My Souvenirs*

T-6101   Mar 65, (March 1, 1965), Adam Faith & The Roulettes, *It's Alright*

T-6102[2]   Mar 65, (March 1, 1965), Manfred Mann, *Manfred Mann Return*

T-6103   (January 11, 1965), The Dave Clark Five, *Across Canada*[3]

T-6104   (February 1, 1965), Bob Whitney, *It's Dance Time*

T-6105   Jan 65, (January 4, 1965), Ed Allen, *It's Ed Allen Time*[4]

KAO-6106   (February 1, 1965), Cliff Richard, *The Cliff Richard Souvenir Album*

T-6107   (January 11, 1965), Gerry & The Pacemakers, *Gerry's Second Album*

(S)T-6108   (December 21, 1964), Malka & Joso, *Introducing*

(S)T-6109   (January 11, 1965[5]), Matt Monro, *Walk Away*

(S)T-6110   Pepe Jaramillo, *Latin World of Pepe Jaramillo*

T-6111   (March 1, 1965), Gerry & The Pacemakers, *Ferry Cross The Mersey*

T-6112   (January 18, 1965), Paddy Butler, *Paddy Butler's Ceili Dance*[6]

T-6113   (March 1, 1965), (History document), *The State Funeral Of Sir Winston Churchill*

(S)KAO 6114   (April 12, 1965), Jimmie Haskell et al., *Sing A Song With The Beatles*

T-6115   Apr 65, (April 12, 1965), Jack London & The Sparrows, *Jack London & The Sparrows*

T-6116   (April 12, 1965), The Dave Clark Five, *Encores!*

T-6117   May 65, (May 17, 1965), Rolf Harris, *All Together Now—Fun Songs For Everyone*

T-6118   (May 17, 1965), Various Artists, *More Smashin'-Smashers*

T-6119   (May 17, 1965), Chad And Jeremy, *What Do You Want With Me*

T-6120   (August 30, 1965), Wes Dakus & The Rebels, *Wes Dakus With The Rebels*

T-6121   May 65, (May 17, 1965), Freddie And The Dreamers, *In Orbit*

T-6122   May 65, (May 17, 1965), Georgie Fame, *Fame At Last, Featuring 'Yeah, Yeah'*

(S)W-6123   (August 30, 1965), The Toronto Symphony/ David Susskind, *Morawez, Matton*

(S)T-6124   (August 30, 1965), Tommy Steele, *So This Is Broadway*

(S)W-6125   (August 30, 1965), Joan Hammond, *On Wings Of Song*

(S)T-6126   (July 26, 1965), Chad & Jeremy, John Barry, *Chad And Jeremy Meet John Barry*

T-6127   (July 26, 1965), The Arrows, *Apache 65*

(S)T-6128   (August 30, 1965), Andy Stewart, *Campbelltown Loch*

(S)T-6129   (July 26, 1965), Malka & Joso, *Mostly Love Songs*

T-6130   Jul 65, (July 26, 1965), Freddie And The Dreamers, *Ready Freddie Go*

(S)T-6131   Aug 65, (August 30, 1965), Matt Monro, *Start Living*

T-6132   (August 30, 1965), (Soundtrack), *Songs From The Movie Seaside Swingers*

T-6133   (July 26, 1965), Claude Ciari, *La Playa*

T-6134   Aug 65, (August 30, 1965), Sounds Incorporated, *Sounds Incorporated*

(S)T-6135   Aug 65, (August 30, 1965), Frank Ifield, *Portrait In Song*

(S)T-6136   (August 30, 1965), Pepe Jaramillo, *The Romantic World Of...*

T-6137   (August 30, 1965), The Dave Clark Five, *Having A Wild Weekend*

T-6138   (July 26, 1965), Ian Whitcomb, *You Turn Me On*

T-6139 Sep 65, (September 6, 1965),
The Yardbirds, *Heart Full Of Soul*

T-6140 (October 4, 1965), Billy J. Kramer,
Trains And Boats And Planes

T-6141 Nov 65, (November 1, 1965),
The Kirkintilloch Childrens Choir,
The Wonderful Songs Of...

T-6142 (September 6, 1966)[7], Various Artists,
Folk Songs Italianissimo

T-6143 Oct 65, (October 4, 1965), The Hollies,
In The Hollies Style

(S)T-6144 Oct 65, (October 4, 1965), The Shadows,
The Sound Of The Shadows

T-6145 Nov 65, (November 1, 1965),
Robert Wilson, *Down In The Glen—
The Favourite Songs Of Robert Wilson*

(S)T-6146 (November 1, 1965), Richard Anthony,
Sings In English

T-6147 (October 4, 1965), Dick Curless,
A Tombstone Every Mile

(S)T-6148 Oct 65, (October 4, 1965), Claude Ciari,
Sensational

(S)T-6149 Nov 65, (November 1, 1965), Cliff Richard,
Love Is Forever

(S)T-6150 (November 1, 1965), Dick Kallman,
Hank Sings!

(S)T-6151 Dec 65, (December 3, 1965), Mrs. Mills
with Geoff Love,
Another Party With Mrs. Mills!

T-6152 Jun 66, (June 6, 1966), The Hollies,
Look Through Any Window[8]

T-6153 Jan 66, (January 3, 1966),
The Dave Clark Five, *Hits*

T-6154 Jan 66, (January 3, 1966), Tom Jones,
Johnny Rivers, Freddie & The Dreamers,
Three At The Top

T-6155 Jan 66, (January 3, 1966),
Gerry & The Pacemakers,
The Hits Of Gerry & The Pacemakers

(S)T-6156 (January 3, 1966), Manuel,
Music Of The Mountains

(S)T-6157 (April 4, 1966), Matt Monro,
As Long As I'm Singing

T-6158 (January 3, 1966), The Staccatos, *Initially*

T-6159 Jun 66, (June 6, 1966), The Swinging
Blue Jeans, *Don't Make Me Over*

(D)T-6160 Jan 66, (January 10, 1966), Dean Martin,
The Lush Years

T-6161 Feb 66, (January 31, 1966), Downliners
Sect, *The New 'In' Sound Country Rock*[9]

(D)T-6162 (May 2, 1966), The Dave Clark Five,
Instrumental Album

T-6163 (January 31, 1966), Rolf Harris,
Man With The Microphone

T-6164 (March 4, 1966), Barry Allen, *Goin' Places*

(S)T-6165 Feb 66, (January 31, 1966), Ken Dodd,
Presenting...

(S)T-6166 (March 7, 1966), The Yardbirds,
Having A Rave Up

T-6167 Feb 66 (March 7, 1966), The Dave Clark
Five, *I Like It Like That/Over And Over*

KAO 6168 (March 7, 1966), The Big Town Boys,
The Big Town Boys

(S)T-6169 (March 14, 1966), Malka And Joso,
Jewish Songs

T-6170 Apr 66, (April 4, 1966), Arthur Wilkinson
Orchestra, etc., *The Beatle Cracker
Suite/Ein Kleine Beatles Musik*

T-6171 (June 6, 1966), Newman Centre
Troubadors, *The Canticle Of The Gift*

T-6172 (April 4, 1966), The Sunrays, *Andrea*

(D)T-6173 (May 2, 1966), Dean Martin, *Relaxin'*

T-6174 (June 6, 1966), Dick Curless,
Travellin' Man

(S)T-6175 May 66, (May 2, 1966), Mrs. Mills,
Especially For You

(S)T-6176 Apr 67, (April 3, 1967), Frank Ifield,
Call Her Your Sweetheart

T-6177 (September 6, 1966), Gary Buck,
Stepping Into The Picture

(S)T-6178 (September 6, 1966), Vince Hill,
Have You Met Vince Hill?

(S)T-6179 May 66, (May 2, 1966), The Mike Sammes
Singers, *The Start Of Something Big*

T-6180 Jun 66, (June 6, 1966),
The Dave Clark Five, *At The Scene*

(S)T-6181 Jan 67, (January 2, 1967),
Gerry & The Pacemakers, *Today!*

T-6182 Sept 66, (September 26, 1966), Robbie
Lane & The Disciples, *It's Happening*

(S)T-6183 Jun 66, (June 6, 1966), The Merrymen,
Caribeat With The Merrymen

T-6184 (June 6, 1966), Cliff Richard,
Blue Turns To Grey

T-6185 Oct 66, (October 24, 1966), Diane Leigh,
Shadows Of Your Heart

T-6186 (June 6, 1966), Dick Curless & Kay Adams,
A Devil Like Me

T-6187 (June 6, 1966), Manfred Mann,
Mann Made

(S)T-6188 Oct 66, (October 3, 1966), Claude Ciari,
Merci Cheri

T-6189 Jun 66, (June 27, 1966), Barry Allen,
Lovedrops

T-6190 (June 27, 1966), Mae West,
Way Out West

T-6191 (September 6, 1966), Ketty Lester,
When A Woman Loves A Man

(S)T-6192 (October 3, 1966), Milo, *Hocus Pocus,
Introducing The Hit Trumpet Of Milo*

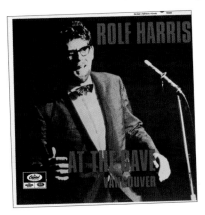

T-6193 (November 28, 1966), Rolf Harris,
At The Cave

(S)T-6194   Nov 66, (October 3, 1966), Cliff Richard, *Kinda Latin*

T-6195   Nov 66, (November 7, 1966), The Hollies, *Bus Stop*

(D)T-6196   Apr 67, (April 3, 1967), The Dave Clark Five, *More Hits*

T-6197   (November 7, 1966), Georgie Fame, *Get Away*

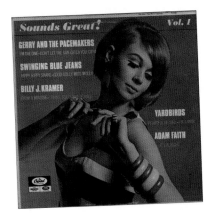

T-6198   Apr 67, (April 3, 1967), Various Artists, *Sounds Great Volume One*

T-6199   (April 3, 1967), Manfred Mann, *Soul Of Mann, Instrumental Hits*

T-6200   Jun 67, (May 29, 1967), Lyn & Graham McCarthy, *Bitter And Sweet*

(S)T-6201   (September 6, 1966), Mario Patron, *Mexican Brass*

(S)T-6202   Sep 66, (September 6, 1966), The Yardbirds, *Over, Under, Sideways, Down*

(S)T-6203   (February 6, 1967), Roy Clark, *Live*

T-6204   (February 6, 1967), The Crusaders, *Make A Joyful Noise With Drums & Guitars*

(S)T-6205   (March 6, 1967), 18th Century Concepts, *In The 20th. Century Bag*

(S)T-6206   (January 2, 1967), Dean Martin, *Happy In Love*

(S)T-6207   Sep 67, (September 4, 1967), The Yardbirds, *Little Games*

(S)T-6208   (September 6, 1966), (Soundtrack) Davie Allen And The Arrows, *The Wild Angels*

T-6209   (November 7, 1966), Ian Whitcomb, *Mod, Mod Music Hall*

(S)T-6210   (January 2, 1967), The Hollies, *Stop! Stop! Stop!*

T-6211   Apr 67, (April 3, 1967), Various Artists, *Sounds Great Volume Two*

(S)T-6212   (April 3, 1967), Andy Stewart & Friends, *At The White Heather Club*

(S)T-6213   (April 3, 1967), The Manhattan Strings, *Play Hits Made Famous By The Monkees*

(D)T-6214   (May 1, 1967), (Soundtrack), *Wild Angels, Volume II*

(S)T-6215   (May 1, 1967), (Soundtrack), *Thunder Alley*

(S)T-6216   (May 1, 1967), Band Of The Royal Horse Guards, *Band Of The Royal Horse Guards*

T-6217   (May 1, 1967), Dick Curless, *All Of Me Belongs To You*

T-6218   (May 15, 1967), The Arrows, *Blues Theme*

(D)T-6219   (May 15, 1967), (Soundtrack), *Devil's Angels*

T-6220   (September 4, 1967), The Dave Clark Five, *You've Got What It Takes*

(S)KAO-6221   (June 12, 1967), Various Artists, *Canada Observed*

(S)T-6222   (July 24, 1967), Gilbert Becaud, *Mon Amour*

(S)T-6223   (June 12, 1967), Vince Hill, *Edelweiss*

(S)T-6224   Jul 67, (July 24, 1967), Cliff Richard, *In A Mod Mood*

(S)T-6225   (July 24, 1967), Andy Stewart, *On Stage*

(S)T-6226   (June 12, 1967), Lee Gagnon, *A La Jazztek*

(S)T-6227   Jul 67, (September 4, 1967), Frank Ifield, *You Came Along*

(D)T-6228   Jul 67, (July 24, 1967), The Hollies, *The Hits Of The Hollies*

(D)T-6229   Oct 67, (October 2, 1967), The Yardbirds, *The Hits Of The Yardbirds*

(D)T-6230   (September 4, 1967), Manfred Mann, *Mann Made Hits*

(D)T-6231   (January 2, 1968), Yvan Landry, *Jazz En Liberte*

(S)T-6232   Sep 67, (September 4, 1967), The Shadows, *Shadows 67*

T-6233   (July 24, 1967), Kim Fowley, *Love Is Alive And Well*

T-6234   (July 24, 1967), Casey Kasem, *Astrology For Young Lovers*

T-6235   (August 14, 1967), Gypsy Boots, *Unpredictable*

(S)T-6236   (November 6, 1967), Adamo, *The Sensational Adamo*

(S)T-6237   (September 18, 1967), (Documentary in Sound), *Makers Of History—Elizabeth The Great*

(S)T-6238   (September 18, 1967), (Documentary in Sound), *Makers Of History Volume 2—King John And The Magna Carta*

(S)T-6239   (September 18, 1967), (Documentary in Sound), *Makers Of History—Abraham Lincoln*

(S)T-6240   (September 18, 1967), (Documentary in Sound), *Makers Of History—Oliver Cromwell*

(D)T-6241   (October 2, 1967), (Soundtrack), *Born Losers*

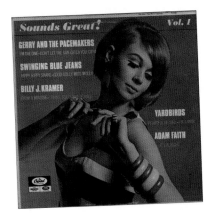

(S)T-6242   Pink Floyd, *The Piper At The Gates Of Dawn*

(S)T-6243   (September 18, 1967), (Documentary in Sound), *Makers Of History—Napoleon & Wellington*

T-6244   (November 6, 1967), Peter Dawson, *A Song For Everyone*

(D)T-6245   Nov 67, (November 6, 1967), The Hollies, *Love N Flowers*

(S)T-6246   (November 6, 1967), (Soundtrack), *The Trip*

(S)T-6247   (November 6, 1967), Various Artists, *Have A Jewish Christmas*

(S)T-6248   (May 6, 1968), Toronto Festival Singers, *Music Of Healy Willan*

T-6249   (January 1, 1968), The Goons, *Goon... But Not Forgotten*

(S)T-6250   (January 1, 1968), Frankie Laine, *Memory Laine*

(D)T-6251   (January 1, 1968), Dean Martin, *Dino—Like Never Before*

(D)T-6252   (January 1, 1968), The Arrows, *Cycle-Delic Sounds*

(S)T-6253   (November 4, 1968), Lee Gagnon, *Le Jazze*

ST-6254   (June 3, 1968), Frank Ifield, *The Singer And The Song*

ST-6255   (July 1, 1968), The Main Attraction, *And Now The Main Attraction*

ST-6256   (June 3, 1968), Eternity's Children, *Eternity's Children*

T-6257   (January 2, 1968), Harry Nilsson, *Spotlight On Nilsson*

(S)T-6258   (January 2, 1968), Festival Singers of Toronto/Elmer Isler, *Music By Poulenc...*

(S)T-6259   (January 2, 1968), Franck Pourcel, *Live For Life*

(S)T-6260   (January 1, 1968), Claude Ciari, *Mood Guitar*

(S)T-6261   (February 5, 1968), Winnipeg Orchestra, *Canadian Light Music*

(S)T-6262   Jan 68, (February 5, 1968), Mr. Paul's Party Band, *Big Piano Beat*

ST-6263   Aug 68, (October 7, 1968), Cliff Richard, *All My Love*

(S)T-6264   (February 5, 1968), David Allan (Soundtrack), *The Glory Stompers*

(S)T-6265   (February 5, 1968), The Dave Clark Five, *Everybody Knows*

(S)T-6266   (March 4, 1968), Simon Dupree & The Big Sound, *Without Reservations*

(S)T-6267   (March 4, 1968), Frankie Vaughan, *There Must Be A Way*

ST-6268   (March 4, 1968), Jake Holmes, *The Above Ground Sound Of Jake Holmes*

DT-6269   (April 1, 1968), (Soundtrack), *Mary Jane*

ST-6270   (April 1, 1968), Des O'Connor, *When You're Smiling*

ST-6271   Apr 68, (April 1, 1968), Franck Pourcel, *Love Is Blue*

ST-6272   (May 6, 1968), Dick Curless, *Long Lonesome Road*

ST-6273   (May 6, 1968), (Soundtrack), *Psych Out*

ST-6274   (May 6, 1968), (Soundtrack), *Hell Cats*

ST-6275   (May 6, 1968), (Soundtrack), *The Wild Racers*

ST-6276   (June 3, 1968), The Love Exchange, *The Love Exchange*

ST-6277   (June 3, 1968), The Smoke, *The Smoke*

ST-6278   (June 3, 1968), Them, *Now And Them*

ST-6279   The Pink Floyd, *A Saucerful Of Secrets*

ST-6280   (June 3, 1968), Mrs. Mills, *Summer Party*

SN-6281   Jul 68, (October 7, 1968), Ivan Romanoff Orchestra & Chorus (CBC), *Continental Rhapsody*

ST-6282   (August 5, 1968), Franck Pourcel, *La La La*

ST-6283   (February 10, 1969), Gary Buck, *Tomorrow Today*

SKAO-6284   (Soundtrack), *Wild In The Streets*

ST-6285   (August 5, 1968), Vera Lynn, *The Best Of Vera Lynn*

SN-6286   (October 7, 1968), Bev Munro, *Hello Operator*

DT-6287   (August 5, 1968), Andy Stewart, *The Best Of Andy Stewart*

SN-6288   (September 3, 1968), Jim Pirie, *Soulero*

SN-6289   (September 3, 1968), Chicho Valle, *Latin Lustre*

SN-6290   Aug 68, (September 3, 1968), The Jimmy Dale Adventure, *Soft And Groovy*

SN-6291   (February 10, 1969), Carl Tapscott Singers, *This Joyful Eastertide*

ST-6292   (July 1, 1969), Franck Pourcel, *The Way It Used To Be*

ST-6293   (August 5, 1968), Matt Monro, *Walk Softly Into Love*

DT-6294   (July 1, 1968), Rolf Harris, *It's A Rolf Harris World*

ST-6295   (August 5, 1968), (Soundtrack), *Angels From Hell*

ST-6296   (September 3, 1968), The Arrows, *The Arrows*

SN-6297   (October 7, 1968), The Carl Tapscott Singers, *Carols for a Family Christmas*

ST-6298   Roslyn, *Portrait Of Roslyn*

SN-6299   (March 1968), Ivan Romanoff Orchestra & Chorus, *Ukranian Rhapsody*

ST-6300   (October 7, 1968), Anne Shelton, *Favourites*

SN-6301   (November 4, 1968), Wally Koster, *Broadway Hit Parade*

ST-6302   (November 4, 1968), Eternity's Children, *Timeless*

ST-6303   (November 4, 1968), Max Frost & The Troopers, *The Shape Of Things To Come*

ST-6304   (August 4, 1969), Mother Tuckers Yellow Duck, *Home Grown Stuff*

SKAO 6305   (vault uses ST-6305) Brian Browne, *The Letter*

ST-6306   (November 4, 1968), Various (Soundtracks), *Best Of The American International Soundtracks*

ST-6307   (January 13, 1969), Claude Ciari, *Mood Guitar Plays The World Hits*

ST-6308   (January 13, 1969), Mrs. Mills, *16 Party Pieces*

DT-6309   (September 1, 1969), Bernard Miles, *Carry On Laughing*

ST-6310   (January 13, 1969), Franck Pourcel, *Those Were The Days*

SN-6311   Feb 69, (January 13, 1969), Louis Bannet, *Atour Du Monde*

ST-6312   (April 7, 1969), Chad And Jeremy (Soundtrack), *Three In The Attic*

ST-6313   (June 2, 1969), (Soundtrack), *The Devil's Eight*

ST-6314   (June 2, 1969), Mike And Brian, *Warm On The Inside*

SN-6315   (June 2, 1969), Johnny Thorson, *The Johnny Thorson Banjo Album*

ST-6316   (June 2, 1969), (Soundtrack), *Hell's Bells*

ST-6317   (November 3, 1969), Mrs. Mills, *Back To The Roaring 20s With Mrs. Mills*

ST-6318   (October 6, 1969), Pink Floyd (Soundtrack), *More*

SN-6319   (October 20, 1969), The Dubliners, *At Home With The Dubliners*

ST-6320   (August 4, 1969), Duane Davis, *Reflections*

ST-6321   (October 6, 1969), Yvan Landry Quartet, *Café Au Lait*

ST-6322   (November 3, 1969), Robert Jacobs, *Ray Bradbury's Dark Carnival*

ST-6323   (August 4, 1969), Festival Singers Of Canada/Elmer Isler, *Trumpets Of Summer*

ST-6324   (1970), Peter Law & The Pacific, *The Sound Of Peter Law & The Pacific*

ST-6325   (October 6, 1969), (Soundtrack), *Angel Angel Down We Go*

ST-6326   (September 1, 1969), Danny Doyle, *Expressions Of Danny Doyle*

ST-6327   (November 4, 1969), The Patmacs, *Open House*

SKAO-6328   (November 17, 1969), Edward Bear, *Bearings*

ST-6329   (September 1, 1969), Danny Doyle, *The Hits Of Danny Doyle*

ST-6330   (November 17, 1969), Anne Murray, *This Way Is My Way*

ST-6331   (September 1, 1969), Valentino, *Sounds Romantic*

ST-6332   (September 1, 1969), Jerry Toth, *Tell Me Now*

ST-6333   (October 4, 1969), Ivan Romanoff, *Ukranian Christmas*

ST-6334   (December 20, 1969), The National Band Of The Canadian Armed Forces, *The National Band Of The Canadian Armed Forces*

ST-6335   (December 29, 1969), Bernard Braden, *Reads Stephen Leacock*

ST-6336   De Sade, *De Sade*

ST-6337   Pierre Lalonde, *The Young Years*

ST-6338   Alan Scott, *When I Needed A Woman*

DT-6339   (December 29, 1969), Paul Robeson, *The Best Of Paul Robeson*

ST-6340   (December 29, 1969), Cliff Richard, *Sincerely*

ST-6341   (March 2, 1970), Andy Stewart, *Sings Harry Lauder*

ST-6342   (February 2, 1970), Gunter Norris, *I Got Rhythm*

ST-6343   (February 2, 1970), Franck Pourcel, *Midnight Cowboy*

ST-6344   (March 2, 1970), Mae West, *Mae West*

ST-6345   (March 2, 1970), B.C. Beefeater Band, *B.C. Beefeater Band*

ST-6346   Donna Ramsay, *Cool Green Waters*

ST-6347   (May 1970), Gary Buck, *Wayward Woman Of The World*

ST-6348   (April 1970), Gene MacLellan, *T.C.I.T.M*

SKAO-6349   (May 1970), Edward Bear, *Eclipse*

ST-6350   (May 1970), Anne Murray, *Honey, Wheat, And Laughter*

ST-6351[10]   The Beatles, *Let It Be*

ST-6352   (May 1970), Mother Tuckers Yellow Duck, *Starting A New Day*

T-6353   (May 1970), The Goons, *Goon Again*

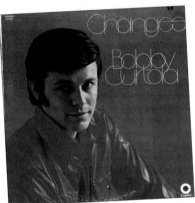

ST-6354   (May 1970), Bobby Curtola, *Changes*

ST-6355   (September 1970), Vince Hill, *Introducing Vince Hill*

SKAO-6356   (November 1970), Tommy Graham & Friends, *Planet Earth*

ST-6357   (January 1971), Franck Pourcel, *Impressions*

T-6358   (February 1971), Paul Robeson, *Encore*

ST-6359   Anne Murray, *Straight, Clean, And Simple*

ST-6360   (March 1971), The Flame, *The Flame*

ST-6361   (March 22, 1971), Bobby Curtola, *Curtola*

ST-6362   (May 1971), Aarons And Ackley, *Aarons And Ackley*

ST-6363   (September 1971), Rolf Harris, *Jake The Peg In Vancouver Town*

ST-6364   (September 1971), Pepper Tree, *You're My People*

ST-6365   (October 1971), Flying Circus, *Prepared In Peace*

ST-6366   (September 1971), Anne Murray, *Talk It Over In The Morning*

ST-6367   (October 1971), Pierre Lalonde, *Pierre Lalonde*

ST-6368   (October 1971), The Goons, *First Men On The Goon*

ST-6369   (October 1971), Rolf Harris, *Instant Music*

ST-6370   (November 1971), Fergus, *All The Right Noises*

ST-6371   (March 1972), Shirley Eikhard, *Shirley Eikhard*

ST-6372   (April 1972), Christopher Kearney, *Christopher Kearney*

ST-6373   (April 1972), John Keating & LSO, *Conducts—Theme From Persuaders, Six Wives Of Henry VIII, etc.*

ST-6374   (April 1972), London Stage Cast, *Harold Fielding's London Production of Showboat*

ST-6375   (May 1972), Franck Pourcel, *San Remo '72*

ST-6376   (April 1972), Anne Murray, *Annie*

ST-6377   (May 1972), Fela Ransome Kuti / Ginger Baker, *Live*

ST-6378   (October 1972), Ronney Abramson, *Ronney Abramson*

ST-6379   (May 1972), Aarons And Ackley, *You And I*

ST-6380   (Soundtrack), *Gone With The Wind*

ST-6381   (September 1972), Mrs. Mills, *Music Hall Party*

ST-6382   (November 1972), Fergus, *Town Of Fergus*

SKAO-6383   (October 1972), Flying Circus, *Gypsy Road*

ST-6384   (November 1972), Bob McBride, *Butterfly Days*

ST-6385   (November 1972), Vera Lynn, *Favourite Sacred Songs*

SW-6386[10]   (November 1972), The Beatles, *Let It Be*

ST-6387   (December 4, 1972), Edward Bear, *Last Song*

ST-6388   (March 13, 1973), Truck, *Truck*

ST-6389   (January 6, 1973), New Potatoes, *New Potatoes*

ST-6390   (June 1974), Paul Kuhn /SFB Big Band, *Berlin Big Band*

ST-6391   (February 1973), Flying Circus

ST-6392   (April 9, 1973), Christopher Kearney, *Pemmican Stash*

ST-6393   (April 9, 1973), Anne Murray, *Danny's Song*

ST-6394   (May 14, 1973), Fela Ransome Kuti, *Afrodesiac*

SKAO-6395   (June 4, 1973), Edward Bear, *Close Your Eyes*

ST-6396   (June 4, 1973), Rolf Harris, *You Name It*

ST-6397   (November 6, 1973), Bob McBride, *Sea Of Dreams*

ST-6398   (May 1973), Bill King, *Goodbye Superdad*

ST-6399   (June 1973), Mandingo, *The Primeval Rhythm of Life*

ST-6400   (September 1973), Flying Circus, *Last Laugh*

SO-6401   (November 19, 1973), (Soundtrack), *The Selfish Giant*

T-6402   (November 19, 1973), Shawn Philips, *First Impressions*

ST-6403   (November 19, 1973), Franck Pourcel, *James Bond's Greatest Hits*

ST-6404   (January 7, 1974), Mandingo, *Sacrifice*

ST-6405   (January 7, 1974), Ron Goodwin, *Spellbound*

ST-6406   (January 7, 1974), Liverpool Spinners, *Liverpool Spinners*

ST-6407   (April 7, 1974), EM, *Time Of Man*

ST-6408   (April 15, 1974), The Shadows, *Rockin' With Curly Leeds*

ST-6409   (February 11, 1974), Anne Murray, *ove Song*

ST-6410   (October 1975), Copperpenny, *Fuse*

ST-6411   (October 1974), Mrs. Mills, *Non Stop Honky Tonk Piano*

T-6412   (August 12, 1974), Shawn Philips, *Favourite Things*

ST-6413   (February 10, 1975), Maneige, *Maneige*

ST-6414   (March 11, 1974), Cockney Rebel, *The Human Menagerie*

ST-6415   (August 12, 1974), Fusion Orchestra, *Skeleton In Armour*

MO-6416   (October 14, 1974), Various, *Children Talking*

SO-6417   (September 9, 1974), (Soundtrack), *The Little Mermaid*

8XT-6418   (May 12, 1975), Hugo Strasser, *Und Sein Orchester*[11]

SKAO-6419   (October 14, 1974), Justin Paige, *Justin Paige*

ST-6420   (January 13, 1975), Mandingo, *A Story Of Survival*

ST-6421   (September 9, 1974), John Keating, *Incorporated*

ST-6422   (June 1974), Bill King, *Dixie Peach*

ST-6423   (January 13, 1975), Peter Donato

ST-6424   (March 10, 1975), Christopher Kearney, *Sweet Water*

ST-6425   (November 11, 1974), Anne Murray, *Country*

SO-6426   (November 11, 1974), (Soundtrack), *The Happy Prince*

ST-6427   (February 10, 1975), Mrs. Mills, *Hollywood Party*

ST-6428   (November 11,1974), Anne Murray, *Highly Prized Possession*

T-6429   (January 13, 1975), The Goons, *The Very Best Of The Goons*

SKAO-6430   (June 9, 1975), Sylvia Tyson, *Woman's World*

SM-6431   (August 11, 1975), Brian Browne, *Morning, Noon, & Night Time Too*

SM-6432 (August 11, 1975), Malka And Joso, *Jewish Songs*

SM-6433 (August 11, 1975), Lee Gagnon, *Discotheque*

ST-6434 (August 11, 1975), The Kings Singers, *Keep On Changing*

ST-6435 (1976), Bette Davis, *Miss Bette Davis*

ST-6436 (November 8, 1975), Hugo Strasser, *Once More With Feeling*

ST-6437 (January 12, 1976), Ann Mortifee, *Baptism*

ST-6438 (November 10, 1975), Maneige, *Les Porches*

ST-6439 (November 24, 1975), Suzanne Stevens, *Love's The Only Game In Town*

ST-6440 (November 10, 1975), Sandy Davis, *Back On My Feet Again*

ST-6441 (September 1976), Sylvia Tyson, *Cool Wind From The North*

ST-6442 (March 8, 1976), Simon Park, *Venus Fly Trap*

ST-6443 (March 8, 1976), Gonzalez, *Our Only Weapon Is Our Music*

ST-6444 Various Artists, *Hits Of The Mersey Era Volume 1*

ST-6445 (September 13, 1976), Cliff Richard, *3 1st. Of February Street*

ST-6446 Various Artists, *Hits Of The Sixties*

ST-6447 (May 10, 1976), Various Artists, *Disco Date*

ST-6448 (November 8, 1976), Pussycat, *Smile*

ST-6449 (February 14, 1977), Gil Ventura, *That's The Way I Like It*

ST-6450 (May 9, 1977), The Albion Dance Band, *The Prospect Before Us*

ST-6451 (September 14, 1976), Rolf Harris, *Turn On*

ST-6452 (August 8, 1977), Vera Lynn, *In Nashville*

ST-6453 (August 8, 1977), Marshall Hain, *Free Ride*

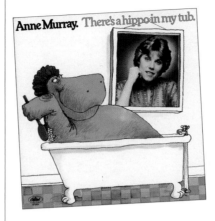

ST-6454 (October 1978), Anne Murray, *There's A Hippo In My Tub*

ST-6455 (release cancelled), Cliff Richard

STAO-6456 (December 1978), Kate Bush, *Lionheart*

ST-6457 (January 1979), Mandingo, *Savage Rite*

ST-6458 (January 1979), Matumbi, *Seven Seals*

ST-6459 (February 12, 1979), Long John Baldry, *Baldry's Out*

ST-6460 Chas And Dave, *Rockney*

ST-6461 (September 1979), Cliff Richard, *Rock & Roll Juvenile*

ST-6462 Pam Ayres

ST-6463 Lisa Dal Bello, *Pretty Girls*

ST-6464 (November 1979), Prism, *Prism*

ST-6465 Prism, *See Forever Eyes*

ST-6466 1979, Prism, *Armageddon*

ST-6467 Surrender

ST-6468 (February 1980), Screen Idols, *Premiere*

ST-6469 (release cancelled), Rambow

ST-6470 (March 1980), The Monks, *Bad Habits*

ST-6471 (March 1980), Matumbi, *Point Of View*

ST-6472 (April 1980), Che And Ray

ST-6473 (June 1980), The Flys

ST-6474 (June 1980), Roy Harper (UK folk artist)

ST-6475 (July 1980), The Start, *Hey You*

STAO-6476 (October 6, 1980), Kate Bush, *Never Forever*

ST-6477 (October 13, 1980), Prism, *Greatest Hits*

ST-6478 Reckless, *Reckless*

ST-6479 Singbird, *No Ordinary Child*

ST-6480 (November 1980), Photograph, *The Photograph Album*

ST-6481 (November 1980), Streetheart, *Drugstore Dancer*

ST-6482 (January 1981), Eloy, *Wings Of Vision*

ST-6483 (March 1981), Shona Laing, *Tied To The Tracks*

ST-6484 (March 1981), The Monks, *Bad Habits*[12]

LT-6485 (April 1981), Fischer Z, *Red Skies Over Paradise*

ST-6486 (July 1981), Chris Hall, *Lifeline*

ST-6487 (September 1981), Klaatu, *Magenta Lake*

ST-6488 (August 1981), Frank Mills, *Prelude To Romance*

CKBB-6489 (January 1982), Leggat, *Illuminations*

ST-6490 (January 1982), Long John Baldry, *Rock With The Best*

ST-6491 (January 1982), Streetheart, *Streetheart*

ST-6492 (March 1982), Bruce Miller, *Magic Night*

ST-6493 (February 1983), Chris Hall, *Hypnotized*

ST-6494 (June 1982), Cliff Richard, *The Early Years*

ST-6495 (not released), Angelic Upstarts, *Still From The Heart*

ST-6496 (August 1982), Frank Mills, *Rondo*

ST-6497 (August 1982), Bob Schneider, *Listen To The Children*

ST-6498 (August 1982), Bob Schneider, *When You Dream A Dream*

ST-6499 (January 1983), Streetheart, *Dancing With Danger*

ST-6500 (March 1983), Helix, *No Rest For The Wicked*

ST-6501 (May 1983), Frank Mills, *Music Box Dancer*

ST-6502 (May 1983), Frank Mills, *Sunday Morning Suite*

ST-6503 (July 1983), David Wilcox, *My Eyes Keep Me In Trouble*

ST-6504 (September 1983), Bob Schneider, *Having A Good Time*

ST-6505 (August 1983), David Wilcox, *Out Of The Woods*

ST-6506 (September 1983), Frank Mills, *A Special Christmas*

ST-6507 (October 1983), Streetheart, *Live After Dark*

ST-6508 (Dec 83), Andrew Powell, *Plays The Best Of The Alan Parsons Project*

ST-6509 (December 1983), Franck Pourcel, *In A Nostalgia Mood*

ST-6510 (release cancelled, US number used), Luba

ST-6511 (February 1984), The Shorts, *Comment Ca Va*

ST-6512 (September 13, 1984), Bruce Murray, *Two Hearts*

ST-6513 (August 1984), David Wilcox, *Bad Reputation*

ST-6514 (November 1984), Streetheart, *Buried Treasure*

STBK-6515 Frank Zappa, *Them Or Us*

SQ-6516 Marillion, *Real To Reel (live)*

ST-6517 (January 1985), Rodney Rude

ST-6518 (March 1985), Frank Zappa, *Francesco*

ST-6519 (June 1985), Bamboo, *Stop All Distractions*

SQ-6520 (June 1985), Various Artists, *Moose Molten Metal*

SKCO-6521 (June 1985, Frank Zappa, *Thing Fish*

ST-6522 (July 1985, David Wilcox, *David Wilcox*

ST-6523 Unused

SQ-6524 Various Artists, *Dance Compilation, Dance Mixes*

ST-6525 Francesca, *(possibly Frank Zappa?, no release date)*

4XQ-6526 Various Artists, *Country Compilation*

ST-6527 Glass Tiger, *The Thin Red Line*

ST-6528 Unused

ST-6529 Saxon, *Strong Arm Of The Law*

ST-6530 Frank Zappa, *Sheik Yerbouti*

ST-6531 Frank Zappa, *Tinseltown Rebellion*

ST-6532 Frank Zappa, *You Are What You Is*

ST-6533 Frank Zappa, *Ship Arriving Too Late To Save A Drowning Witch*

ST-6534 Frank Zappa, *The Man From Utopia*

ST-6535 Frank Zappa, *Vs. The Mothers Of Prevention*

ST-6536 Saxon, *Saxon*

ST-6537 Saxon, *Denim And Leather*

ST-6538 Saxon, *Wheels Of Steel*

ST-6539 Unused

SQ-6540 Various Artists, *Moose Molten Metal Volume 2*

ST-6541 Zappacosta, *A To Z*

ST-6542 Talk Talk, *It's My Mix*

ST-6543 The Partland Brothers, *Electric Honey*

ST-6544 (Soundtrack), *Mona Lisa*

ST-6545 Fate, *Fate*

ST-6546 Vicious Pink, *Vicious Pink*

ST-6547 Strange Cruise, *Strange Cruise*

ST-6548 Frank Mills, *Transitions*

ST-6549 Les Immer Essen, *Tally-Ho*

ST-6550 Johnny Clegg /Savuka, *Third World Child*

ST-6551 Daniel Lavoie, *Tips*

ST-6552 The Partland Brothers, *American*

ST-6553 Frank Zappa, *Jazz From Hell*

ST-6554 Queen, *Live Magic*

ST-6555 Rock And Hyde, *Under The Volcano*

ST-6556 Hot Chocolate, *The Very Best Of Hot Chocolate*

ST-6557 The Hollies, *Twenty Golden Greats*

ST-6558 The Saints, *All Fools Day*

ST-6559 Unused

ST-6560 Roxette, *Pearls Of Passion*

ST-6561 Unused

ST-6562 Unused

ST-6563 Unused

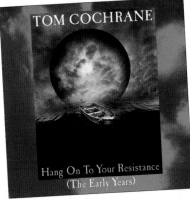

CLT-6564 (last disc issued on the 6000 series), Tom Cochrane, *Hang On To Your Resistance*

Piers Hemmingsen gratefully acknowledges assistance from Randall Haslett, Matt Hemmingsen, Bob Harrold, John Puffer, John Potter, Chris Crisco Probert, Pontus Von Tell, Doug Hinman, Paul Floyd, Steve Clifford, Ron Martin, Bruce Spizer, Brian Schofield, Andre Gibeault, Ron Hall, Jim De Simone, Andrew Croft (Beatlology Magazine), Fraser Hill (EMI), David MacMillan (EMI), Barry Norris, Paul Shaffer, Richard Green, David Watmough, Graham Newton (RCA/CHUM), Denny Doherty, Kal Raudoja, Peter Dunn (Vinyl Museum), Jim Levitt (Discovery Records), Gerry Miskolczi (All That Rocks), Doug Thompson (CHUM), Martin Koppel (Kop's/Vortex), Barb Ellenson (Driftwood Music), Around Again, David Nolan (Legend Records), Open City, Rick's Recollections, Vortex and Paul White.

[1] Vault records show title "Little Children"

[2] Vault records show title *5-4-3-2-1*; also have same T-6102 number assigned to a Hollies LP, *We're Through*

[3] Vault records show title *Coast to Coast with The Dave Clark Five*

[4] Vault records show title *The Ed Allen Exercise Album*

[5] Vault records show release date of January 11, 1964

[6] Vault records show the title *Paddy Butler's Cork Dance*

[7] Release date likely September 6, 1965

[8] Vault records show the title *I Can't Let Go*

[9] Vault records show the title *The Country Rock Sound Of The Downliner's Sect*

[10] Rear sleeve notes original released as SOAL-6351

[11] 8-track tape

[12] Re-issue of 6470

BIBLIOGRAPHY

The author relied on a large number of newspapers and periodicals for research, including *Billboard, The Canadian Composer, Downbeat, The Globe and Mail, High Fidelity, Maclean's, Music Express, Music World, Newsweek, The New Yorker, RPM, The Record, Record Week, Time, The Toronto Star* and *The Toronto Telegram.*

In addition, the following books were consulted:

Hall, Ron, *The CHUM Chart Book, 1957-1986*, Stardust Productions, 1990.

Jennings, Nicholas, *Before the Gold Rush: Flashbacks to the Dawn of the Canadian Sound*, Viking, 1997; Penguin, 1998.

Kendall, Brian, *Our Hearts Went Boom: The Beatles' Invasion of Canada*, Viking, 1997.

Kennedy, Ted, *Canada Top 40: RPM and The Record*, Canadian Chart Research.

Livingstone, David, *Anne Murray: The Story So Far*, Prentice-Hall, 1981.

Melhuish, Martin, *Oh What a Feeling: A Vital History of Canadian Music*, Quarry Press, 1996.

Pevere, Geoff and Dymond, Greig, *Mondo Canuck: A Canadian Pop Culture Odyssey*, Prentice Hall Canada, 1996.

Pritchard, David and Lysaght, Alan, *The Beatles: An Oral History*, Stoddart, 1998.

Yorke, Ritchie, *Axes, Chops and Hot Licks: The Canadian Rock Music Scene*, Hurtig Publishers, 1971.

Photo Credits

Although every effort has been made to ensure that permissions for all material were obtained, those sources not formally acknowledged here should contact EMI Music Canada for inclusion in all future editions of this book.

INDEX

Note: Italicized numbers indicate captions

Aarons & Ackley, 54
Aboriginal recordings. *See* Native music
AC/DC, 93
Adams, Bryan, 68, 89-90, 93, 96, 108,114, 129
Addams, Victoria, 132
Adderly, Cannonball, 38
Aerosmith, 98, 106
A Foot in Coldwater, 55, 81, *81*
Aglukark, Susan, 117, *118,* 120, 126
    profile, 124
Air Canada Centre (Toronto), 142
Aizelwood, John, 77
Al Trace and his Orchestra, 3
The Alan Parsons Project, *57,* 61
Alert Music, 92, 116
Alex Sherman Enterprises Ltd., 30, 53
    (*see also* Sherman Music Centres)
Allen, Barry, 27, 28
    profile, 31
Allen, Bruce, 86, 96, 127
Allen, Woody, 38
Almeida, Laurindo, 15, *18*
Alpert, Herb, 60
A&M [Records], 60, 86, 98, 138
"American Bandstand," 23
American Country Music Association, 65
American Music Publishing, 77
Amesbury, Bill, 58, 60
Amnesty International, 136
Ampex Records, 72
Andes, Mark, 105, *105*
Anderson, Cleve, 99
Anderson, Eric, 66
Anderson, Joel, *113*
The Andrew Sisters, 14
Andrews, Punch, 80
Andruchow, Al, 56, 57, 78, *144*
Anthem Records, *60, 161,* 144
Angel [Records], 10, 91
The Animals, 33, *46,* 47
Anka, Paul, 64
Anne Murray Centre (Springhill, N.S.), 68
Anthem Records, 61, 85, 89, 110
    profile, 109
Anthony, Ray, 10
Antonioni, Michelangelo, 79
Apartheid, 136
Apple Records, 30, 45, 54, 57, 73,116
April Wine, 61, 85, *86,* 91, 109
Aquarius Records, 61, 85, 88, 89, 91, 101, 115, 116
    profile, 109
Arboit, Ric, 144
Arc Records, 65, 66
Arden, Jann, 68
Arista Records, 57, 58, 61
Armstrong, Louis, 11
Arnez, Desi, *14*
Ashgrove Club (L.A.), 15
Asmit, Jay, 120
Atkinson, Shirley, *60*
Atlantic Records, 71, 100
Attic Records, 24
Auf der Maur, Melissa, 141
Averre, Berton, 106
Axton, Hoyt, 76
Aykroyd, Dan, 126
Ayre, Art, 35
Aysworth, Allan, 3
Aznavour, Charles, *118*

Babe Ruth [band], 56
Bachman, Randy, 31, *128*
Baker, Carroll, 34
Baker, Ginger, *90*
Baldry, Long John, 61, 85
Ball, Lucille, *14*
Balmer, Carol Ann, *43*
Bamboo (Toronto), 116
Bamford, Joe, 93
The Band, 29, 30, 49, 54, 92, 132
    profile, 32
The Band of the Irish Guard, 23
Bangs, Lester, 67
Banham, Bill, 142, 143
Bannon, Bill, 24, 28, 44, 68
Barenaked Ladies, *127,* 130
Barnett, Charlie, 12
Baron, Natalie, 29
Barrett, Syd, 79
Bartel, Roger, 133
Basso, Guido, 50, 63
Bateman, Jeff, 95
Battle, Kathleen, 91
Battle of the New Sounds, 31, 33
Baxter, David, 99
Baxter, Les, *7, 20*
Bay City Rollers, *57,* 58
BBC, 24, 82
B.B. Gabor, 109
The Beach Boys, 25, 28, 33, *33,* 37,77, 86
    profile, 39-40
The Beastie Boys, 74
Beal, Chuck, *28*
Beard, Chris, 50
Beatlemania [phenomenon] 25, 42, 42-44, 117
Beatlemania! [album], 25, 33, 41, 44
The Beatles, 25, 25-26, *25, 26,* 27, 28, 29, 30, 32, 33, 35, 40, 46, 48, 49, 53, 55, 106, 117, 118
    profiles, 41-45, 73-76
Beatles-inspired records, 44-45
Beau Dommage, 57, 64
    profile, 62
Beck, 139
Bed-In [for peace, 1969; Lennon/Ono], 30, 73
Beechwood Music, 28, 58, 66
Beker, Jeanie, 88
Belafonte, Harry, 20
Bell, Bruce, 81
Bell, Michael [Luba], 94
Bell, Mike [The Staccatos], *37*
Bell Records, 57
Bell, Rick, 37, *37*
Belly, 139
Benatar, Pat, 86, 94, 106
Bennett, Willie P., 69
Benny, Jack, 14, *14,* 50
Bergen, Polly, 14
Bernstein, Leonard, 12
Berry, Chuck, 23, 32, 73, 81, 142
Berry, Jerry, 117
Berry, Ken, 115, 120
Berry, Tom, 92, 144
Bertrand, Pierre, 62, *62*
Bibby, Richard, 42
Bickert, Ed, 50
Big bands, 12, 17, 81
Big Bop Nouveau Band, 12
Biggs, John, 15
The Big Town Boys, 54
Bilingual stars. *See*
    French-English crossover acts
Billboard, 18, 26, 42, 48, 50, 54, 56, 61, 70, 63, 99, 106, 133
Bill Haley and the Comets, 8

Billy J. Kramer & the Dakotas, 46, 47
Birdland (N.Y.), 11
B Kool, 113
Black, Clint, 114, 129
The Black Dyke Mills Brass Band, 45
Blaine, Hal, 38
Blakey, Art, 145
Blondie, 61, *61,* 106
Blood, Sweat & Tears, 32
Blue Angel (N.Y.), 20
Blue Note Records, 116, 119, 120, 140
    profile, 145
The Bluenote (Toronto), 71
Blue Rodeo, 99
Blur, 118
BMI Canada, 10
Bo Diddley, 71, 73
Bobby "O," 107
Bogart, Frank, 23
Bonnycastle, L.C., 3
The Boomtown Rats, 89
Boot Records, 126, 146
La Bottine Souriante, *122,* 123
Bower, Johnny, 50, 146
Bowie, David, 85, 86
    profile, 103
The Box, 92, 144
Boynton, Peter, 97
Boys Brigade, 109
Brady, Paul, 140
Branson, Richard, 115, 142
Brave Belt, 55
Brennan, Walter, 50
The Brian Browne Trio, 29
Bridges, Lloyd, 50
Brightman, Sarah, 119
British invasion, profile, 46-47
    (*See also* New British invasion)
The British Modbeats, 45
British new wave, 85
Britten, Terry, 108
Brodie, Paul, 25
Brooks, Bob, 114
Brooks, Bonnie, 50
Brooks, Diane, 64, 71
Brooks, Garth, 113, 114, 118-19
    profile, 134-35
Brooks, Rob, 130
Brower, John, 30
Brown, Keith, 109
Brown, Melanie, 143
Brown, Sawyer, 116
Browne, Jackson, 140
Buck, Gary, 28, *28, 31,* 53, 55, *55*
Buffalo Springfield, 35
The Buggles, 84
Bunnett, Jane, 145
Bunton, Emma, 143
Burns, George, *14*
Burr, H.F., 29
Burrows, Jeff, *116,* 133
Bush, Kate, 85, 118
Bust It Records, 137
Butterfield, Paul, 63
The Byrds, 32

Cadell, Meryn, 115
Les Cailloux, 28, 70
Calgary Sun, 102, 127
Callas, Maria, 119
Calypso, 20
Cameron, Deane, 58, 59, 61, 67-68, *67,* 81, 85, 87, 90, 91, 92, 94, 95, 97, 106, 109, 112, 113, 114, 116, 118, 119, 121, *121,* 126, 137, 147

50th-anniversary speech, excerpt, 121, 123
Campbell, Glen, *33,* 38, 39, 54, 57, 59, 66, 68, 113
    profile, 77
Campbell, Taylor, 44
Canada Bear Ltd., 63
Canada Observed, 50
Canadian Academy of Recording
    Arts and Science. *See* CARAS
Canadian Beatle Fan Club, 42
The Canadian Composer, 55, 62, 63, 102
Canadian content. *See* CanCon
Canadian Country Music Association, 65, 124
Canadian Music Hall of Fame, 11, 68, 71, 116, 119, 132
Canadian Musician, 93, 124
Canadian National Exhibition, 126
Canadian nationalism, 65, 82, 126, 146
Canadian Pacific Railway, *2, 3,* 6
Canadian Radio-television and
    Telecommunications Commission.
    See CRTC
Canadian Recording Industry Association, 91
CanCon, 29-30, 52-53, 54, 55, 63, 81, 110, 126
Capitol-EMI:
    affiliate labels. *See* Profiles, Record
      labels
    A&R dept. merge with Cap.U.S., 58
    changes name to EMI Music Canada, 115
    creates urban music dept., 112
    and domestic signings, 57, *58,* 62, 64, 86, 90-91
    issues first CDs, 84, 87
    musicians, profiles. *See* Profiles,
      musicians
    novelty records. *See* Profiles,
      Novelty music
    opens pressing plant, 59, *59, 60*
    and retail chains, 58
    technological advances, 85-86
Capitol Industries Inc., 60, 92
Capitol Nashville, 134
Capitol Record Club of Canada, 9
Capitol Record Distributors of Canada, 7
Capitol Records of America, 2, 6, 7, 8, 28, 53, 57, 58, 61
Capitol Records of Canada:
    affiliate labels. *See* Profiles, Record labels
    American Drive offices (1967), 28-29, *29, 30*
    birth of, 2-6
    corporate culture of, 6, 56
    and domestic signings, 2, 28, 29-30, 34, 52-53, 54, 55-56, 81
    EMI takover of, 8
    move to Queen St. (Toronto), 8-9
    musicians, profiles. *See* Profiles,
      musicians
    novelty music. *See* Profiles, Novelty music
    promotional tactics, 7, 10, 24
    renamed. *See* Capitol-EMI
    and retail chains, 30, 53
    6000 series (LPs), 148-56
Capitol Records-EMI of Canada. *See* Capitol-
    EMI
*Capitol Records Guide to Canadian Content
    Programming,* 54
Capitol U.S. *See* Capitol Records of America
CARAS, 81, 91
Card, Graeme, 82
Caroline Records, 141
Carmassi, Denny, 105, *105*
Carson, Brian, *57*
Carson, Johnny, 36, 38, 39

Casa Loma (Toronto), 17
Cash, Peter, 115
Cashbox, 42, 48, 50
Cassette tapes, 57, 86
Caymi, Dori, 36
CBC, 27, 31, 38, 65, 70, 82, 95
CBC Radio, 7, 14, 64, 124, 126, 129
CBS [broadcasting], 13, 14, 138
CBS Records, 62
Cee, Joey, 40
Celebrity recordings, 20
CEMA, 118
Centennial:
    anthem, 38
    celebration, 28, 50, 65
CFPL (London, Ont.), 10
CFRB (Toronto), 10
CFTM-TV (Montreal), 64
CFUN (Vancouver), 23, 24, 39, 45
Chamberlain, Jimmy, 141
The Champs, 77
The Chantels, 41
Chapin Carpenter, Mary, 131
Chapman, Mike, 106
Chapman, Tracy, 136
Chappell, Doug, 115
Charisma [Records], 116
Chartrand, Christine, 57
The Chatter Box, 7, 7
Chatwood, Stuart, *116,* 133
Chen, Wei, *135*
Cher, 45
Cherry Beach Rehearsal Rooms (Toronto), 133
Chess Records, 71
Chick Corea, 12
Chisholm, Melanie, 143
Choclair, 120
Chrétien, Jean, *115, 118*
Chris and Cosey, 90
Christgau, Robert, 78
Christy, June, *7, 17*
Chrysalis [Records], 58, 61, 114, 115
CHUM (Toronto), 19, 24, 31, 35, 37, 44, 45, 46, 49, 50
Church, Cindy, 69
CITI-FM (Winnipeg), 88
Citytv, 84, 88 (*See also* MuchMusic)
CJMS (Montreal), *45*
CKEY (Toronto), 7, 44
CKLB (Oshawa), 41
CKLW (Windsor, Ont.), 80
Clancy, King, 43
Clapton, Eric, 73
Clark, Alex, 65-66
Clark, Dick, 23, 33
Clark, Petula, 73
Clark, Terri, 146
Clarke, Harvey, 7, 10, 121, *121, 123, 123*
Claude, Renée, 70
Claude Thornhill Orchestra, 11
Clegg, Johnny, 114, 136
Cliff Richard & the Shadows, 24, 33, 48
Cline, Patsy, 34, 69
Clovis, New Mexico (studios), 31
Cobo Hall (Detroit), 80
Coca-Cola, 9, 37
Cochran, Eddie, 37
Cochran, Hank, 34
Cochran, Murray, 3
Cochrane, Tom, 81, 89, 91, 92, 95, *95,* 97, 114, *115,* 120, 146
    profile, 125
Cockburn, Bruce, 68, 69, 114, 125